# EFFECTIVE COMMUNICATION DURING DISASTERS

## Making Use of Technology, Media, and Human Resources

# EFFECTIVE COMMUNICATION DURING DISASTERS

## Making Use of Technology, Media, and Human Resources

*Edited by*
**Girish Bobby Kapur, MD, MPH,**
**Sarah Bezek, MD, and Jonathan Dyal, MD, MPH**

Apple Academic Press Inc.   Apple Academic Press Inc.
3333 Mistwell Crescent   9 Spinnaker Way
Oakville, ON L6L 0A2   Waretown, NJ 08758
Canada   USA

©2017 by Apple Academic Press, Inc.

First issued in paperback 2021

No claim to original U.S. Government works

ISBN 13: 978-1-77-463679-4 (pbk)
ISBN 13: 978-1-77-188511-9 (hbk)

---

### Library and Archives Canada Cataloguing in Publication

---

Effective communication during disasters : making use of technology, media, and human resources / edited by Girish Bobby Kapur, Jonathan Dyal, and Sarah Bezek.
Includes bibliographical references and index.

Issued in print and electronic formats.
ISBN 978-1-77188-511-9 (hardcover).--ISBN 978-1-77188-512-6 (pdf)

1. Emergency management--Technological innovations. 2. Communication in crisis management--Technological innovations. 3. Disaster relief--Technological innovations. 4. Emergency communication systems.  I. Kapur, Girish Bobby, author, editor II. Bezek, Sarah, editor  III. Dyal, Jonathan, editor

| HV551.2.E34 2016 | 363.34'8 | C2016-906569-3 | C2016-906570-7 |

..................................................................................................................................................

CIP data on file with US Library of Congress

..................................................................................................................................................

Apple Academic Press also publishes its books in a variety of electronic formats. Some content that appears in print may not be available in electronic format. For information about Apple Academic Press products, visit our website at **www.appleacademicpress.com** and the CRC Press website at **www.crcpress.com**

# About the Editors

---

**GIRISH BOBBY KAPUR, MD, MPH**

Girish Bobby Kapur, MD, MPH, is the Chief of the Department of Emergency Medicine at Jackson Memorial Hospital (JMH) in Miami, Florida, and was recruited in 2015 to bring transformative change in the delivery of high-quality acute patient care at one of the nation's busiest emergency centers. In addition, Dr. Kapur is launching an academic platform with his colleagues at JMH based on clinical excellence, innovative education, translational research, and public health outreach at the Jackson Health System and the University of Miami Miller School of Medicine. Dr. Kapur is an internationally recognized emergency physician and public health expert who previously served as the Associate Chief for Academic Affairs and the Founding Residency Program Director in the Section of Emergency Medicine and an Associate Professor of Medicine and Pediatrics at Baylor College of Medicine (BCM) from 2009–2015.

Based on his international and academic accomplishments, Dr. Kapur was also appointed by BCM President Paul Klotman as the Founding Director of the Center for Globalization at Baylor College of Medicine. For two years, Dr. Kapur helped guide the College's global initiatives and worked with the BCM faculty, residents, and students to fulfill BCM's mission to be an international leader in academic medicine. In September 2014, Dr. Kapur led a six-person team that trained nearly 1,500 people in Ebola preparedness and response in Nigeria during the middle of the epidemic in the country. Dr. Kapur was also a co-investigator on the USAID grant "Fighting Ebola: A Grand Challenge" that was one of twelve grants awarded from over 1,500 submissions. Before his roles at BCM, Dr. Kapur directed global health training programs and international projects at the Ronald Reagan Institute for Emergency Medicine at George Washington University (GWU) from 2004–2009. At GWU, Dr. Kapur established multiple academic training programs and acute healthcare systems with partners in India, China, Latin America and the Middle East. In addition, Dr. Kapur implemented a countrywide project to improve emergency services in Turkey that trained more than 2,000 physicians providing emergency care in Turkey's national hospitals.

Dr. Kapur received his Bachelor of Arts degree in English Literature and Policy Studies from Rice University and his Medical Doctor degree from Baylor College of Medicine. He then completed his residency in Emergency Medicine from Yale School of Medicine, followed by a fellowship in international emergency medicine and global health from Brigham and Women's Hospital and Harvard School of Medicine. He also completed his Master in Public Health from the Harvard School of Public Health.

Dr. Kapur has published multiple peer-reviewed papers and is the senior editor for the first textbook in the field of emergency public health titled *Emergency Public Health: Preparedness and Response.*

Dr. Kapur has served as the Chair of the International Committee for both the American College of Emergency Physicians and the Society for Academic Emergency Medicine. In June 2012, Dr. Kapur was awarded the Order of the International Federation of Emergency Medicine for his contributions to global health and emergency medicine, an honor given to only two US emergency physicians every two years.

### SARAH BEZEK, MD

Sarah K. Bezek, MD, is an Assistant Professor in the Department of Medicine and Section of Emergency Medicine at Baylor College of Medicine in Houston, Texas. She is a graduate of Texas Tech University Health Sciences Center and trained in Emergency Medicine at Yale University. She has been practicing emergency medicine as a board-certified physician working predominantly with underserved populations.

She is on faculty at the National School of Tropical Medicine in Houston, Texas, with special emphasis on education, acute care and trauma in low/middle income countries, and neglected diseases of poverty. She has given lectures both locally and internationally regarding emerging infectious diseases. She has also worked on research in the area of new malarial diagnostics.

She has been awarded for her work with mentorship and medical student education.

## JONATHAN DYAL, MD, MPH

Jonathan Dyal's interest in disaster response began while studying emerging infectious diseases at Stanford University. His commitment to emergency disaster management was solidified by medical relief trips to Bolivia, Ghana, Tanzania, and Uganda.

Dr. Dyal began his career in international disaster response by pursuing his MD at Johns Hopkins University School of Medicine. While enrolled at Johns Hopkins, he worked with the distinguished faculty of the Center for Global Health to conduct research in Pune, India, on Cryptococcal Meningitis. Before beginning his clinical training, he earned his Master's in Public Health at the Johns Hopkins University Bloomberg School of Public Health. His thesis focused on the origins of an outbreak of syphilis among high-risk groups around Lake Victoria.

After graduating from the School of Public Health, Dr. Dyal was awarded a Doris Duke Global Health Fellowship. As a Doris Duke Fellow, he spent a year studying emerging zoonotic diseases and viral hemorrhagic fevers in Uganda. During this time he also enrolled in the University of Minnesota's Global Health Course. In addition to studying disaster management in low resource settings, this experience prepared him to pursue a Certificate in Tropical Medicine, which was awarded by the American Society for Tropical Medicine and Hygiene in June, 2015.

Dr. Dyal is currently an Emergency Medicine resident at Baylor College of Medicine. As a resident, Dr. Dyal has collaborated with many of the global health and disaster management faculty at Baylor. He has published several articles on emerging infectious diseases, including Chikungunya virus and leptospirosis. Upon graduation, his future plans include working with the Center for Disease Control's Epidemic Intelligence Service and a Disaster Medicine Fellowship in Emergency Medicine.

# Contents

# Acknowledgment and How to Cite

The editors and publisher thank each of the authors who contributed to this book. The chapters in this book were previously published elsewhere. To cite the work contained in this book and to view the individual permissions, please refer to the citation at the beginning of each chapter. Each chapter was carefully selected by the editors; the result is a book that looks at communication during natural disasters from a variety of perspectives. The chapters included are broken into five sections, which describe the following topics:

We have divided this topic into four parts. In Part 1, "Overview of Communication Challenges and Best-Practice Analyses," we consider these topics:

- In chapter 1, recommendations to build communications capacity prior to a disaster, which include pre-writing public service announcements in multiple languages on questions that frequently arise during disasters; maintaining a database of statistics for different regions and types of disaster; maintaining lists of the locally trusted sources of information for frequently affected countries and regions; maintaining email listservs of employees, international media outlet contacts, and government and non-governmental organization contacts that can be used to rapidly disseminate information; developing a global network with 24-hour cross-coverage by participants from each time zone; and creating a central electronic sharepoint where all of these materials can be accessed by communications officers around the globe.
- Models of information dissemination presented in chapter 2 for six typical information media, including short message service (SMS), microblogs, news portals, cell phones, television, and oral communication. Then, the information dissemination capability of each medium concerning individuals of different ages, genders, and residential areas was simulated, and the dissemination characteristics were studied. Finally, radar graphs were used to illustrate comprehensive assessments of the six media; these graphs show directly the information dissemination characteristics of all media. The models and the results are essential for improving the efficiency of information dissemination for the purpose of disaster pre-warning and for

formulating emergency plans which help to reduce the possibility of injuries, deaths and other losses in a disaster.

- In chapter 3, intervention studies of disaster risk communication and an overview of the contemporary literature. The authors highlight the need for high-quality randomized trials and appropriately analyzed cluster randomized trials in the field of disaster risk communication where these can be conducted within an appropriate research ethics framework.
- An argument in chapter 4 that there is an opportunity to conduct analysis while the response is operational due to the increasing availability of information within hours and days of a disaster event. The authors offer a classification scheme for the disaster information needs of the public and best observed practice standards for content and timeliness. By comparing the information shared with the public within days of a disaster to these standards, the authors identify potential deficiencies in communicating critical disaster response information to the public at a time when they can still be corrected.

In Part 2, "The Internet and Social Media," we look at:

- In chapter 5, insights from a workshop that was conducted at the 2014 Australian and New Zealand Disaster and Emergency Management Conference, during which participants discussed the current strengths and limitations of social media use in the context of emergencies, the future of social media use and the associated barriers and enablers.
- A disaster resilient network in chapter 6 that integrates various wireless networks into a cognitive wireless network that users can use as an access network to the Internet at the serious disaster occurrence. The authors designed and developed the disaster resilient network based on software defined network (SDN) technology to automatically select the best network link and route among the possible access networks to the Internet by periodically monitoring their network states and evaluate those using extended AHP method.
- In chapter 7, an Internet-based emergency response system that integrates Internet social networking and information communication technology into central government disaster management system. Web-based networking provides two-way communication that establishes a reliable and accessible tunnel for proximal and distal users in disaster preparedness and management.

In Part 3, "Mobile Phones and Other Technology," we discuss:

- In chapter 8, mobile devices limitations for effective communication and coordination of help in emergency situations and ways to overcome some of these limitations in the future by the incorporation of features to increase their resilience and effectiveness as aid tools at relatively low cost. The authors discuss improvements in autonomous energy generation and use, based on existing and rapidly emerging technologies, as well as further improvements in physical durability and off-line operability are encouraged, and they identify the possibility to combine capabilities from other devices, such as space-based telecommunication systems and traditional two-way radios, to enhance the utility of mobile devices for these applications. The solutions the authors propose could help millions of citizens around the world to manage the risks and impacts of natural and health-related hazards.

- In chapter 9, the features of messages that are associated with their retransmission, focusing on message content, style, and structure, as well as the networked relationships of message senders to answer the question: what characteristics of a terse message sent under conditions of imminent threat predict its retransmission among members of the public?

Ultimately, in Part 4, "Understanding the Challenges to Effective Communication," we turn to this final issue:

- In chapter 10, mothers needs after a nuclear disaster for information on radiation risks as they impact on decisions related to relocations, concerns for child safety, and experiences with interpersonal conflicts within the family owing to differing risk perceptions.
- In chapter 11, non-compliance during Do-Not Drink notices, which were traced to the public's limited knowledge of water notices and their folk beliefs about the protection offered from boiling water. The authors suggest that future information dissemination plans reduce reliance on official leaflets and maximize the potential of local media and personal networks. Current public health education programs are recommended to attend to insufficient and incorrect public knowledge about precautionary actions.

# List of Contributors

**Wladimir J. Alonso**
Fogarty International Center, National Institutes of Health (NIH) and Origem Scientifica

**Olga Anikeeva**
Torrens Resilience Institute at Flinders University

**Ghassem R. Asrar**
Joint Global Change Research Institute, Pacific Northwest National Laboratory, University of Maryland

**Paul Arbon**
Director of Torrens Resilience Institute at Flinders University and current President of the World Association for Disaster and Emergency Medicine

**Declan T. Bradley**
Public Health Agency and Queen's University Belfast, Belfast, Northern Ireland, United Kingdom

**Susan A. Brink**
Center for Disaster Management and Risk Reduction Technology, Karlsruhe Institute of Technology

**Carter T. Butts**
Department of Sociology, Department of Statistics, Department of Electrical Engineering and Computer Science, and Institute for Mathematical Behavioral Sciences, University of California Irvine, Irvine, CA, United States of America

**Edward Chan**
International Injury Research Unit, Department of International Health, Johns Hopkins Bloomberg School of Public Health, 615 North Wolfe Street, Suite E-8132, Baltimore, Maryland, 21205, USA

**Mike Clarke**
Director, All Ireland Hub for Trials Methodology Research; Evidence Aid

**James E. Daniell**
Center for Disaster Management and Risk Reduction Technology, Karlsruhe Institute of Technology

**Sean M. Fitzhugh**
Department of Sociology, University of California Irvine, Irvine, CA, United States of America

**C. Ben Gibson**
Department of Sociology, University of California Irvine, Irvine, CA, United States of America

**Trevor Girard**
Center for Disaster Management and Risk Reduction Technology, Karlsruhe Institute of Technology

**Aya Goto**
Department of Public Health, Fukushima Medical University School of Medicine, Hikarigaoka 1, Fukushima-City, Fukushima 960-1295, Japan and Takemi Program in International Health, Harvard School of Public Health (at time of manuscript writing), 665 Huntington Avenue, Boston, MA 02115, USA

**Donald D. Halstead**
Office for Educational Programs, Harvard School of Public Health, 665 Huntington Avenue, Boston, MA 02115, USA

**Cheng-Min Huang**
International Injury Research Unit, Department of International Health, Johns Hopkins Bloomberg School of Public Health, 615 North Wolfe Street, Suite E-8132, Baltimore, Maryland, 21205, USA

**Hong Huang**
Institute of Public Safety Research, Department of Engineering Physics, Tsinghua University, Beijing, China

**Paul R. Hunter**
School of Medicine, Health Policy and Practice, University of East Anglia, Norwich NR4 7TJ, UK

**Adnan A. Hyder**
International Injury Research Unit, Department of International Health, Johns Hopkins Bloomberg School of Public Health, 615 North Wolfe Street, Suite E-8132, Baltimore, Maryland, 21205, USA

**G. Bobby Kapur**
Chief, Department of Emergency Medicine, Jackson Memorial Hospital (JMH), Miami, Florida

**Bijan Khazai**
Center for Disaster Management and Risk Reduction Technology, Karlsruhe Institute of Technology

**Olivia Knapton**
Department of Education and Professional Studies, King's College London, Waterloo Bridge Wing, Waterloo Road, London SE1 9NH, UK

**Tina Kunz-Plapp**
Center for Disaster Management and Risk Reduction Technology, Karlsruhe Institute of Technology

**Alden Y. Lai**
Department of Health Communication, School of Public Health, The University of Tokyo (at time of manuscript writing), 7-3-1 Bunkyo-ku, Hongo, Tokyo 113-8654, Japan

**Cedar League**
Trauma, Health and Hazards Center, University of Colorado, Colorado Springs, CO, United States of America

**Marie McFarland**
Belfast Health and Social Care Trust, Department of Pathology, Belfast, Northern Ireland, United Kingdom

**Laura N. Medford-Davis**
Section of Emergency Medicine, Baylor College of Medicine, Ben Taub General Hospital Emergency Center, Houston TX, USA

**Michael R. Reich**
Department of Global Health and Population, Harvard School of Public Health, 665 Huntington Avenue, Boston, MA 02115, USA

**Rima E. Rudd**
Department of Social and Behavioral Sciences, Harvard School of Public Health, 677 Huntington Avenue, Boston, MA 02115, USA

**Gabriella Rundblad**
Department of Education and Professional Studies, King's College London, Waterloo Bridge Wing, Waterloo Road, London SE1 9NH, UK

**Goshi Sato**
Iwate Prefectural University, 152-52 Takizawa, Iwate 0200173, Japan

**Cynthia Schuck-Paim**
Origem Scientifica

**Yoshitaka Shibata**
Iwate Prefectural University, 152-52 Takizawa, Iwate 0200173, Japan

**Emma S. Spiro**
Information School, University of Washington, Seattle, WA, United States of America

**Malinda Steenkamp**
Torrens Resilience Institute at Flinders University

**Boni Su**
Institute of Public Safety Research, Department of Engineering Physics, Tsinghua University, Beijing, China

**Jeannette Sutton**
Department of Communication, University of Kentucky, Lexington, KY, United States of America

**Yuu Suzuki**
Department of Public Health, Fukushima Medical University School of Medicine, Hikarigaoka 1, Fukushima-City, Fukushima 960-1295, Japan

**Noriki Uchida**
Saitama Institute of Technology, Fukaya, Saitama Prefecture 369-0203, Japan

**Friedemann Wenzel**
Center for Disaster Management and Risk Reduction Technology, Karlsruhe Institute of Technology

**Kazuki Yoshida**
Department of Public Health, Fukushima Medical University School of Medicine, Hikarigaoka 1, Fukushima-City, Fukushima 960-1295, Japan

**Hiromi Yoshida-Komiya**
Gender-Specific Medicine Center, Fukushima Medical University School of Medicine, Hikarigaoka 1, Fukushima-city, Fukushima 960-1295, Japan

**Bo Zhang**
Institute of Public Safety Research, Department of Engineering Physics, Tsinghua University, Beijing, China

**Nan Zhang**
Institute of Public Safety Research, Department of Engineering Physics, Tsinghua University, Beijing, China

**Jinlong Zhao**
Institute of Public Safety Research, Department of Engineering Physics, Tsinghua University, Beijing, China

# Introduction

Communication during and immediately after a disaster situation is a vital component of response and recovery. Effective communication connects first responders, support systems, and family members with the communities and individuals immersed in the disaster. Reliable communication also plays a key role in a community's resilience.

In today's world, there are new opportunities for disaster communications through modern technology and social media. Social network applications like Facebook, Twitter, and Instagram can connect friends, family, first responders, and those providing relief and assistance. However, social media and other modern communication tools have their limitations. They can be affected by disaster situations where there are power outages or interrupted cellular service.

The research contained in this compendium offers much-needed information for emergency responders, utility companies, relief organizations, and governments as they invest in infrastructure to support post-disaster communications. In order to make use of modern communication methods, as well as fully utilize more traditional communication networks, it is imperative that we understand how people actually communicate in the wake of a disaster situation and how various communication strategies can best be utilized.

— Girish Bobby Kapur, Jonathan Dyal, and Sarah Bezek

One hundred ninety-four member nations turn to the World Health Organization (WHO) for guidance and assistance during disasters. Purposes of disaster communication include preventing panic, promoting appropriate health behaviors, coordinating response among stakeholders, advocating for affected populations, and mobilizing resources. In Chapter 1,

Medford-Davis and Kapur undertook a quality improvement project to gather expert consensus on best practices that could be used to improve WHO protocols for disaster communication. Open-ended surveys of 26 WHO Communications Officers with disaster response experience were conducted. Responses were categorized to determine the common themes of disaster response communication and areas for practice improvement. Disasters where the participants had experience included 29 outbreaks of 13 different diseases in 16 countries, 18 natural disasters of 6 different types in 15 countries, 2 technical disasters in 2 countries, and ten conflicts in 10 countries. Recommendations to build communications capacity prior to a disaster include pre-writing public service announcements in multiple languages on questions that frequently arise during disasters; maintaining a database of statistics for different regions and types of disaster; maintaining lists of the locally trusted sources of information for frequently affected countries and regions; maintaining email listservs of employees, international media outlet contacts, and government and non-governmental organization contacts that can be used to rapidly disseminate information; developing a global network with 24-h cross-coverage by participants from each time zone; and creating a central electronic sharepoint where all of these materials can be accessed by communications officers around the globe.

Knowing the information dissemination mechanisms of different media and having an efficient information dissemination plan for disaster pre-warning plays a very important role in reducing losses and ensuring the safety of human beings. In Chapter 2, Zhang and colleagues established models of information dissemination for six typical information media, including short message service (SMS), microblogs, news portals, cell phones, television, and oral communication. Then, the information dissemination capability of each medium concerning individuals of different ages, genders, and residential areas was simulated, and the dissemination characteristics were studied. Finally, radar graphs were used to illustrate comprehensive assessments of the six media; these graphs show directly the information dissemination characteristics of all media. The models and the results are essential for improving the efficiency of information dissemination for the purpose of disaster pre-warning and for formulating emergency plans which help to reduce the possibility of injuries, deaths and other losses in a disaster.

A disaster is a serious disruption to the functioning of a community that exceeds its capacity to cope within its own resources. Risk communication in disasters aims to prevent and mitigate harm from disasters, prepare the population before a disaster, disseminate information during disasters and aid subsequent recovery. The aim of Chapter 3, by Bradley and colleagues, is to identify, appraise and synthesise the findings of studies of the effects of risk communication interventions during four stages of the disaster cycle. The authors searched the Cochrane Central Register of Controlled Trials, Embase, MEDLINE, PsycInfo, Sociological Abstracts, Web of Science and grey literature sources for randomised trials, cluster randomised trials, controlled and uncontrolled before and after studies, interrupted time series studies and qualitative studies of any method of disaster risk communication to at-risk populations. Outcome criteria were disaster-related knowledge and behaviour, and health outcomes. Searches yielded 5,224 unique articles, of which 100 were judged to be potentially relevant. Twenty-five studies met the inclusion criteria, and two additional studies were identified from other searching. The studies evaluated interventions in all four stages of the disaster cycle, included a variety of man-made, natural and infectious disease disasters, and were conducted in many disparate settings. Only one randomised trial and one cluster randomised trial were identified, with less robust designs used in the other studies. Several studies reported improvements in disaster-related knowledge and behaviour. The authors identified and appraised intervention studies of disaster risk communication and present an overview of the contemporary literature. Most studies used non-randomised designs that make interpretation challenging. The article does not make specific recommendations for practice but highlight the need for high-quality randomised trials and appropriately-analysed cluster randomised trials in the field of disaster risk communication where these can be conducted within an appropriate research ethics framework.

Analysis of a disaster event can identify strengths and weaknesses of the response implemented by the disaster management system; however, analysis does not typically occur until after the response phase is over. The result is that knowledge gained can only benefit future responses rather than the response under investigation. Chapter 4, by Girard and colleagues, argues that there is an opportunity to conduct analysis while the response is operational due to the increasing availability of information within hours and days of a disaster event. Hence, this article introduces a methodology for analyzing publicly communicated disaster response information in near-real-time. A classification scheme for the disaster information needs of the public has been developed to facilitate analysis and has led to the establishment of best observed practice standards for content and timeliness. By comparing the information shared with the public within days of a disaster to these standards, information gaps are revealed that can be investigated further. The result is identification of potential deficiencies in communicating critical disaster response information to the public at a time when they can still be corrected.

Social media is becoming an important source of information during disasters and other emergency events. In recent years, both in Australia and internationally, an increasing number of people have turned to social media, both to find relevant and up-to-date information and to voice their concerns and experiences of emergency events. Similarly, emergency services and response agencies have been using social media platforms, primarily for the purpose of communicating updates and other essential material to their respective networks. Chapter 5, by Anikeeva and colleagues, discusses insights from a workshop that was conducted at the 2014 Australian and New Zealand Disaster and Emergency Management Conference, during which participants discussed the current strengths and limitations of social media use in the context of emergencies, the future of social media use and the associated barriers and enablers.

In order to temporally recover the information network infrastructure in disaster areas from the Great East Japan Earthquake in 2011, various wireless network technologies such as satellite IP network, 3G, and Wi-Fi were effectively used. However, since those wireless networks are individually introduced and installed but not totally integrated, some of networks were congested due to the sudden network traffic generation and unbalanced traffic distribution, and eventually the total network could not effectively function. In Chapter 6, Sato and colleagues propose a disaster resilient network which integrates various wireless networks into a cognitive wireless network that users can use as an access network to the Internet at the serious disaster occurrence. The authors designed and developed the disaster resilient network based on software defined network (SDN) technology to automatically select the best network link and route among the possible access networks to the Internet by periodically monitoring their network states and evaluate those using extended AHP method. In order to verify the usefulness of our proposed system, a prototype system is constructed and its performance is evaluated.

Internet social networking tools and the emerging web 2.0 technologies are providing a new way for web users and health workers in information sharing and knowledge dissemination. Based on the characters of immediate, two-way and large scale of impact, the internet social networking tools have been utilized as a solution in emergency response during disasters. Chapter 7, by Huang and colleagues, highlights the use of internet social networking in disaster emergency response and public health management of disasters by focusing on a case study of the typhoon Morakot disaster in Taiwan. In the case of typhoon disaster in Taiwan, internet social networking and mobile technology were found to be helpful for community residents, professional emergency rescuers, and government agencies in gathering and disseminating real-time information, regarding volunteer recruitment and relief supplies allocation. The authors noted that if internet tools are to be integrated in the development of emergency response system, the accessibility, accuracy, validity, feasibility, privacy and the scalability of itself should be carefully considered especially in the effort of applying it in resource poor settings. This paper seeks to promote an internet-based emergency response system by integrating internet social networking and information communication technology into central government disaster management system. Web-based networking provides two-way communication which establishes a reliable and accessible tunnel for proximal and distal users in disaster preparedness and management.

Despite the increasingly positive role of portable communication technologies for socioeconomic development and their growing use in global health and other emergency contexts, several challenges still hinder exploring the full potential of mobile phones as effective mitigation tools in natural disasters, public health emergencies and in the aftermath of extreme disruptive events. Mobile devices are designed and advertised to withstand predominantly the demands of normal daily situations, being fraught with fragilities that limit their utility for effective communication and coordination of help in emergency situations. In Chapter 8, Alonso and colleague discuss ways to overcome some of these limitations in the future by the incorporation of features to increase their resilience and effectiveness as aid tools at relatively low cost. Improvements in autonomous energy generation and use, based on existing and rapidly emerging technologies, as well as further improvements in physical durability and off-line operability are encouraged. The authors also identify the possibility to combine capabilities from other devices, such as space-based telecommunication systems and traditional two-way radios, to enhance the utility of mobile devices for these applications. The solutions the article proposes can help millions of citizens around the world to manage the risks and impacts of natural and health-related hazards. They should also promote further resilience to avoiding and recovering from such events, especially in vulnerable regions with limited infrastructure.

Message retransmission is a central aspect of information diffusion. In a disaster context, the passing on of official warning messages by members of the public also serves as a behavioral indicator of message salience, suggesting that particular messages are (or are not) perceived by the public to be both noteworthy and valuable enough to share with others. Chapter 9, by Sutton and colleagues, provides the first examination of terse message retransmission of official warning messages in response to a domestic terrorist attack, the Boston Marathon Bombing in 2013. Using messages posted from public officials' Twitter accounts that were active during the period of the Boston Marathon bombing and manhunt, the authors examine the features of messages that are associated with their retransmission. The article focuss on message content, style, and structure, as well as the networked relationships of message senders to answer the question: what characteristics of a terse message sent under conditions of imminent threat predict its retransmission among members of the public? They employ a negative binomial model to examine how message characteristics affect message retransmission. The authors find that, rather than any single effect dominating the process, retransmission of official Tweets during the Boston bombing response was jointly influenced by various message content, style, and sender characteristics. These findings suggest the need for more work that investigates impact of multiple factors on the allocation of attention and on message retransmission during hazard events.

Local public health nurses (PHNs) have been recognized as the main health service providers in communities in Japan. The Fukushima nuclear disaster in 2011 has, however, created a major challenge for them in responding to mothers' concerns. This was in part due to difficulties in assessing, understanding and communicating health risks on low-dose radiation exposure. In order to guide the development of risk communication plans, Chapter 10, by Goto and colleagues, sought to investigate mothers' primary concerns and possible solutions perceived by a core healthcare profession like the PHNs. A total of 150 records from parenting counseling sessions conducted between PHNs and mothers who have attended mandatory 18-month health checkups for their children at the Fukushima City Health and Welfare Center in 2010, 2011 (year of disaster) and 2012 were examined. Discussion notes of three peer discussions among PHNs organized in response to the nuclear disaster in 2012 and 2013 were also analyzed. All transcribed data were first subjected to text mining to list the words according to their frequencies and inter-relationships. The Steps Coding and Theorization method was then undertaken as a framework for qualitative analysis. PHNs noted mothers to have considerable needs for information on radiation risks as they impact on decisions related to relocations, concerns for child safety, and experiences with interpersonal conflicts within the family owing to differing risk perceptions. PHNs identified themselves as the information channels in the community, recommended the building of their risk communication capacities to support residents in making well-informed decisions, and advocated for self-measurement of radiation levels to increase residents' sense of control. PHNs also suggested a more standardized form of information dissemination and an expansion of community-based counseling services. Inadequate risk communication on radiation in the Fukushima nuclear incident has resulted in multiple repercussions for mothers in the community. Empowerment of local residents to assume more active roles in the understanding of their environment, increasing PHNs' capacity in communication, and an expansion of health services such as counseling will together better address risk communication challenges in post-disaster recovery efforts.

During times of public health emergencies, effective communication between the emergency response agencies and the affected public is important to ensure that people protect themselves from injury or disease. In order to investigate compliance with public health advice during natural disasters, Chapter 11, by Rundblad and colleagues, examined consumer behaviour during two water notices that were issued as a result of serious flooding. During the summer of 2007, 140,000 homes in Gloucestershire, United Kingdom, that are supplied water from Mythe treatment works, lost their drinking water for up to 17 days. Consumers were issued a "Do Not Drink" notice when the water was restored, which was subsequently replaced with a "Boil Water" notice. The rare occurrence of two water notices provided a unique opportunity to compare compliance with public health advice. Information source use and other factors that may affect consumer perception and behaviour were also explored. A postal questionnaire was sent to 1,000 randomly selected households. Chi-square, ANOVA, MANOVA and generalised estimating equation (with and without prior factor analysis) were used for quantitative analysis. In terms of information sources, the authors found high use of and clear preference for the local radio throughout the incident, but family/friends/neighbours also proved crucial at the onset. Local newspapers and the water company were associated with clarity of advice and feeling informed, respectively. Older consumers and those in paid employment were particularly unlikely to read the official information leaflets. They also found a high degree of confusion regarding which notice was in place at which time, with correct recall varying between 23.2%-26.7%, and a great number of consumers believed two notices were in place simultaneously. In terms of behaviour, overall non-compliance levels were significantly higher for the "Do Not Drink" notice (62.9%) compared to the "Boil Water" notice (48.3%); consumers in paid employment were not likely to comply with advice. Non-compliance with the general advice to boil bowser water was noticeably lower (27.3%). Higher non-compliance during the "Do Not Drink" notice was traced to the public's limited knowledge of water notices and their folk beliefs about the protection offered from boiling water. The article suggests that future information dissemination plans reduce reliance on official leaflets and maximise the potential of local media and personal networks. Current public health education programmes are recommended to attend to insufficient and incorrect public knowledge about precautionary actions.

# PART I

# OVERVIEW OF
# COMMUNICATION CHALLENGES
# AND BEST-PRACTICE ANALYSES

# Preparing for Effective Communications During Disasters: Lessons from a World Health Organization Quality Improvement Project

LAURA N. MEDFORD-DAVIS AND G. BOBBY KAPUR

## 1.1 BACKGROUND

During and after a disaster, effective communications must coordinate response efforts in order to limit secondary morbidity and disease [1]. Organizations must communicate early and frequently with multiple stakeholders to prevent panic and implement an orderly response plan [2]. The government and other decision makers need to know what response efforts are ongoing, and what type of further assistance is required where in order to coordinate relief. Health professionals want to know which health risks or diseases are increased in the current environment, how best to advise their patients, and how they can stay informed of emerging disease trends while working in the field. The public wants to know how to obtain assistance, what ongoing personal risks they face, and how they can protect themselves and their families [3]. Platforms for this type of health messaging include press releases and media interviews, Internet articles and social media, town hall forums, and frequent timely communication among responders.

**TABLE 1:** Crisis types

| Characterization | N (Percent) |
|---|---|
| Crisis length | |
| Acute | 21 (81%) |
| Chronic | 5 (19%) |
| Crisis type | |
| Natural disaster | 13 (50%) |
| Outbreak | 11 (42%) |
| Conflict | 2 (8%) |
| Deployment location | |
| Field | 10 (39%) |
| Country office | 7 (27%) |
| Field and country office | 5 (19%) |
| Regional office | 3 (11%) |
| Headquarters | 1 (4%) |
| Arrived how long after crisis started | |
| First 72 h | 3 (12%) |
| 3 days–1 week | 6 (23%) |
| 1 week–1 month | 6 (23%) |
| Greater than 1 month | 11 (42%) |

Each disaster serves as a learning opportunity for how to communicate better in the next disaster. Several retrospective studies have tried to document these lessons by determining how the public understood the messages that were communicated to them during a recent disaster [4-11]. Gaps in a disaster communication plan such as technical or complex instructions [4] can leave groups vulnerable to misunderstanding the message, while methods of dissemination [5-8] and demographics [7,9] can result in the message never reaching certain target populations. Other studies have focused on learning lessons from the groups responding to the disaster, including healthcare professionals [8,10] and US governmental agencies [11].

A large body of risk communications literature has gone beyond the piecemeal focus on each individual disaster to educate on overarching best methods of health messaging [12,13]. However disaster communications has been criticized because communications preparedness remains underdeveloped [14]. An expert Delphi study published in 2012 came to the consensus that despite all the existing literature, there is still a lack of understanding about communication, identifying communication as a top three priority area for further disaster management research [15].

## 1.2 METHODS

The primary author interviewed WHO Communications Officers who had responded to prior disasters using an open-ended survey. The primary author was employed by WHO and based in Switzerland at the time of survey administration and data review. This quality improvement project represents a non-sensitive survey approved by the WHO Communications Department Head, which was used for internal evaluation and improvement of existing WHO procedures, and as such was subject to the regulations of WHO, which does not have an IRB for internal projects.

A communications officer at WHO is responsible for developing and publishing communication and advocacy material for the organization, serving as a spokesperson for the organization, developing and implementing a strategic corporate communication plan, and supporting member countries to develop and implement communications. The communications officers work for WHO offices primarily leading daily communications activities (e.g., World Health Day campaign, release of new WHO guidelines, etc.), but in the case of a disaster may be deployed to support disaster communications in the affected area.

**TABLE 2:** Suggested communications role for WHO during a disaster response

| Communications role | N (percent) |
| --- | --- |
| Disseminate information and products of communication | 26 (100%) |
| Develop and maintain internal and external contact lists | 3 (11.5%) |
| Take meeting minutes; share information between WHO team members | 13 (50%) |
| Send daily updates to RO and HQ | 17 (65%) |
| Write situation reports | 19 (73%) |
| Develop a communications strategy | 24 (92%) |
| Media liaison | 26 (100%) |
| Draft talking points and Q&As | 17 (65%) |
| Draft press releases | 14 (54%) |
| Organize press conferences | 13 (50%) |
| Respond to media queries | 10 (38%) |
| Media monitoring | 5 (19%) |
| Advocacy and resource mobilization | 17 (65%) |
| Document the crisis response | 13 (50%) |
| Develop feature stories | 11 (42%) |
| Update the website | 9 (35%) |
| Write donor reports | 3 (11.5%) |
| Write grant proposals | 1 (4%) |
| Liaison to Ministry of Health | 13 (50%) |
| Provide technical support for government communications; give public visibility to government response efforts | 7 (27%) |
| Coordinate data and communications strategy | 6 (23%) |
| Health promotion and social mobilization | 12 (46%) |

A senior WHO employee with extensive communications and disaster experience at WHO contributed an initial list of 15 potential participants. Participants were then asked to refer other participants with disaster experience using snowball sampling methodology. A total of 31 potential participants were identified and contacted via corporate email to request their participation. Twenty-eight people responded; 2 were excluded due to scheduling conflicts and 26 were formally interviewed by phone, by video conference, or in person.

**TABLE 3:** Recommended skillset for a disaster communications expert

| Recommendations | N (percent) |
| --- | --- |
| Professional skills | |
| Managerial skills: able to lead a communications team to coordinate a communications strategy | 18 (70%) |
| Effective writing and editing skills | 15 (58%) |
| Media relations experience | 12 (46%) |
| Analytical skills: able to synthesize large volumes of technical information into concise common language | 3 (12%) |
| Technical skills | |
| Photography and videography: able to record and edit | 24 (92%) |
| Public health literacy | 12 (46%) |
| Computer proficiency | 6 (23%) |
| Working use of English and preferably the local language | 7 (27%) |
| Interpersonal skills and helpful personality traits | |
| Team player: able to work on a team with people from diverse cultural and professional backgrounds | 14 (54%) |
| Diplomatic and respectful in complex socio-cultural-political contexts | 12 (46%) |
| Remains calm under stress | 10 (38%) |
| Willing to work in hardship conditions | 10 (38%) |
| Flexible | 8 (31%) |
| Proactive | 6 (23%) |
| Able to multi-task | 6 (23%) |
| Resourceful, able to improvise | 4 (15%) |
| Able to quickly assess a rapidly evolving situation and act quickly and decisively | 4 (15%) |

In-depth interviews were conducted in English. Participants were asked a series of closed- and open-ended questions from a structured survey template about their experiences responding to disasters as communications officers on behalf of WHO (Additional file 1). Interviews lasted approximately 75-90 min. All of the interviews were digitally audio-recorded with the participants' permission. Data were entered into a Microsoft Excel spreadsheet, version 14.0.6129.5000 (Microsoft Corp., Redmond, WA, USA).

Analysis included: (1) descriptive statistical analysis to objectively characterize the incidence of different types of disaster experience; (2) a careful re-listening to the interview recording to fully understand participant's perspectives; (3) coding of the responses to each open-ended question into different thematic categories based on word repetitions and key words in context [16]; (4) extraction of data using pawing [16] to determine the most frequently reported barriers and augmenters of effective disaster communication; (5) extraction of data using pawing to determine the most commonly reported themes of disaster communications that represent transferable knowledge between different disasters. Some participants gave responses that did not fit into the key word themes of any other participants; these were recorded as new themes at a frequency of one to exhaust all possible themes. Themes were ranked in importance based on their frequency of appearance in the responses, with the addition of one single-frequency recommendation theme determined to be important based on the researchers' prior literature review of the topic and knowledge of the structure of the WHO. Results were used by the WHO Communications Department to develop new protocols for future WHO disaster response communications.

## 1.3 RESULTS

Twenty-six WHO Communication Officers from Headquarters (HQ) in Geneva, all 6 regional offices (RO), and 11 country offices (CO) participated. The majority (N=22; 85%) had experience in multiple disasters. Participants had responded to both acute and chronic disasters, defined as whether the disaster had happened less or more than 3 months prior to deployment. Most communications officers were deployed close to the disaster epicenter: to the field, to the nearest country office, or to a combination of both. Half were deployed within 3 days to 1 month after the disaster began, but just three arrived within the first 72 h after the disaster (Table 1). The disasters where they had worked included 29 disease outbreaks of 13 different diseases in 5 regions and 16 countries, 18 natural disasters of 6 different types (e.g., tsunami, earthquake, flood, etc.) in 5 regions and 15 countries, 2 technical disasters in 2 regions and 2 countries, and 10 conflicts in 3 regions and 10 countries.

**TABLE 4:** Trainings for a communications officer prior to deployment

| Recommendations | N (Percent) |
| --- | --- |
| Communications | 12 (46%) |
|   Designing a crisis communications strategy | |
|   How to manage and coordinate an emergency communications team | |
|   Presentation and media spokesperson skills | 7 (27%) |
|   Humanizing statistics for a general audience | |
|   Simulation in a rapidly evolving, high-stress environment | |
| Disaster standards and guidelines | 7 (27%) |
|   Sphere Handbook | |
|   OSHA | |
|   UN and health cluster structure | |
| Public health | 8 (31%) |
|   Epidemiology, basic statistics | |
|   Types of disasters and their health consequences | |
|   Myths and realities of health during a disaster | |
| Personal effectiveness | 6 (23%) |
|   Basic life support and first aid | |
|   Security precautions | |
|   Coping with stress | |
| IT | 3 (12%) |
|   How to use a satellite phone | |
|   Establishing phone and internet connections in remote locations | |

Qualitative responses from the communications officers resulted in a list of core communications priorities for WHO during a disaster response (Table 2), recommendations for hiring a competent communications officer who can be deployed for disaster response (Table 3), and recommendations for trainings a communications officer should receive prior to deployment (Table 4). In addition, the communications officers provided recommendations for methods to build communications capacity that could be undertaken prior to a disaster to improve preparedness (Table 5).

**TABLE 5:** Recommendations to improve communications capacity prior to a crisis

| Recommendation | N (percent) |
|---|---|
| Develop and pre-write or pre-record common public service announcements in multiple languages on questions that frequently arise during crises | 7 (26%) |
| Maintain a database of statistics for various regions and types of crisis | 2 (8%) |
| Maintain lists for all frequently affected countries and regions of the locally trusted media outlets and sources of information | 3 (12%) |
| Maintain email listservs that can be used to rapidly disseminate information to your organization's employees, international media outlet contacts, government Ministries of Health, and non-governmental organization contacts | 3 (12%) |
| Develop a global network with 24-h cross-coverage by participants from each time zone | 2 (8%) |
| Create a central electronic sharepoint where all of these materials can be accessed by communications officers around the globe when crisis strikes | 1 (4%) |

## 1.4 DISCUSSION

One hundred ninety-four member states turn to WHO for guidance and assistance in response to disasters that include not only disease outbreaks, but also natural disasters, man-made disasters, and conflicts [17]. Post-disaster communication is one area of expertise for which WHO provides support to member countries. WHO also convenes international experts to reach public consensus on priority topics, and it recently convened an expert panel on the topic of communications during disease outbreaks [18].

WHO Headquarters is subdivided into clusters that operate relatively independently [19]. Different clusters respond to different types of disasters and sometimes even to different aspects of the same disaster. For example, the Humanitarian Action in Crisis (HAC) cluster responds to natural disasters and conflicts, while the Global Alert and Response Network (GAR) responds to disease outbreaks. After the earthquake in Haiti in 2010, HAC initially responded, but GAR joined relief efforts later that year when a cholera outbreak began. In addition, WHO consists of six regions each coordinated from a RO (Figure 1) [20]. At the regional level there are also clusters, although their specific titles and functions vary from region to region. Finally, COs have large variations in the number and specialized scope of staff. Countries with larger WHO operations have larger offices, while some countries do not house an in-country office at all.

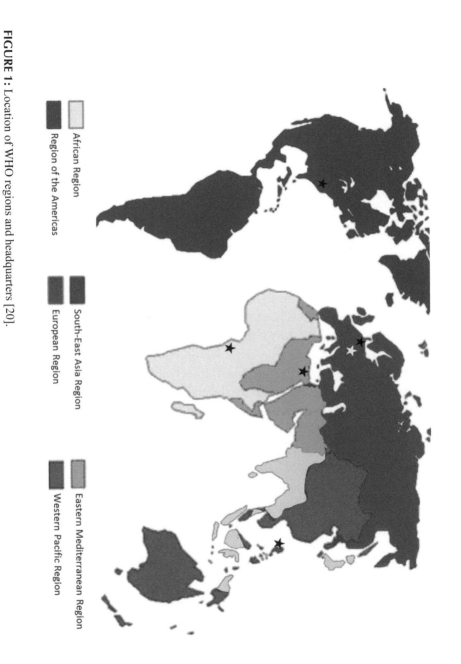

**FIGURE 1:** Location of WHO regions and headquarters [20].

A small number of communications officers working at different levels (country, regional, or headquarters) and in the different clusters are consistently deployed throughout this global network to respond to disasters. Usually the CO where the disaster occurred requests additional support from their RO or HQ if they do not have their own communications officer or if there is too much work for one officer. Each individual officer possesses vast experiential knowledge about disaster response and communications during disasters in particular. This study was organized by the Department of Communications (DCO) cluster, which leads communications at HQ. Its objective was to gather and utilize this experiential knowledge to formulate best practices for communication during a disaster that could be used to develop WHO policies and procedures, as well as to develop a training program to improve preparedness for deployment of WHO Communications Officers to disasters.

WHO's main role during a disaster is to support the local government's Ministry of Health (MoH) and to co-chair the United Nations Health Cluster along with the local MoH. In this role, WHO communications officers are responsible for sharing information about the response efforts among the different member organizations of the Health Cluster. They create and update a detailed situation report and distribute it frequently to all cluster members. The report maps which organizations are providing which health services to each affected area, where gaps still remain in services, and the joint action plan to fill those gaps. For this role, it is helpful to have the contacts at each major health cluster organization included in electronic listservs so that a communications leader can rapidly send an internal message to government partners at the Ministry of Health and to non-governmental organization partners who are participating in the response effort.

Where possible and depending on the size of an organization, additional team members can be assigned to support the communications activities of those in the field through a global network with 24-h cross-coverage from offices in other time zones. While those working in the field sleep, communications officers at a headquarters in another time zone where it is still daylight can respond to international media queries on their behalf. Current WHO practice is to hold daily teleconferences between the communications officer in the field or CO and the other communications officers supporting them from the RO and/or HQ to summarize the situation and assign the work that needs to be completed. Additional communications occur as needed throughout the day via email and/or telephone. Raw photo or video footage from the field can be emailed to the office-based staff for editing prior to further distribution.

**TABLE 6:** Examples of disaster messages to prepare in advance

|  | Storms (hurricane, tornado) | Floods (Tsunamis) | Conflicts | Disease outbreak | Chemical disaster |
|---|---|---|---|---|---|
| Dead bodies killed by natural disaster and conflict do not carry disease | X | X | X |  |  |
| Avoiding waterborne illness; sterilizing water | X | X |  | X | X |
| Basic wound care and first aid | X | X | X |  |  |
| Vaccines and immunizations | X | X | X | X |  |
| Personal protective equipment to avoid secondary injury | X | X |  | X | X |
| Power outage safety: staying warm (or cool depending on the local weather conditions) | X | X | X |  |  |
| Power outage safety: carbon monoxide poisoning | X | X | X |  |  |
| Safety around loose power lines | X | X |  |  |  |
| Identifying and avoiding gas leaks | X | X |  |  |  |
| Do not send bulk donations; wait for specific requests | X | X | X |  |  |

Perhaps the most interesting and broadly applicable finding of this study is the recommendation for how to prepare disaster communications ahead of time, which included several useful and novel methods that can be adapted by any organization. Respondents noted that similar questions arose in seemingly different disasters and suggested preparing the answers to the most common problems in advance. One example is allaying the public's fear of dead bodies spreading disease, since several experts pointed out that bodies do not pose an imminent risk when killed by a natural disaster or conflict rather than an infectious disease. Another example is a message to the international public to refrain from sending bulk donations of used goods and instead to wait for a request of which specific goods are needed and where. Additional examples include warnings about generator use to prevent carbon monoxide poisoning, and messages about safe handling of waste and how to sanitize water when plumbing has been compromised. Such public health messages could be written and recorded for television, radio, and social media in multiple languages ahead of time (Table 6).

Developing a databank of basic statistics about the local population, health status, and disaster risk for areas most frequently affected by disaster was also suggested. Pairing each statistic with a brief descriptor written in human factor terminology makes it ready for immediate use in communications. As an example of human factor terminology, in an area commonly afflicted by flooding, rather than stating that the incidence of floods is 21% per lifetime, it is better to state that one of every five persons will be affected by a flood in their lifetime.

For those regions frequently affected by particular disaster types, media surveillance should be undertaken regularly as to which sources of information the local public trusts. These sources may include a particular television network, radio station, or even a community leader or religious authority. Text messaging and/or social media can also augment the number of people reached. During a disaster, these trusted sources are the outlets that should be targeted when disseminating health messages to the public to ensure that no group misses the message. Listservs of these local media and community contacts should be created and maintained in advance of any disaster for quick dissemination of press releases and public health messages.

Another recommendation to improve future coordination within WHO was to store all of the documents mentioned above including common messages, statistics, and listservs with important contacts in a central electronic repository utilizing "cloud technology" such as Sharepoint, Google Docs, or Dropbox where they can be readily accessed and updated by all of the organization's officers working from around the globe. Other areas which were identified for improvement that are more specific to internal WHO processes included the lack of a defined on-call system for deployment and the lack of a formal briefing or debriefing process. The need to develop more formal training to expand the list of experts qualified for deployment led to a list of suggested trainings that would help prepare a communications officer for first-time deployment (Table 4).

### 1.4.1 LIMITATIONS

This is a retrospective study composed of a convenience snowball sample rather than a randomized sample of all possible participants. Because people were asked very open-ended questions without prompting, the few responses that were offered by nearly 100% of respondents likely indicate a very strong relevance, but it is difficult to draw scientific conclusions about responses given by <50% of respondents since other respondents might have agreed had they been specifically questioned on the value of these ideas. This is a preliminary data-gathering project that presents interesting ideas that should be further evaluated in a more rigorous study, ideally convening disaster communications experts from a variety of organizations.

### 1.5 CONCLUSIONS

Many communications tasks can and should be undertaken prior to a disaster to improve preparedness. Some of these tasks represent common sense, while others may be more novel. Investing time and manpower now to improve an organization's communications capacity can save time in disseminating key messages to minimize chaos and coordinate stakeholders once disaster strikes.

# REFERENCES

1. Sellnow TL, Sellnow DD, Lane DR, Littlefield RS: The value of instructional communication in crisis situations: restoring order to chaos. Risk Anal 2012, 32(4):633-643.

2. Perko T: Importance of risk communication during and after a nuclear accident. Integr Environ Assess Manag 2011, 7(3):388-392.

3. Rubin GJ, Amlot R, Page L: The London polonium incident: lessons in risk communications. Health Phys 2011, 101(5):545-550.

4. Sugerman DE, Keir JM, Dee DL, Lipman H, Waterman SH, Ginsberg M, Fishbein DB: Emergency health risk communication during the 2007 San Diego wildfires: comprehension, compliance, and recall. J Health Commun 2012, 17(6):698-712.

5. Wang CJ, Little AA, Holliman JB, NG CY, Barrero-Castillero A, Fu CM, Zuckerman B, Bauchner H: Communication of urgent public health messages to urban populations: lessons from the Massachusetts water main break. Disaster Med Public Health Prep 2011, 5(3):235-241.

6. Paek HJ, Hilyard K, Freimuth V, Barge JK, Mindlin M: Theory-based approaches to understanding public emergency preparedness: implications for effective health and risk communication. J Health Commun 2010, 15(4):428-444.

7. Rundblad G, Knapton O, Hunter PR: Communication, perception and behaviour during a natural disaster involving a 'Do Not Drink' and subsequent 'Boil Water' notice: a postal questionnaire study. BMC Public Health 2010, 10:641.

8. Zhou H, Shi L, Mao Y, Tang J, Zeng Y: Diffusion of new technology, health services and information after a crisis: a focus group study of the Sichuan "5.12" Earthquake. Int J Health Plann Manage 2012. doi:10.1002/hpm.2137

9. Taylor-Clark KA, Viswanath K, Blendon RJ: Communication inequalities during Public Health disasters: Katrina's wake. Health Commun 2010, 25(3):221-229.

10. Seidl IA, Johnson AJ, Mantel P, Aitken P: A strategy for real time improvement (RTI) in communication during the H1N1 emergency response. Aust Health Rev 2010, 34(4):493-498.

11. Miller CW, McCurley MC: Federal interagency communication strategies for addressing radiation emergencies and other public health crises. Health Phys 2011, 101(5):559-561.

12. Covello VT: Best practice in public health risk and crisis communication. J Health Commun 2003, 8(Suppl 1):5.

13. The Peter M Sandman Risk Communication Website http://www.psandman.com

14. Becker SM: Risk communication and radiological/nuclear terrorism: a strategic view. Health Phys 2011, 101(5):551-558.

15. Mackway-Jones K, Carley S: An international expert delphi study to determine research needs in major incident management. Prehosp Disaster Med 2012, 27(4):351-358.

16. Ryan GW, Bernard HR: Techniques to identify themes. Field Methods 2003, 15(1):85-109.

17. WHO - Countries http://www.who.int/countries/en/

18. World Health Organization: Outbreak communication: Best practices for communicating with the public during an outbreak. http://www.who.int/csr/resources/publications/WHO_CDS_2005_32/en/

19. WHO - its people and its offices http://www.who.int/about/structure/en/index.html

20. WHO Regional Offices http://www.who.int/about/regions/en/index.html

*There is one supplemental file that is not available in this version of the article. To view this additional information, please use the citation on the first page of this chapter.*

# CHAPTER 2

# Information Dissemination Analysis of Different Media towards the Application for Disaster Pre-Warning

NAN ZHANG, HONG HUANG , BONI SU, JINLONG ZHAO, AND BO ZHANG

## 2.1 INTRODUCTION

Natural and man-made disasters seriously threaten human life and property. A more reliable and efficient pre-warning information dissemination system could improve public emergency responses, and enable people to evacuate and take protective measures before and during a disaster [1]. In the Indian Coast, for example, more than one hundred people could be saved because a scientist, using his cell phone, managed to warn about an imminent serious tsunami caused by an 8.7 magnitude earthquake [2]. Moreover, victims easily survived in an effective and efficient way if they have more detailed information [3]. Therefore, the research on information dissemination is of great theoretical and practical value. This paper focuses on information dissemination relating to disaster pre-warning; it does not concern itself with research subjects such as economic-geographic development [4].

Information media can be divided into social and traditional media. Social media including short messages, microblogs, and news portals, because of their high impact and coverage ratio made possible by developments in information technology [5]–[6], are becoming increasingly popular and therefore critical tools of information dissemination [7]. For instance, they can enhance the decision-making process since more data is provided than it is the case with traditional media [8]. However, some traditional media, including cell phones, television, and oral communication, also play important roles in information dissemination. In some serious disaster cases, when all electronic networks are paralyzed, traditional media such as oral communication, albeit slower, can still be employed [9].

The different characteristics of each information dissemination medium have been studied in different fields. Sattler found that an effective message could be issued by a credible source and transmitted in a quick and stable way through warning message transmission by cell phone and e-mail [10]. Wei analyzed the optimal combination of television broadcasting sequences which ensured the best information dissemination to television viewers [11]. Whittaker researched information management of emails and found habits of email users in information management [12].

Furthermore, there are some studies that looked at information dissemination media in disasters and emergencies. Odeny found that short message services could improve the attendance at post-operative clinic visits after adult male circumcision for HIV prevention [13]. Zhang established that different information media, including cell phones, television and emails, have different information dissemination characteristics in disaster's pre-warning [14]. Shim used wireless TV to improve disaster management and to provide communications for respondents during a natural or man-made disaster [15]. Katada created a simulation model and built a general-purpose system for the efficient study of the dissemination of information concerning disasters and scenarios of information transmission [16]. Zhang used sound trucks to transmit information in an optimal path in the case of network paralysis caused by a serious disaster [17].

Analysis of recent studies reveals that most works focus on a single medium, but neglect detailed comparisons of different media. However, in actual situations, a single information medium cannot ensure the dissemination of large amounts of information. Therefore, each medium should be analyzed and compared to other media to improve overall efficiency of information dissemination.

In this study, information dissemination models of six information media, including short message service (SMS), microblogs, news portals, cell phones, television, and oral communication were developed and the information dissemination characteristics were studied and compared. The capabilities and mechanisms of these information dissemination media were also studied concerning people of different ages, genders and residential areas. The developed models were applied to the city of Beijing. Based on the simulation and effectiveness analysis of all information media, optimized plans and suggestions were put forward to improve the effectiveness of information dissemination during emergencies. The results of this research are useful in the development of a comprehensive information dissemination system to transmit emergency information in an effective way.

## 2.2 METHOD

In this study we use the following evaluation indices to compare the different information dissemination characteristics: total coverage of information reception, the time it takes for half of the population to believe the information, frequency of media usage and time, the degree of trust, total cost, and delay time. Among these indices, the degree of trust and frequency of media usage and time can be directly obtained through questionnaires and the total cost can be obtained from the internet: Taobao (the most famous electronic mall in China; URL: www.taobao.com). Another three indices need to be calculated by the computational simulation based on information dissemination models. The models are established considering special information dissemination characteristics such as dissemination mechanisms and individual preference for different media. Some required parameters in the models such as average forwarding times were also collected by questionnaires which were distributed on site. The simulation allows the calculation of the total coverage of information reception, the time it takes for half of the population to believe the information and the delay time. All the parameters mentioned above are obtained from questionnaires and the internet. Different information dissemination models are described below:

## 2.2.1 BASIC PARAMETERS IN INFORMATION DISSEMINATION

### 2.2.1.1 BRIEF INTRODUCTION OF BASIC PARAMETERS

In the information dissemination process effective information dissemination probability and delay time are two important factors. Effective information dissemination probability expresses the probability of a recipient receiving and believing the information after a message is distributed from an information source. Delay time is the time difference between information reception by media and by recipients.

Effective information dissemination probability and delay time are related to service usage and the degree of trust which reflects the probability that people believe the media. For service usage, media usage frequency, media coverage ratio, and forwarding number are thought to be three important components. To obtain the above data, a questionnaire is considered to be a useful tool.

### 2.2.1.2 QUESTIONNAIRES

In this study 370 questionnaires were filled out (350 of them were available) in May and June, 2013. In the period of disaster pre-warning, individual differences are very obvious in information acquisition and dissemination. The questionnaires include six multiple-choice questions and twenty-nine fill-in questions. We collected the following data: age, gender, educational background, vocation, media usage number ($N_{use}$) and times per day ($T_{use}$), information forwarding number ($n_{fw}$) and probability ($p_{fw}$), and the degree of trust of each of the six information media. All respondents were between the ages of 10 and 80. About half of questionnaires derived from urban areas while the rest were filled out in rural areas.

The questionnaires allowed a detailed analysis of the degree of trust and service usage for short messages, microblogs, news portals, cell phones, television and oral communication. The data are presented in Table.1

**TABLE 1:** Comparison of the degree of trust and service condition of six media.

|  | The degree of trust (%) | Media coverage (%) | Usage frequency (times/day) or (minutes/day) | Average forward-ing number (persons) |
|---|---|---|---|---|
| SMS | 41.3 | 97.2 | >10 times | 11.8 |
| Microblog | 48.3 | 66.5 | 7.5 times | 132 |
| News portal | 57.7 | 85.0 | 84.5 min | 0 |
| Cell phone | 43.3 | 99.0 | >10 times | 9.7 |
| Television | 79.0 | 91.7 | 99.9 min | 0 |
| Oral | 38.91 | 100.0 |  | 3.9 |

The degree of trust in an information medium reflects its importance, and is crucial in information dissemination [18]. The questionnaires suggest that television, news portals, and microblogs have the three highest degrees of trust (79.0%, 57.7%, and 48.3% respectively); they are followed by cell phones (43.3%), short messages (41.3%) and oral communication (38.91%). Television and news portals have the highest degrees of trust among the six media because these two media are managed by the government.

Media coverage ratio determines whether the media could be used in information dissemination for pre-warning of a disaster. Oral communication, cell phones, and short messages as the top three (100%, 99%, and 97% respectively) had the top three coverage ratios; reflecting our dependence on these media in our daily lives. Microblogs rank at the bottom of the six media types (66%) which is due to personal preference. The analysis of the data on media coverage ratios reveals that the usage coverage is very high although the degree of trust of some media is low.

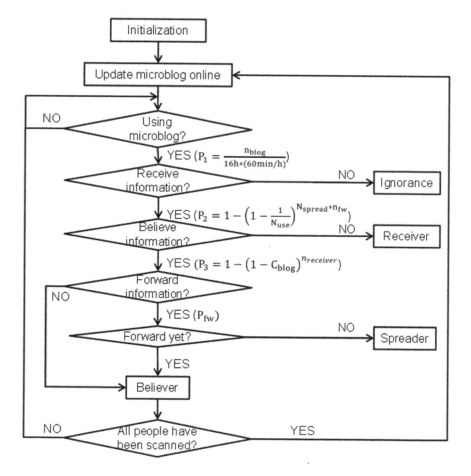

**FIGURE 1:** Microblog information dissemination process.

The frequency of media usage is an important factor, reflects the popularity of the respective medium, and determines the difficulty of information acquisition. Oral communication is the most frequently used medium in our daily lives. Cell phone and short messaging forms of communication come second as they are used more than 10 times per day. Television and news portals as mass media have lower usage numbers but longer watching times. Microblogs are very popular as well (7.5 usage times per day).

Forwarding number indicates the speed of information dissemination from person to person. Strong forwarding capability could lead to rapid information acquisition [19]. Microblogs had the highest average forwarding number (132); followed by short messaging (11.8), cell phone (9.7) and oral communication (3.9). However, television and news portals are one way media transmitting information from a public organization to a wide audience, and cannot be used for forwarding information person to person.

The detailed results of effective information dissemination probability and delay time are introduced and calculated below.

## 2.2.2 MODEL ESTABLISHMENT

The models of six typical information media including short messages, microblogs, news portals, cell phones, television and oral communication could be divided into three types. The first type was based on person to person without geographical limitation, including short messages and cell phones, the initial stage of which may present an exponential growth in recipients. The second type was based on person to person with geographical limitation such as oral communication where information can be disseminated only within a limited distance. In addition, television and news portals can transmit information from a mass media to person with a logarithmic growth in recipients which were defined as the third type. In order to establish the information dissemination model of the media, we assigned three statuses to the people who are facing the disaster: "ignorance", "receiver", and "believer". "Ignorance" is assigned to people who have not received information about the disaster; "receiver" refers to people who get the information but do not believe it; "believer" designates people who have received the information and believed it.

In this study the information dissemination models of microblogs, oral communication and television were taken as the representative media to analyze. The effective information dissemination probability and delay time of each information medium were obtained through process analysis and data calculation.

## 2.2.2.1 MICROBLOG

Due to fast speed and convenient operation in information dissemination, microblogs have become increasingly popular in recent years. Fig. 1 shows the information dissemination process of a microblog and the probability of a person being assigned to the status of ignorance, receiver or believer. In Fig. 1 $P_{1(b)}$ expresses the probability of microblog users using a microblog per minute, and $n_{blog}$ is the average usage number of microblog users (16 hours are the effective time per day). $P_{2(b)}$ is the probability of ignorant users receiving information and $N_{use}$ is the number of people using a microblog. $N_{sp(b)}$ is the number of spreaders $N_{sp(b)} = N_{bel(b)} * P_{fw(b)}$, $N_{bel(b)}$ is the number of information believers and $n_{fw(b)}$ is the average number of microblog fans (The parameter nblog, $N_{use(b)}$, $n_{fw(b)}$ and $p_{fw(b)}$ can be directly obtained from questionnaires). $P_{3(b)}$ is the probability of that those people who received information believe the same; it is related to the degree of trust of the microblog and received information numbers in the time interval (nrec(b) can be obtained by computational simulation). The detailed simulation process is listed below:

1.  Set all the parameters which are obtained from questionnaires to target people and create 5 initiative believers which are regarded as the information sources forwarding the information through microblog.
2.  Search for the target people who have qualification to forward microblogs in this step. These target people should follow four conditions:
    - The person is using microblog at this step

- The person is the information believer
- The person wants to forward the microblog
- The person hasn't forward the microblog yet

3. Update all the microblog online users.
4. The microblog user i checks the blog.

With the increase of received information number and the degree of trust, the probability will also rise. $P_{fw(b)}$ is the average forwarding probability from believers to spreaders.

Based on Fig. 1, the effective information dissemination probability Pblog is expressed by Equation 1.

$$
\begin{aligned}
P_{blog} &= P_{1(b)} \cdot P_{2(b)} \cdot P_{3(b)} \\
&= \frac{n_{blog}}{16 \cdot 60min} \left( 1 - \left( 1 - \frac{1}{N_{use(b)}} \right) N_{sp(b)} \cdot n_{fw(b)} \right) \\
&\quad \cdot \left( 1 - (1 - C_{blog})^{n_{rec(b)}} \right)
\end{aligned}
\tag{1}
$$

Fig. 2 shows the calculation of delay time of a microblog $T_{blog}$. Users are hypothesized not to check microblogs at night (midnight to 8 a.m.). Based on the usage number of microblogs per day, people check microblogs n times between 8 a.m. to midnight with the same interval $16/(n+1)$. In Fig. 2 period 1 is the checking time and period 2 is the rest time without checking microblogs.

**Microblog (received information at period 1)**

$$
T_{1,blog}(t_1, t_2) = P_{1,blog} \int_{t_1}^{t_2} f_{1,blog}(t) \cdot p_{1,blog}(dt)
\tag{2}
$$

Here $T_{1,blog}$ is the total delay time, $P_{1,blog}$ denotes the proportion of period 1 to 24 hours; $f_{1,blog}$ is the function of delay time; $P_{1,blog}$ represents the time weight of dt.

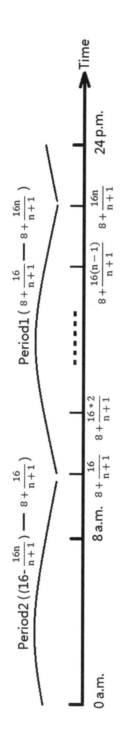

**FIGURE 2:** Microblog delay time calculation

$$T_{1,blog}(n) = \frac{\frac{16}{n+1}(n-1)}{24} \int_0^{\frac{16}{n+1}} \left(\frac{16}{n+1} - t\right) \cdot \frac{dt}{\frac{16}{n+1}} = \frac{2(n-1)}{3(n+1)} \cdot \frac{1}{2} \cdot \left(\frac{16}{(n+1)}\right)$$

$$= \frac{16(n-1)^2}{3(n+1)^2}$$

(3)

**Microblog (received information at period 2)**

$$T_{2,blog}(t_3, t_4) = P_{2,blog} \int_{t_3}^{t_4} f_{2,blog}(t) \cdot p_{2,blog}(dt)$$

(4)

where $T_{2,blog}$ is the total delay time, $P_{1,blog}$ is the proportion of period 2 to 24 hours; $f_{2,blog}$ shows the function of delay time; $P_{2,blog}(dt)$ expresses the time weight of $dt$

$$T_{2,blog}(n) = \frac{n+5}{3(n+1)} \int_0^{8+2 \cdot \frac{16}{n+1}} \left(8 + 2 \cdot \frac{16}{n+1} - t\right) \cdot \frac{dt}{8 + 2 \cdot \frac{16}{n+1}} = \frac{4(n+5)^2}{3(n+1)^2}$$

(5)

$$T_{blog}(n) = T_{1,blog}(n) + T_{2,blog}(n) = \frac{16(n-1)}{3(n+1)^2} + \frac{4(n+5)^2}{3(n+1)^2} = \frac{4((n+1)^2 - 28)}{3(n+1)^2}$$

(6)

$$T_{blog}(n) = \begin{cases} \dfrac{12}{n} & n < 1 \\[2mm] \dfrac{4((n+7)^2 - 28)}{3(n+1)^2} & n \geq 1 \end{cases}$$

(7)

If the usage frequency is less than 1 ($n<1$), i.e., the microblog user will not check the microblog every day, the average delay time is easy to calculate. Equation 7 is the comprehensive calculation of average delay time of microblog $T_{blog}$ where n is the usage number of the microblogs per day.

Effective information dissemination probability can be obtained through the same analysis since the information dissemination models of short messaging and cell phones are very similar to that of a microblog. The delay time for short messaging was directly obtained through questionnaires. The delay time of cell phones was acquired by conducting 150 calling experiments covering different situations, including answering the phone, busy line, powering off, and hanging up. The models for cell phones and short messages are given in the Appendix A and B of Appendix S1 respectively (information dissemination characteristics curves are shown in Fig. S1 and Fig. S2).


## 2.2.2.2 ORAL COMMUNICATION.

Oral communication is a very universal and flexible information dissemination form. However, the distance over which information can be transmitted is very limited. Because of this limitation, population density is the most important influencing factor in information dissemination. Beijing's population density decreases from the center to the periphery in concentric circles. Fig. 3 illustrates this population distribution pattern by dividing Beijing into 16 annular regions. In the urban areas depicted by the center annular region, the population density is 23000 persons/km$^2$, while the outermost annular region has a population density of just 200 persons/km2 (All data were taken from the 2010 Beijing census.). In addition, the speed of information dissemination will decrease as the distance from the central area increases.

An over 100 times difference in population density among different areas leads to an obvious difference in information dissemination speed between urban areas and rural areas. Considering that the positioning of information sources will strongly influence information dissemination, the Monte Carlo method was used to simulate the information dissemination process. It was calculated that the information believers would notify on average 3.87 target people within a range of 90 m. seventy-nine percent of target people would be notified within the distance of 30 m, 14.6% in the range between 30–60 m, and 6.4% within a greater distance [20]. Therefore, the simulation grid was set to be 30 m*30 m and the Beijing area was divided into more than 20 million grids. The dissemination distance and the number of notified people were then obtained. The information dissemination time in one grid was set to one minute, i.e., all people in this grid can obtain within one minute any information disseminated by sources located in the same grid. The effective information dissemination probability, which is the product of probability of information reception, degree of trust, and average delay time, can be obtained through computational calculation.

## 2.2.2.3 TELEVISION.

Television is a mass medium with strong influence and high degree of trust that transmits information from medium to person using images and sound. In this study the television-watching period was divided into 8 phases with 3 hour intervals. Fig. 4 shows the television watching time at different time periods based, on questionnaires. The average time of TV watching peaked at 73 minutes after 6 p.m. which indicates that the majority of people choose to watch TV in the evening. This means that television may be a very good choice for disaster information dissemination during the evening.

Fig. 5 shows the information dissemination process of TV. The information is assumed to be broadcast once every hour. Among the processes, $P_{1,TV}$ is the ratio of watching TV in each time period. $P_{2,TV}$ expresses the probability of a TV watcher getting the information from a TV station. A person should get the information at least once during a 60 minute period. $P_{2,TV}$ is therefore a piecewise function related to the duration of watching time $t_i$. Finally, the probability that television viewers believe the information $P_{3,TV}$ is calculated through the degree of trust of TV (CTV) and receiving times of information. In summary, the effective information dissemination probability P, is calculated by Equation 8.

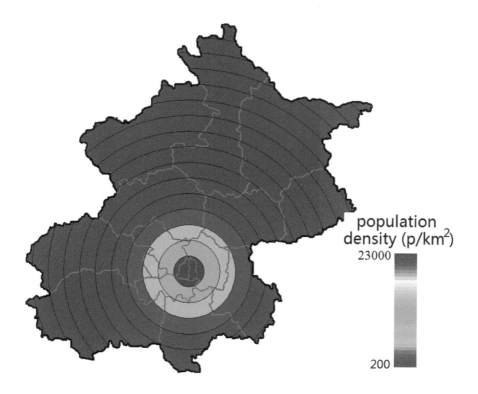

**FIGURE 3:** The approximate population distribution map of Beijing.

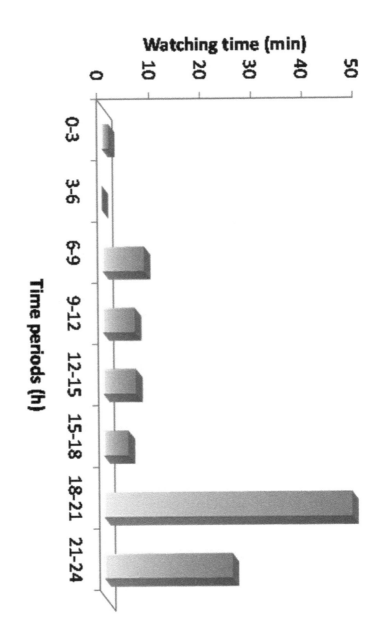

**FIGURE 4:** Television watching time distribution.

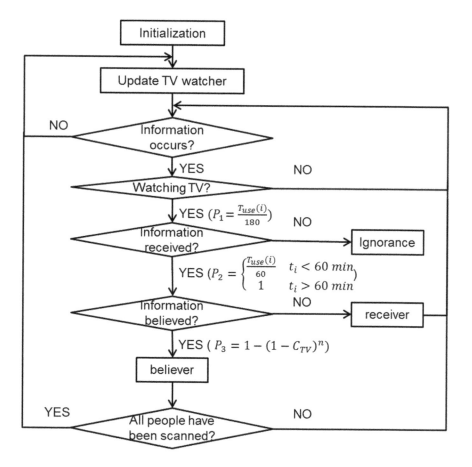

**FIGURE 5:** Television information dissemination process.

$$P_{TV} = P_{1,TV} \cdot P_{2,TV} \cdot P_{3,TV} = \begin{cases} \dfrac{T_{use}(i)}{180} \cdot \dfrac{T_{use}(i)}{60} \cdot (1 - (1 - C_{TV})^n) & t_i < 60\ min \\[3mm] \dfrac{T_{use}(i)}{180} \cdot (1 - (1 - C_{TV})^n) & t_i > 60\ min \end{cases}$$

$$(8)$$

In contrast to a microblog, watching television is a continuous activity. In Fig. 6, the shaded color expresses the continuing watching time periods. For example, $t_1$ shows that the watcher watched TV $t_1$ minutes between midnight and 3 a.m. When an information source is broadcast during period 1, the average delay time is calculated based on Equation 9.

$$T_{1,TV}(t_2, t_2) = P_{1,TV} \int_{t1}^{t2} f_{1,TV}(t) \cdot p_{1,TV}(dt)$$

$$(9)$$

where $T_{1,TV}$ expresses the delay time; $P_{1,TV}$ denotes the proportion of a 24 hour period; $f_{1,TV}(x)$ is a function of delay time; $P_{1,TV}(dt)$ represents the time weight of dt. The comprehensive function is calculated by Equation 10 considering different delay times from period 1 to period 8.

$$T_{TV} = \frac{1}{48} \left[ \sum_{i=2}^{8} \left( \frac{t(n-1)}{2} + \frac{t(n)}{2} - 3 \right)^2 + \left( \frac{t_1}{2} + \frac{t_8}{2} - 3 \right)^2 \right]$$

$$(10)$$

The television model could also be used to simulate the dissemination of information by a news portal because the information dissemination mechanism of a news portal is similar to that of television. The model of a news portal is given in the Appendix C in Appendix S1 (the information dissemination characteristics curve is shown in Fig. S3).

**FIGURE 6:** Television delay time calculation.

## 2.3 RESULTS

### *2.3.1 CAPABILITY ANALYSIS*
### *OF INFORMATION DISSEMINATION*

Simulations were performed concerning all the models mentioned above; and different curves were drawn to judge their capability to disseminate information, taking into account typical influencing factors such as age, gender, and residential area. In this study the information dissemination capability is reflected by the number of information believers within a fixed time period. Since the majority of children and elders acquire information from their families, the sample size of this population is small. Thus, we have set the age range from 16 to 55. According to census data [21], there are about 25 million people in Beijing. Using all the data from the simulations, detailed results of information dissemination are analyzed below:

**Information media 1: short messages**
Fig. 7 shows the information dissemination of short messaging with different influencing factors. The curves indicate that short messages can be sent very rapidly. Statistical data analysis reveals that the information dissemination of SMS accords with equation 11.

$$N_{SMS}(t) = \frac{1}{6.11 \times 10^{-8} + 0.0002609 \times e^{-t/7.663}} \tag{11}$$

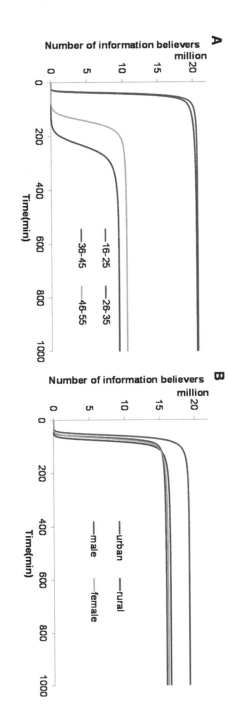
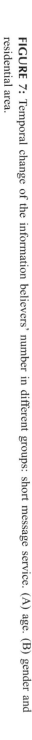

**FIGURE 7:** Temporal change of the information believers' number in different groups: short message service. (A) age. (B) gender and residential area.

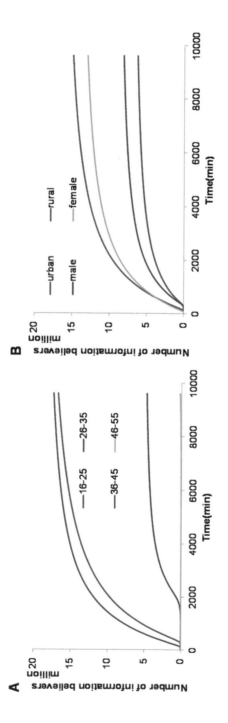

**FIGURE 8:** Temporal change of the information believers' number in different groups: microblog. (A) age. (B) gender and residential area.

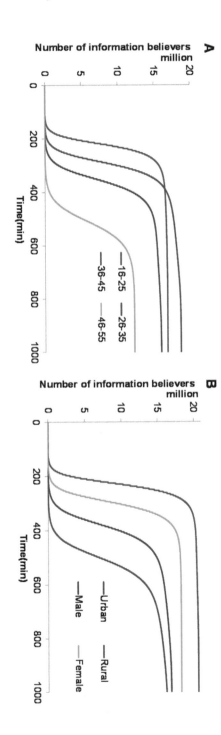

**FIGURE 9:** Temporal change of the information believers' number in different groups: cell phone. (A) age. (B) gender and residential area.

In eq. 11, t is the time for information dissemination and $N_{SMS}(t)$ is the total number of information believers. This curve follow the logistic distribution which $R^2=0.9963$.

Fig. 7 (A) discloses that the capability of disseminating information of the younger group (16–35) is much greater than that of the middle-aged group (36–55). The delay time and usage time are two key factors that explain the difference between various age groups. According to Fig. 7 (B), about 18 million people will receive and believe the information within five hours of information dissemination in the urban area. Fig. 7 (B) also illustrates that the efficiency of information dissemination via short message relies more on the distribution of residential while the impact of gender can be ignored. It can be concluded that increasing short message usage frequency and usage time of people living in rural areas would greatly improve total information dissemination efficiency.

**Information media 2: microblogs**

Fig. 8 demonstrates the information dissemination of a microblog which obeys logarithmic growth. Information source can be transmitted in a short time because there are many microblog fans. Furthermore, the number of people who believe information just reaches about 11 million because of a low degree of trust and low usage. In Fig. 8 (A) we see that the information dissemination effectiveness is low in the group aged 36–55. In contrast, the younger group shows a strong capability in information dissemination. Fig. 8 (B) illustrates that the capability of information dissemination in the urban and female groups is stronger than that in the rural and male group.

**Information media 3: cell phone**

Cell phones are the most common information dissemination media used in our daily lives. Fig. 9 reveals that the information dissemination curves of cell phones also fit a logistic distribution with a slow initial dissemination speed. According to our statistical data analysis, the information dissemination of cell phone accords with equation 12.

$$N_{phone}(t) = \frac{1}{6.075\times10^{-8} + 0.0001548\times e^{-t/34.06}}$$

(12)

where t is the time for information dissemination and $N_{phone}(t)$ is the total number of information believers. This curve follow the logistic distribution which $R^2=0.9987$.

Fig. 9 shows that more than 10 million people can be informed via cell phone communication within 6 hours after the curves abruptly became flat due to busy lines and powering off of cell phones. Fig. 9 (A) demonstrates that cell phone usage by young people (16–35) is obviously higher than that of middle-aged people (36–55). Fig. 9 (B) shows that after about 16 hours the final value reached 16.8 million, while the rest 8.2 million people had not changed into information believers because of the low degree of trust in cell phones and the usage ratio of rural areas. The unusual continuous increase should be attributed to the long communication time periods via cell phones (about three hours). It also can be seen that females have a higher capability of information dissemination by cell phone than males. In addition, inhabitants in urban areas use cell phones frequently, which means this medium has a better information dissemination capability there than in rural areas immediately before a disaster situation.

**Information media 4: Oral communication**

Fig. 10 shows that an increase in the degree of trust and forwarding number results in an increase of both the growth rate and the final number of information believers. The curves were drawn under different conditions, including different residential areas, forwarding people numbers, and degrees of trust. However, because of the geographical limitation of information dissemination via oral communication, continued increase of forwarding numbers did not result in a significant improvement. A comparison of the black to the brown line shows that, consistent with the law of population density distribution, the speed of information dissemination in urban areas is much higher than in rural areas. Considering that the position of an information source is the main factor determining the speed of information dissemination via oral communication, the Monte Carlo method was employed to improve the accuracy of results and to avoid the uncertainty caused by different information distribution sources. In this case the simulation time is set to 100.

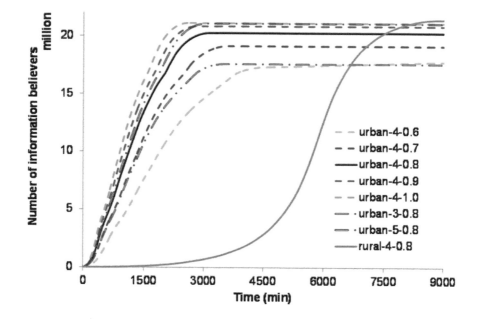

**FIGURE 10:** Temporal change of the information believers' number: oral communication.

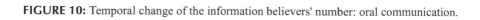

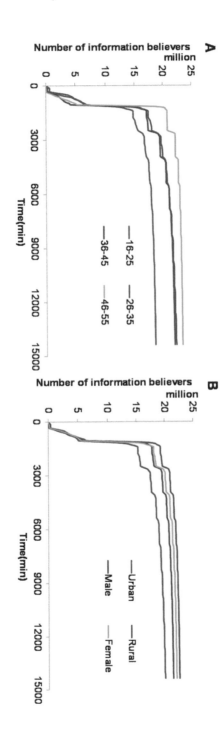

**FIGURE 11:** Temporal change of the information believers' number in different groups: television. (A) age. (B) gender and residential area.

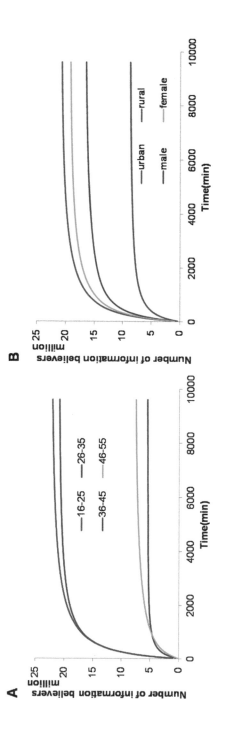

FIGURE 12: Temporal change of the information believers' number in different groups: news portal. (A) age. (B) gender and residential area.

**Information media 5: Television**
Fig. 11 shows the information dissemination by television with different influencing factors. We can conclude that the speed of information dissemination of TV is strongly related to particular time periods: A large number of people are accustomed to watching TV between 6 p.m. and midnight; at other times the speed of information dissemination is more limited. According to the curves of information dissemination, in the first day (1440 min), about 17 million people received the information, and over the following few days the slope of the curve declined. Finally, after ten days, about 22 million people would have been informed via TV because of the high degree of trust. As shown in Fig. 11 (A), the length of time watching TV increases with increasing age, and the speed of information acquisition via TV is faster. Fig. 11 (B) shows that the capability of information dissemination of television in rural areas is, in contrast to all the other five media, stronger than in urban areas. In addition, the effect of gender is very small. Furthermore, the very high information coverage leads to the dominance of TV with regard to information dissemination.

**Information media 6: News portal**
The information dissemination of a news portal with three influencing factors is shown in Fig. 12. Statistical data analysis shows that the information dissemination of news portal accords with equation 13.

$$N_{portal}(t) = -1.531 \times 10^7 e^{-0.001618t} + 1.705 \times 10^7 \qquad (13)$$

where t is the time for information dissemination and $N_{portal}(t)$ is the total number of information believers. This curve follow the logistic distribution which $R^2 = 0.9587$.

Fig. 12 (A) demonstrates that age is the most important influencing factor. The fact that information acquisition of the younger group (16–35) is much greater than that of the middle-aged group (36–55) shows that information on news portals can be quickly disseminated among young people. Fig. 12 (B) shows that, considering the influencing factors of gender and residential area, a news portal is very fast at disseminating information, potentially reaching 15 million people in just 1700 minutes. However, due to the lower degree of trust, the final number of information believers reached only 17.8 million.

The analysis of the six media under study increases our understanding of different information characteristics. When a serious disaster is approaching, a single information medium cannot manage the dissemination of a large amount of information. A combination of several information dissemination media which is tailored to the specific situation can increase the efficiency of information dissemination and provide people with more time and more accurate information to be informed and make better decisions. Furthermore, governments can make scientific and correct decisions to transmit information, based on different criteria such as information source and characteristics of disaster carriers.

## 2.3.2 COMPREHENSIVE ASSESSMENT OF EACH INFORMATION DISSEMINATION MECHANISM

Fig. 13 shows the change in the number of information believers over time when using short messages, microblogs, cell phones, television, news portals, and oral communication. In the initial 30 minutes, the news portal is the fastest regarding information dissemination because a large number of users can receive the information at the same time. Between 30 and 500 minutes after information dissemination short messages rank first (ignoring the maximum load carrying ability of the base station). The speed of information dissemination can reach exponential growth in the initial period since messages are transmitted from person to person in a short time. After a period of about 100 minutes, the number of information believers will reach a constant value of 16 million. Cell phones have a lower speed of information dissemination than short message services because information cannot be forwarded to many people in a short time. Fig. 13 shows a logistic curve and illustrates that cell phones increased the number of information believers to 16 million within 720 minutes. Television plays an important role in the evening when the majority of people are watching TV at home. With the highest degree of trust and coverage ratio, TV can inform as many people as possible. The information dissemination ability of a microblog is not high due to a lower coverage ratio and degree of trust. It can be used as an auxiliary tool in information dissemination. Oral communication, albeit slow, is a very important information dissemination medium in disaster situations, particularly in the case of network paralysis. A combination of different information media will improve the effectiveness and speed of information dissemination.

In this paper six information media were studied. Six indices were established to evaluate the comprehensive capability of each medium regarding information dissemination: total coverage of information reception (TCIR); the time it takes for half of the population to believe the information (THB); frequency of media usage and time (FMU); the degree of trust (TD); total cost (TC); and delay time (DT).

TCIR is defined as the ratio of the number of people who received the information to the total number of people over a long enough period. THB is the time at which half of the people received and believed the information, and it represents the speed of information dissemination during the initial time. TCIR and THB can be calculated using the model process mentioned above. FMU indicates the popularity of the media. Information from official information media has a high degree of trust. The data for these two indices can be directly obtained from questionnaires. The total cost of each information medium was calculated through a price investigation on Taobao which has more than 70% of electronic commerce market share in China [22]. The delay time of the six information media are calculated by the equations mentioned above.

The final scores of the six media are computed using a Min-Max Normalization; they are listed in Table.2. Six indices are classified into two categories. One is positive (+) (capability of information dissemination increases when the value of the index increases), the other is negative (−) (the value is subtracted by 1). According to these six indices, the comprehensive expression of each information medium is reflected in the radar graph shown in Fig. 14.

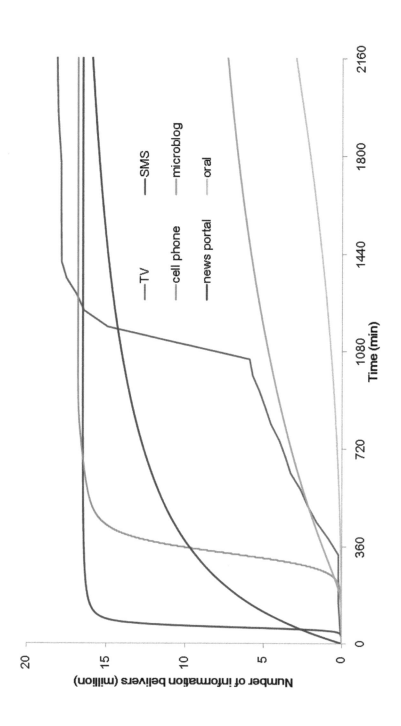

**FIGURE 13:** Comprehensive information dissemination comparison of six media.

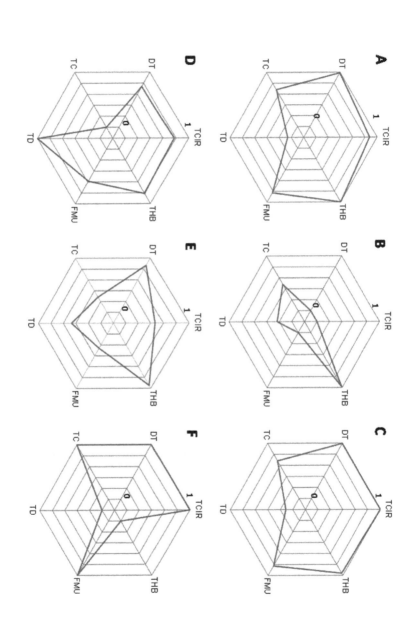

**FIGURE 14:** Radar graphs of comprehensive information dissemination assessment of each media. (A) Short message service; (B) Microblog; (C) Cell phone; (D) Television; (E) News portal; (F) Oral communication.

**TABLE 2:** Value of six indices of different information media.

|       |     | SMS   | Microblog | Cell phone | Television | News portal | Oral  |
|-------|-----|-------|-----------|------------|------------|-------------|-------|
| TCIR  | (+) | 0.879 | 0         | 1.000      | 0.773      | 0.472       | 1.000 |
| THB   | (−) | 1.000 | 0.986     | 0.961      | 0.814      | 0.947       | 0     |
| FMU   | (+) | 0.826 | 0         | 0.826      | 0.583      | 0.261       | 1.000 |
| TD    | (+) | 0.059 | 0.235     | 0.110      | 1.000      | 0.468       | 0     |
| TC    | (−) | 0.682 | 0.482     | 0.681      | 0          | 0.283       | 1.000 |
| DT    | (−) | 0.990 | 0         | 0.994      | 0.737      | 0.867       | 1.000 |

The radar graphs express the information dissemination capability of the six media and the comprehensive characteristics directly. Data analysis reveals that short messages, cell phones, and TV have a higher comprehensive information dissemination capability. Short messages and cell phones have a shorter delay time and higher information coverage ratio as well as information dissemination speed, but the degree of trust in them is lower. Television has the highest degree of trust but longer delay time. Microblogs, which have a very long delay time and moderate degrees of trust and information coverage ratio, have a fast initial information dissemination speed. News portals, as a very popular network media, are a very fast method of information dissemination, particularly during the early periods. Oral communication is also a very important information dissemination medium (no cost, ease of use), especially in high population density areas. Different lengths of pre-warning times allow different choices of information dissemination media. For instance, if the pre-warning time is limited, short messages and news portals should be used. Ultimately, the combination of different media can improve the efficiency of information dissemination. The results above can be useful in making an emergency plan that ensures the safety of lives and properties during a disaster.

## 2.3.3 INFORMATION MEDIA IN DISASTER PRE-WARNING

Developing information dissemination technology and understanding the mechanisms of each information medium are crucial for disaster pre-warning and management. Tailored to the specific disaster situation, government and victims can use different information dissemination strategies. Cell phones, SMS, microblogs, news portals, and TV usually play the most important role in some conventional disaster pre-warning such as rainstorm and frost because they feature a higher information dissemination effectiveness. However, when a serious earthquake strikes, the majority of networking and station bases will paralyze and the majority of electronic network media cannot be used. Here, oral communication will disseminate emergency information with few words or sentences. A large number of victims would try to notify all the people around them. Our analysis of oral communication mentioned above suggests that information sources positioning strongly determined the effectiveness of information dissemination. Governments can set the optimal source position to improve the information dissemination speed; they also can assess the spreading time through the analysis introduced above to help improve disaster management and save more lives. Data analysis also revealed that TV has a higher degree of trust and that it also has a higher information dissemination effectiveness in the evening. Governments should put their attention to TV rather than microblog or news portal to spread the warning information if a serious disaster occurs in the evening. Generally speaking, by combining different information media characteristics governments can improve disaster pre-warning and reduce casualties and damage to properties in an effective way, and victims can acquire more information to make informed decisions. Summing up, there is a need to analyze information dissemination characteristics of different media to ensure that warning information can be spread to every person with short delay times in a reliable manner.

## 2.4 CONCLUSIONS

In this study models of six information dissemination media, including short messages, microblogs, cell phones, television, news portals, and oral communication, were established. The capabilities of each medium to disseminate information were assessed, using data obtained from the dissemination models, statistical data, and questionnaires collected in Beijing. Based on the information dissemination capability analysis and taking into consideration factors such as age, gender, and residential area, different characteristics of the six media were summarized. Our analysis shows that SMSs have the highest speed while cell phones can disseminate more detailed information because verbal communication allows better explanation of complex situations. People's habits suggest the employment of television be emphasized in the evening.

In case of serious disasters such as earthquakes, electronic networks are prone to paralyze and oral communication will play an important role to disseminate information in a reliable manner. To directly compare and analyze different aspects of the information dissemination capabilities of the six media radar graphs considering six indices were drawn. Short message services and cell phones have more comprehensive information dissemination capabilities than other information media but they have lower degrees of trust. Television is also a good information dissemination medium; it has a higher information coverage and the highest degree of trust. Compared to other information media, oral communication is not outstanding in information dissemination speed; however, it possesses convenience. News portals and microblogs can be used as auxiliary tools, but their information coverage is not very large. Each of the six media has different strength and limitations; therefore, to help improve dissemination of information, reduce losses, and ensure the safety of disaster carriers, their combination should be tailored to the specific disaster situation. The models and simulation methods can be applied to many other regions.

In future works, more ways of information dissemination and more influencing factors will be considered, including the maximum information carrying capacity and the vulnerability of each medium in a disaster. An integrated system covering all recommendable combinations of media will be established to disseminate emergency information timely and accurately under various circumstances.

## REFERENCES

1. Basher R (2006) Global early warning systems for natural hazards: systematic and people-centred. Philos Trans R Soc A-Math Phys Eng Sci 364(1845): 2167–2182. doi: 10.1098/rsta.2006.1819

2.  Chenglan B (2005) Tsunami Disaster and Its Pre-warning System. Recent Dev World Seismol 1: 14–18.

3.  Preis T, Moat HS, Bishop SR, Treleaven P, Stanley HE (2013) Quantifying the digital traces of Hurricane Sandy on Flickr. Sci Rep 1–3.

4.  Li Q, Yang T, Zhao E, Xia X, Han ZG (2013) The Impacts of Information-Sharing Mechanisms on Spatial Market Formation Based on Agent-Based Modeling. PloS One 8(3): e58270. doi: 10.1371/journal.pone.0058270

5.  Kaplan AM, Haenlein M (2010) Users of the world, unite! The challenges and opportunities of social media. Bus Horiz 53(1): 59–68. doi: 10.1016/j.bushor.2009.09.003

6.  Macilwain C (2013) Sharing information is preferable to patenting. Nat 498: 273. doi: 10.1038/498273a

7.  Allen HG, Stanton TR, Di Pietro F, Moseley GL (2013) Social media release increases dissemination of original articles in the clinical pain sciences. PloS One 8(7): e68914. doi: 10.1371/journal.pone.0068914

8.  Lengel RH, Daft RL (1988) The selection of communication media as an executive skill. Acad Manag Exec 2(3): 225–232. doi: 10.5465/ame.1988.4277259

9.  Uchida N, Takahata K, Shibata Y, Shiratori N (2011) Never Die Network Extended with Cognitive Wireless Network for Disaster Information System. Complex, Intell Softw Intensive Syst (CISIS), 2011 International Conference on. IEEE 24–31.

10. Sattler DN, Larpenteur K, Shipley G (2011) Active shooter on campus: evaluating text and e-mail warning message effectiveness. J Homel Secur Emerg Manag 8(1).

11. Wei J, Zhao D, Yang F, Du S, Marinova D (2010) Timing crisis information release via television. Disasters 34(4): 1013–1030. doi: 10.1111/j.1467-7717.2010.01180.x

12. Whittaker S, Bellotti V, Gwizdka J (2006) Microblog in personal information management. Commun ACM 49(1): 68–73. doi: 10.1145/1107458.1107494

13. Odeny TA, Bailey RC, Bukusi EA, Simoni JM, Tapia KA, et al. (2012) Text messaging to improve attendance at post-operative clinic visits after adult male circumcision for HIV prevention: a randomized controlled trial. PloS One 7(9): e43832. doi: 10.1371/journal.pone.0043832

14. Zhang N, Huang H, Su B, Zhang B (2013) Analysis of different information dissemination ways for disaster pre-warning: A Case Study of Beijing. Proc 3rd Int Conf Multimedia Technol (ICMT 2013). Springer Berlin Heidelberg: 183–192.

15. Shim JP, Varshney U, Dekleva S, Nickerson RC (2007) Wireless telecommunications issues: Cell phone TV, wireless networks in disaster management, ubiquitous computing, and adoption of future wireless applications. Commun Assoc Inf Syst 20: 442–456.

16. Katada T, Asada J, Kuwasawa N, Oikawa Y (2000) Development of practical scenario simulator for dissemination of disaster information. J Civ Eng Inf Process Syst 9: 129–136.

17. Zhang N, Huang H, Su B, Zhang H (2013) Population evacuation analysis: considering dynamic population vulnerability distribution and disaster information dissemination. Nat Hazards 69(3): 1629–1646. doi: 10.1007/s11069-013-0767-y

18. Lang SY (2012) Research on portal websites of china sports news media credibility—Take the university students audience groups for example. Beijing: Capital University of Physical Education and Sports.

19. Eugster PT, Guerraoui R, Kermarrec AM, Massoulié L (2004) Epidemic informa-
    tion dissemination in distributed systems. Comput 37(5): 60–67. doi: 10.1109/
    mc.2004.1297243

20. Katada T, Oikawa Y, Tanaka T (1999) Development of simulation model for evaluat-
    ing the efficiency of disaster information dissemination. J Jpn Soc Civ Eng: 1–14.

21. Beijing Bureau of Statistics (2009) Census information of Beijing: China statistics
    Press.

22. Li D, Li J, Lin Z (2008) Online consumer-to-consumer market in China–a com-
    parative study of Taobao and eBay. Electron Commer Res Appl 7(1): 55–67. doi:
    10.1016/j.elerap.2007.02.010

*There are several supplemental files that are not available in this version
of the article. To view this additional information, please use the citation
on the first page of this chapter.*

# CHAPTER 3

# The Effectiveness of Disaster Risk Communication: A Systematic Review of Intervention Studies

DECLAN T. BRADLEY, MARIE MCFARLAND, AND MIKE CLARKE

## 3.1 INTRODUCTION

A disaster is a "serious disruption of the functioning of a community or a society involving widespread human, material, economic or environmental losses and impacts, which exceeds the ability of the affected community or society to cope using its own resources." [1] Four stages of a 'disaster cycle' have been identified: Mitigation and prevention, preparedness, response, and recovery. [2,3] Communication between authorities and the public about disasters occurs in all stages of the cycle, with different aims at each stage. Communication is a potentially valuable way of avoiding and reducing harm caused by disasters.

*The Effectiveness of Disaster Risk Communication: A Systematic Review of Intervention Studies.*
*© Bradley DT, McFarland M, and Clarke M.* PLOS Currents: Disasters *(2014). doi: 10.1371/currents.*
*dis.349062e0db1048bb9fc3a3fa67d8a4f8. Licensed under a Creative Commons Attribution License,*
*http://creativecommons.org/licenses/by/3.0/.*

Risk communication aims to provide the public with information about the effects of an event, and how actions may affect the outcome of the event. [4] Crisis and Emergency Risk Communication (CERC) is the use of risk communication in emergencies to inform the public about an event or issue to empower members of a community to protect themselves. [4] In this review, we focus on CERC in the context of disasters, at all stages of the disaster cycle. Risk communication in disasters has historically been a one-way transfer of information from authorities to the public, rather than an interactive flow of information. [5] Disaster risk communication may take place through many different channels, including some that have been recently developed or expanded. Potential channels of communication include face-to face conversations, telephone calls, group meetings, mass media such as television, tailored mass media such as reverse 911 services and interactive social media such as Twitter.

The effectiveness of risk communication interventions could be evaluated by assessing many possible outcomes. We chose to focus on knowledge, behaviour and incidence of health outcomes (e.g. injuries, deaths), which are particularly likely to be measured and reported, and also might be considered the most important outcomes.

As well as seeking to estimate the effects of different types of disaster risk communication, we aim to identify gaps in knowledge or evidence that would benefit from future research. Lastly, we aim to identify lessons from the literature that will help inform the design of future research.

## 3.2 METHODS

### 3.2.1 PROTOCOL AND REGISTRATION

This project was undertaken as part of one author's Masters in Public Health degree (DTB) and was not externally registered in advance. The review is reported according to the PRISMA statement (PRISMA checklist is shown in Appendix 1).

## 3.2.2 ELIGIBILITY CRITERIA AND OUTCOMES

The following intervention study types were included: Randomised trials, cluster randomised trials, quasi-randomised trials, controlled before-and-after studies, uncontrolled before-and-after studies, post-intervention only studies if the pre-intervention state could reasonably be assumed, interrupted time series and qualitative research.

The populations included were people or communities, before, during or following a disaster, who were at risk of being affected by a public health problem. Groups of people considered more vulnerable to disasters because of their language or other characteristics (e.g. disability) were included in the review. Communications must have been made from public authorities to communities or populations. Studies of communication with or between groups of professionals involved in disaster response were excluded from the review.

The interventions included were face-to-face, television, radio, Internet or telephone communication, or any other method of risk communication aimed at informing the public about a potential disaster situation to enable people to make informed choices that benefit their health on or after 1 January 2000. Risk communication interventions were aimed at producing desired knowledge, behavioural or health outcomes. This time limit was chosen because of recent development in electronic communications.

The United Nations International Strategy for Disaster Reduction definition of disaster was adhered to. [1] The HIV pandemic was excluded from this review because an extensive body of literature exists for this specific topic, which has been reviewed several times in recent years. If it was not clear from the article whether a study took place in the context of a disaster or if the intervention was not described in sufficient detail to be assessed, the study was categorised as 'unclear'.

The outcomes included in this review were: 1. Incidence of health-related events related to the disaster/possible disaster; 2. Health-related behaviour (self-reported or observed) relating to the disaster/possible disaster; 3. Health-related knowledge about the disaster/possible disaster.

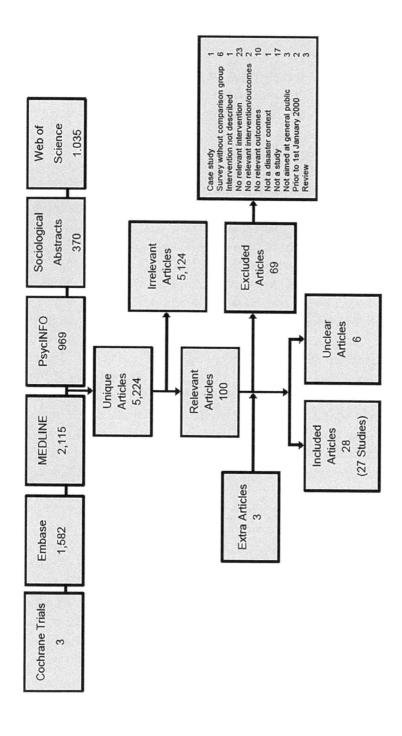

**FIGURE 1:** Review Flowchart. Flowchart showing results of systematic review process.

| First Author | Year | Phase | Disaster | Setting | Interventions | Study Type |
|---|---|---|---|---|---|---|
| Ardalan[27] | 2009 | Preparedness | Flood | Iran | Village disaster teams trained population | Cluster Non-randomised Trial |
| Beaudoin[10] | 2008 | Recovery | Hurricane | USA | Radio media campaign and telephone helpline about mental health issues following disaster | Interrupted Time Series |
| Beaudoin[11] | 2009 | Recovery | Hurricane | USA | Radio media campaign and telephone helpline about mental health issues following disaster | Cluster Uncontrolled Before and After Study and Interrupted Time Series |
| Blando[12] | 2008 | Preparedness | Radiation | USA | Educational materials provided with KI tablets | Controlled Before and After Study |
| Chan[20] | 2007 | Response | SARS epidemic | Hong Kong | Telephone-delivered education | Uncontrolled Before and After Study |
| Clerveaux[31] | 2009 | Preparedness | Hurricane, flood, volcanic eruption, landslide and mud flow | St. Vincent and the Grenadines; Turks and Caicos Islands | Workshop and board game | Cluster Uncontrolled Before and After Study |
| Colindres[32] | 2007 | Response | Water supply | Haiti | Community demonstration | Cluster Uncontrolled before and after survey |
| Dumais[7] | 2009 | Preparedness | Pandemic influenza | Canada | School-based lecture and discussion | Cluster Uncontrolled Before and After Study. |
| Eastwood[6] | 2009 | Mitigation | Pandemic influenza | Australia | Telephone-delivered education | Uncontrolled Before and After Study |
| Eisenman[13] | 2009 | Preparedness | General disaster preparedness | USA | Small-group discussions or written information | Randomised Trial |
| Farahat[26] | 2010 | Response | Pandemic influenza | Egypt | School-based lectures, role-play and discussion | Cluster Uncontrolled Before and After Study |
| Frank[14] | 2006 | Recovery | Terrorist attack | USA | Mass media campaign | Interrupted Time Series |
| Galarce[15] | 2012 | Response | Water supply | USA | Mass media campaign and personal communication | Cluster Uncontrolled Before and After Study |
| Karan[23] | 2007 | Response | SARS epidemic | Singapore | Mass media campaign and personal communication | Cluster Uncontrolled Before and After Study |
| Olsen[21] | 2005 | Response | Avian influenza | Thailand | Mass media campaign and telephone helpline | Cluster Uncontrolled Before and After Study |
| Pang[25] | 2003 | Response | SARS epidemic | China | Mass media campaign, seminars and telephone helpline | Interrupted Time Series |
| Perry[29] | 2007 | Early warning | Tsunami | Mauritius | Telephone, radio and television | Cluster Uncontrolled Before and After Study |
| Roess[28] | 2011 | Mitigation | Infectious disease outbreak | Republic of Congo | Community showing of videos and discussion | Cluster Uncontrolled Before and After Study |
| Rundblad[8] | 2010 | Response | Water supply | UK | Written notices and local radio | Cluster Uncontrolled Before and After Study |
| Sharma[30] | 2009 | Early warning | Cyclone | India | Telegram, fax, telephone, radio and oral communication | Cluster Uncontrolled Before and After Study |
| Strawderman[16] | 2012 | Early warning | Wildfire | USA | Reverse 911 | Uncontrolled Before and After Study |
| Sugerman[17] | 2012 | Response | Wildfire | USA | Mass media campaign | Uncontrolled Before and After Study |
| Tanes[18] | 2012 | Preparedness | Earthquake | USA | Computer game | Cluster Randomised Trial |
| Taylor-Robinson[9] | 2010 | Response | Infectious disease outbreak | UK | Hand-delivered letters, radio and briefing | Cluster Uncontrolled Before and After Study and Qualitative Study |
| Wang[19] | 2011 | Response | Water supply | USA | Mass media campaign | Uncontrolled Before and After study |
| Yasunari[24] | 2011 | Preparedness | General disaster preparedness | Japan | Ante-natal classes | Cluster Non-randomised Trial |
| Yen[22] | 2009 | Response | Infectious disease outbreak | Taiwan | Mass SMS text messaging and mass media campaign | Interrupted Time Series and Cluster Uncontrolled Before and After Study |

**FIGURE 2:** Summary characteristics of included studies

### 3.2.3 INFORMATION SOURCES

We searched the following databases: Cochrane Central Register of Controlled Trials (CENTRAL; 2000 to present); Embase (Ovid, 2000 to present); MEDLINE (Ovid, 2000 to present); PsycInfo (Ovid, 2000 to present); Sociological Abstracts (Proquest, 2000 to present) and Web of Science (Web of Knowledge, 2000 to present). These online databases were searched for relevant articles on 18 June 2013. Searches were not limited by language or country of origin but were limited to manuscripts published on or after 1 of January 2000. The search strategy was constructed from a combination of disaster-related search terms and communication-related search terms. Outcomes were not specified in the search in order to avoid excluding relevant studies. Database selection and the principles of the search strategy were discussed with a subject librarian. Full search strategy for all databases is shown in Appendix 2.

Further articles were identified from references of potentially relevant studies. The websites of the Centers for Disease Control and Prevention, Public Health England, European Centre for Disease Control, the World Health Organisation, The United Nations Office for Disaster Risk Reduction and the World Bank were searched for documents relevant to disaster communication. The New York Academy of Medicine's Grey Literature Report was also searched for "disaster communication."

### 3.2.4 DATA COLLECTION AND ASSESSMENT

Search results were merged and duplicates removed. Two reviewers (DTB and MM) independently read the retrieved titles and abstracts and assessed them for relevance. Reports identified as potentially relevant by either reviewer were retrieved in full and independently assessed for inclusion by two reviewers (DTB and MM), with a discussion to resolve discordances. Published data were extracted by one reviewer (DTB) using a standardised form. No unpublished data were sought.

Data Items collected were: Disaster cycle phase (mitigation, preparedness, response or recovery); Disaster type (infectious disease, natural or man-made); Study type; Geographical setting; Population characteristics and numbers; Randomisation method if applicable; Allocation method if applicable; Blinding; Attrition if applicable; Details of intervention; Outcomes reported; Results.

Study-level assessment for bias was performed with the Cochrane Collaboration's 'Assessment for bias' tool. The tool was not ideally suited to the non-randomised studies. The assessment tool was used to catalogue the characteristics of the study without attempting to make an overall summary categorisation of study bias as their very diverse natures, contexts and methods made most studies not directly comparable, even in terms of bias.

All relevant knowledge, behaviour and incidence outcomes were included in the review in the manner that they were originally reported. Due to the disparate nature of the studies, no formal assessment of risk of bias across studies was considered. No additional analyses were performed.

## 3.3 RESULTS

### 3.3.1 STUDY SELECTION

The electronic searches yielded 5,224 unique articles. Of these, 100 were judged to be potentially relevant by at least one reviewer and were obtained in full. Of these 100 articles, 25 were judged to meet the inclusion criteria, and for a further six studies were judged not to clearly meet the inclusion criteria due to insufficient information. Two additional studies were found from references of other papers, and one additional paper providing extra information about an already included study was also identified (Figure 1). Full study characteristics and assessment for bias for included reports are shown in Appendix 3, references to excluded studies with reasons for exclusion are shown in Appendix 4 and references to studies for which an assessment could not be made are shown in Appendix 5.

### 3.3.2 STUDY CHARACTERISTICS

Summary characteristics of the studies are shown (Figure 2). One study took place in Australia, [6] one in Canada, [7] two in the United Kingdom [8,9] and ten in the United States of America. [10,11,12,13,14,15,16,17,18,19] One was conducted in Hong Kong, [20] one in Thailand, [21] one in Taiwan, [22] one in Singapore, [23] one in Japan, [24] and one in China. [25] One study took place in Egypt, [26] one in Iran, [27] one in Republic of the Congo, [28] one in Mauritius, [29] one in India, [30] one in Haiti [31] and one took place on two Caribbean islands: St. Vincent and the Grenadines, and Turks and Caicos Islands. [32]

Two studies focused on general disaster preparedness, [13,24] one focused on five natural hazards, [31] two on hurricanes only, [10,11] one on a cyclone, [30] one on floods only, [27] two on wildfires, [16,17] one on earthquakes [18] and one on a terrorist attack. [14] Four studies dealt with water supply disasters. [8,14,19,32] One dealt with radiation. [12] The remaining studies focused on infectious disease disasters: Three studied pandemic influenza, [6,7,26] three focused on the SARS epidemic, [20,23,25] one on an outbreak of avian influenza, [21] one on an epidemic of acute haemorrhagic conjunctivitis, [22] one followed an outbreak of monkeypox [28] and one dealt with an outbreak of meningococcal disease. [9]

There were several different types of communication method used in these studies. Mitigation and preparedness interventions used face-to-face group participation and education in eight studies, [6,7,12,13,24,27,28,31] one of which included the use of a specially designed board game. [31] Two early warning alerts used several communication channels [29,30] and another used Reverse-911. [16] Mitigation and preparedness studies that did not use face-to-face communication used a telephone intervention, [6] and a computer game. [18] The response phase interventions were multi-channel information campaigns (with different methods and balance of methods between studies) [8,9, 15,17,19,20,21,22,23,25,32] and a school-based participatory intensive education programme. [26] The three recovery phase interventions used media campaigns to encourage members of the public to access telephone help lines for mental health problems and to undertake healthy behaviours following disasters. [10,11,14]

The objectives of the interventions were to improve the health knowledge and behaviour in relation to disasters, and to decrease the incidence of negative health events. The studies were chosen on that basis, and several studies reported additional outcomes that were outside the scope of this review. The knowledge, behaviour and incidence outcomes are described in detail in Appendix 3 (characteristics and results of included studies).

## 3.4 RESULTS OF INDIVIDUAL STUDIES

### 3.4.1 EFFECT OF RISK COMMUNICATION INTERVENTIONS TO PROMOTE DISASTER MITIGATION AND PREPAREDNESS

#### 3.4.1.1 COMMUNICATION TO PROMOTE MITIGATION AND PREPAREDNESS FOR INFECTIOUS DISEASE DISASTERS

##### 3.4.1.1.1 Setting

Two studies for pandemic influenza took place in high-income countries (Canada [7] and Australia [6]), and one study for monkeypox took place in a low-income country (Republic of the Congo). [28] Both studies of interventions for pandemic influenza took place in 2008, before the 2009 H1N1 pandemic. The study of an intervention for monkeypox took place in 2009, six years after an outbreak in Republic of the Congo, and subsequent to a serological survey that suggested that past infection was widespread. Monkeypox is a potentially fatal disease that is related to smallpox, incidence of which is thought to have increased following the discontinuation of the smallpox vaccine in 1980. [28]

##### 3.4.1.1.2 Participants

The Australian study by Eastwood et al. of a pandemic influenza mitigation intervention included 1,166 individuals (62% female) who were contacted by telephone (58% response rate). [6] Dumais et al. reported an educational intervention in a class of 35 female year 10 students in a private school in Canada. [7] The intervention in Republic of the Congo was delivered on a much greater scale: approximately 23,860 people in 16 towns and villages received the intervention over a period of 90 days. [28] Evaluation was by a survey of 271 people (57% male; mean age 33 years) before and after the intervention. [28]

### 3.4.1.1.3 Description of Interventions

The Eastwood et al. intervention for pandemic influenza was a simple telephone conversation, with a researcher delivering a short script explaining the nature and effects of an influenza pandemic. [6] The Dumais et al. intervention was developed by conducting a pre-intervention survey of students' understanding of viruses and forming an education programme based on revealed insufficiencies. [7] The intervention took place in an 80 minute session involving a lecture and discussion, and addressed shortfalls in knowledge about virus biology. The aim of this intervention was to improve understanding of viruses to facilitate response to risk communication about pandemic and epidemic influenza. The Roess et al. intervention was an outreach education programme in villages in the Republic of Congo. [28] Small group sessions were conducted using two specially made educational videos and discussions about monkeypox in each village.

### 3.4.1.1.4 Results

All three studies were uncontrolled before and after studies. The Eastwood et al. study of pandemic influenza revealed that the Australian public reported themselves to be largely willing to comply with the public health measures proposed, such as self-quarantine and social distancing. Following the information intervention, they were even more likely to report their willingness to self-isolate (94.1% before to 97.5% after), avoid public events (94.2% to 98.3%) and postpone gatherings (90.7% to 97.2%). [6] Participants in the Canadian study of influenza increased their knowledge scores between a pre- and post-intervention test (with a significant change in mean score from 0.2 to 1.3, where 2.0 was the maximum possible score). [7] Roess et al. analysed their before and after study using paired analyses. [28] Significant improvements were noted in outcomes related to recognising monkeypox and knowledge of how it is transmitted. The numbers of people who knew at least one symptom increased from 49% to 95%, named rash and fever as symptoms increased from 11% to 32%, and knew that the rash occurs on palms and soles increased from 14% to 51%. The numbers of people who knew that the disease could be transmitted by contact with an ill person increased 28% to 58%, by fomites (2% to 14%), by contact with an ill animal (24% to 64%) and contact with a dead animal (7% to 19%). There were significant improvements in four appropriate behavioural actions. Whilst there was a reduction in the number of who would eat or sell found rodent carcasses (eating, 33% to 16%; selling 7% to 3%), there was no reduction in the number who would eat or sell primate carcasses (eat, 11%; sell, 4%). [28] The authors noted that the programme had shown effectiveness in increasing knowledge, and might encourage participants to seek healthcare if monkeypox was suspected, but suggested that future strategies should focus on prevention of risk behaviours. The design used in all three infectious disease mitigation or preparedness studies means that inferring causality from the reports is difficult. Alternative explanations for the improvements in knowledge and behaviour include an observer effect, which might influence self-reported behaviour in the study of monkeypox and the Australian study of pandemic influenza. [6]

## 3.4.1.2 COMMUNICATION TO PROMOTE PREPAREDNESS FOR NATURAL DISASTERS

### 3.4.1.2.1 Setting

Five studies of preparedness for natural disasters were identified. Two studies took place in the USA, [13,18] one in Japan, [24] one in Iran [27] and one on the Carribean islands of St. Vincent and the Grenadines, and Turks and Caicos. [31] Two studies were aimed at general preparedness, [13,24] one preparedness for flash floods, [27] one for earthquakes, [18] and one for five natural hazards. [31]

## 3.4.1.2.2 Participants

Eisenman et al. reported a randomised trial of 231 Latino people who lived in Los Angeles County, California, USA, of whom 187 completed the study (a per protocol analysis was presented; mean age was 37 years; both groups were approximately two thirds female). [13] Yasunari et al. reported a cluster non-randomised trial at different hospital sites with 99 primiparous women (mean age 31 years; mean gestation 22.9 weeks) in the intervention group (of 993 who attended these sessions) and 104 primiparous women (mean age 31 years; mean gestational 24.7 weeks) in the control group (of 1,010 who attended the control sessions). [24] Tanes reported a cluster randomised trial of 250 college students (62% male) from "a large Midwestern university". [18,33] Students selected a time slot to attend for the intervention, and the time slots were randomly assigned to an intervention. Clerveaux et al. conducted an uncontrolled cluster before and after study with 42 grade 5 pupils, with mean age 11 years, from St. Vincent and the Grenadines, and 33 Grade 5 pupils, with mean age 10 years, from Turks and Caicos. [31] Ardalan conducted a cluster non-randomised trial in two rural flood-prone areas of Golestan Provence, Iran using independent pre- and post-intervention samples in each area. [27] The intervention group included 1,163 participants pre-intervention and 1,159 post-intervention. The control group included 1,200 pre-intervention and 1,210 post-intervention. The mean age for each group was between 27 and 29 years, and females were slightly more numerous in each group (52% to 59%). [27]

## 3.4.1.2.3 Description of Interventions

Ardalan et al. used a community participation approach to preparedness and mitigation of flood disasters. [27] Village disaster teams were developed, were trained, and then conducted training for local people that included identifying areas at risk of flooding, developing personalised plans, developing an early warning system and conducting evacuation exercises over three months. [27] Eisenman et al. used a randomised trial to compare small group discussions with community health promotion officers lasting one hour (high-intensity intervention) compared to simply receiving written information (low-intensity intervention) for Latino residents of Los Angeles County, USA. [13] A study of pregnant women in Japan offered six 15-minute disaster preparedness classes as part of normal antenatal classes in a cluster non-randomised trial. [24] Participants in the intervention group were instructed about preparedness, communication and receiving medical attention in disasters. Controls received normal antenatal care. [24] Two studies used games to educate participants about disaster preparedness. One used a specially developed board game, the Disaster Awareness Game, to inform school children about disaster preparedness for floods, hurricanes, volcanoes, landslides and mud flows. [31] The intervention took place over two days and included discussion of the topics raised by the game. Tanes used an existing computer game, Beat the Quake, developed in California, which was designed to educate people about appropriate steps to take in the event of an earthquake. [18,33]

### 3.4.1.2.4 Results

Community flood risk preparedness programme participants were much more likely to have taken the recommended preparedness steps than people who lived in areas without the intervention. [27] Adjusted odds ratios for the intervention group ranged from 6 to 50 for outcomes such as having a family preparedness meeting, risk mapping, having emergency supplies, having a plan for vulnerable people and having an evacuation drill. Control group odds ratios (comparing before and after) for the same measures ranged from 0.4 to 2.7. [27] Latino people who took part in a community-based preparedness discussion with a health promoter and people who received written information made significant improvements in disaster preparedness according to a self-reported checklist. [13] The platica (discussion) group was slightly better prepared for ten of 13 measures before the intervention. Overall preparedness score for the written information group increased from 29% to 52%, and for the platica group increased from 38% to 76%. [13] In the Yasunari et al. study of disaster education with antenatal care,

the intervention and control groups both showed non-statistically significant improvements in knowledge on all outcome measures, but no
direct statistical comparison of the two groups was reported. [24] The
intervention group improved in knowledge of the emergency telephone
line (69.7% to 82.8%), the disaster message board (51.5% to 67.7%),
local alternative maternity clinics (52.5% to 68.7%), evacuation sites
(47.5% to 67.7%) and being explain about own health status (86.9%
to 97%). [24] They also were more likely to have discussed communication plan with family (20.2% to 43.4%), be able to find out family
contact methods (46.5% to 70.7%), take measures to prevent furniture
turning over (33.3% to 48.5%) and objects falling (20.2% to 34.3%).
[24] The control group significantly improved in only taking measures
to prevent objects falling (9.6% to 20.2%). [24] The inclusion criteria
for this study were altered post hoc when it was found that the demographics of the intervention and control groups (conducted on different
hospital sites) were markedly different. [24] Both game interventions
led to increases in knowledge about hazards. The Disaster Awareness
Game, played in schools on Caribbean islands, and supplemented with
additional discussion, promoted increases in knowledge about all the
natural hazards presented, as well as increases in knowledge about how
to prepare, evacuate and recover from disasters. No statistical comparisons were made of the before and after comparisons, however. Among
St. Vincent and the Grenadines participants, knowledge (measured by
game score) of the hazard of flooding increased from 65% to 87%, and
hurricanes from 65% to 83%. [31] Among Turks and Caicos Islands participants, knowledge for the five tested hazards also increased (floods,
69% to 75%; hurricanes, 75% to 83%; volcano, 54% to 80%; landslide
51% to 92%; mudflow 43% to 83%). [31] The Beat the Quake game increased knowledge about how to respond to an imminent earthquake according to scores on multiple choice questions, compared to not playing
the game. [18,33] The study evaluated more complex variations of the
game involving comparing goal-setting by researchers or participants
themselves, but no significant differences between these variations was
noted. [18,33]

## 3.4.1.3 COMMUNICATION TO PROMOTE PREPAREDNESS FOR MAN-MADE DISASTERS

### 3.4.1.3.1 Setting

One study of communication for preparedness for man-made disasters was found. [12]

### 3.4.1.3.2 Participants

The participants who are relevant to this review were 421 people who attended voluntary clinics to receive potassium iodide (KI) prophylaxis and information, and 286 individuals who did not attend these clinics, all of whom lived within 10 km of a nuclear power plant. [12] The participants had themselves chosen whether to acquire potassium iodide, and therefore the characteristics of the two groups were likely to be systematically different.

### 3.4.1.3.3 Description of Interventions

The New Jersey Department of Health and Senior Services organised distribution of KI to protect against thyroid cancer in the event of a nuclear or radiation incident. Voluntary clinics offered the pills and information to people within a 10km radius of a nuclear power plant. Information was written at Flesch Kincaid Grade level of 6.5 and pilot tested. [12]

### 3.4.1.3.4 Results

Individuals who received KI and information scored an average of 46% on a knowledge test, while those who did not receive KI or information scored an average of 15%. [12] Due to the fact that the self-selection, it is difficult to evaluate the effect of the intervention, since those with better knowledge of radiation might have been more likely to seek KI, and therefore the intervention group might have had better knowledge anyway.

### 3.4.1.4 COMMUNICATIONS TO PROVIDE EARLY WARNINGS OF NATURAL DISASTERS

### 3.4.1.4.1 Setting

Three studies evaluated the effect of early warning of impending natural disasters. One evaluated the response to a warning of the Indian Ocean Tsunami on the island of Mauritius, [29] and the second evaluated the effect of a warning of a cyclone on the east coast of India. [30] A third study evaluated the response to an evacuation order during a wildfire event in San Diego, California, USA, in 2007. [16]

### 3.4.1.4.2 Participants

The survey in Mauritius reached 319 respondents (including 19 of whom outside the target area; proportion of each gender not reported) out of 1,484 attempted contacts. [29] Sharma (2009) contacted 44 'decision-makers' (59% male) from individual households in Indian villages that were at risk of harm from a cyclone. Strawderman et al. interviewed 1,020 individuals (mean age 54 years; 37% male) who lived in a zone that was evacuated during the San Diego wildfire (of 12,204 telephone numbers attempted). [16,16]

### 3.4.1.4.3 Description of interventions

Perry evaluated the effects of the early warning of the Indian Ocean Tsunami on the inhabitants of Mauritius. [29] Perry describes how the local authorities learned of the tsunami from international news outlets and began to issue warnings to inhabitants and tourists during the time period that the tsunami effects were already being observed. [29] This included the meteorological service contacting police, coastguard, local radio and television channels and directly phoning hotels to warn them of the imminent danger. Perry reported that the information issued may have understated the necessary action required by individuals. [29] Sharma et al. presented a study of the public's response to a warning of a cyclone on the east coast of India that occurred in December 2003. [30] The intervention was a technical report warning of the impending cyclone and the likely effects. This was disseminated from national to local level through several layers of government, translated into local languages at district level and locally disseminated orally. The warning itself covered a large geographic area and did not advise on whether evacuation was necessary. The decision to advise people whether to evacuate was made by administrators at a district level in light of the information provided. Strawderman et al. sought to evaluate a recently-installed public address system called 'Reverse 911', which automatically dials all telephone numbers in a specified area and delivers a recorded emergency message. [16] The warning messages were also spread through television, radio, interpersonal communication and police. [16]

### 3.4.1.4.4 Results

Perry reported that the Mauritius Meteorological Service learned of the tsunami just over two hours before its first effects reached the island. [29] At the onset of the wave effects, 10% of people knew about the expected tsunami, and by the time the effects finished, approximately three hours later, only 42% knew about the warning. Upon hearing of it, most people continued their normal business (64%), while only 25% took action to protect themselves and 15% did the opposite of what was advised and went to watch the waves at the coast. [29] In the study of a cyclone in India 345 of the villagers reported that they evacuated voluntarily, 20% were 'forced' to evacuate and 46% did not evacuate. [30] In the San Diego wildfire, 53% of residents in the evacuation zone received the 'Reverse 911' evacuation message, and 80% who received it evacuated, including 100% of those for whom evacuation was judged necessary. [16] However, only 66% of those who received it reported the message to be the reason why they evacuated. Some people who did not need to evacuate did so anyway because of the message. [16] Information acquired through the Internet had the highest correct rejection rate, and the lowest false alarm rate, suggesting that residents were able to judge their own situation most accurately using it as a source. [16] In the Mauritian tsunami study and the Indian cyclone study there was a low level of compliance with the advice to take protective action against the imminent natural hazards. Factors relating to personal circumstances, beliefs and attitudes, societal response, and the characteristics of the authorities may have influenced whether individuals chose to evacuate. [30] In the San Diego wildfire, 69% of people in the evacuation zone did evacuate, which is much higher than in the other two studies. [16] This may relate to the characteristics of the disaster (fire), the setting (rural USA), the communication methods, or the society. The 'Reverse 911' alert was relatively widely received and acted upon by a majority of recipients. Use of the Internet allowed people to make even more personalised decisions. [16] The studies were all conceived retrospectively and relied on recall by participants. Some studies also assessed aetiological factors, and though the studies focused on the intervention of the evacuation warnings, they were not under the control of the researchers. It is difficult to assess the effectiveness of early warning information whenever it is not necessarily correct to attribute all subsequent evacuations to the warning, since some may occur independently of warnings.

## 3.4.2 EFFECT OF RISK COMMUNICATION INTERVENTIONS TO IMPROVE DISASTER RESPONSE

### 3.4.2.1 COMMUNICATION TO PROMOTE RESPONSE TO INFECTIOUS DISEASE DISASTERS

#### 3.4.2.1.1 Setting

Seven studies of communication interventions during infectious disease disasters were identified. One was in the UK, [9] one was in Egypt, [26] and five were in Asian countries: one in each of China, [25] Thailand, [21] Taiwan, [22] Singapore [23] and Hong Kong. [20] Three studies took place in the context of the SARS epidemic, [20,23,25] one during the 2009-2010 influenza pandemic, [26] one during an avian influenza outbreak, [21] one involved an epidemic of viral conjunctivitis [22] and one was set during a small outbreak of meningococcal disease in a school. [9]

## 3.4.2.1.2 Participants

Farahat et al. studied 420 school pupils (mean age 16 years; 46% male) during the influenza pandemic. [26] Olsen et al. reported a study of 200 participants (median age 50 years; 72% female) during an avian influenza outbreak in Nakhon Phanom, Thailand. [21] Three SARS studies took place in Asia. Pang et al. reported outcomes for 1,860 people in China who were hospitalised with SARS infection. [25] A study by Chan et al. included 122 (63% female) people in Hong Kong aged 55 years or over. [20] The study by Karan et al. included 300 individuals (51% male) in Singapore, 61% of whom were aged between 20 and 39 years. [23] During an outbreak of viral acute haemorrhagic conjunctivitis in Taiwan, comparisons were made between two interventions by directing public health messages at the inhabitants of two affected cities, Taipei (population 2,632,242) and Keelung (population 390,084). [22] Schoolchildren were the population that was mainly affected (Taipei City had 277,159 schoolchildren and Keelung City had 41,244). [22] During an outbreak of meningococcal disease in a secondary-level school in England, 88 school pupils (63% male) aged 16-17 years were surveyed (of 198 who were invited) to investigate their response to the communications. [9]

## 3.4.2.1.3 Description of Interventions

One study used an intensive health education programme consisting of lectures, role-play and group discussion aided by photos, posters, pamphlets and a 'data show' about influenza H1N1 held every other day in schools for two weeks. [26] During the avian influenza outbreak, a multimedia response was conducted, including a telephone help line with prevention information, a web site, newspaper, radio and television information broadcasts, the distribution of education videos to health officers and a booklet sent directly to members of the public. [21] During the SARS epidemic in Beijing, the health ministry announced the outbreak in a press conference on 20 April 2003. [25] Subsequently there were four further ministry press conferences, nine municipal government press conferences, a billboard campaign, bus advertisements, banners, a daily two-hour educational television programme, a telephone help line, 6,672 SARS community seminars and delivery of 8,280,000 copies of educational materials to citizens. [25] In Hong Kong, Chan et al. conducted a telephone intervention with pre-test and post-test surveys. [20] The intervention was delivered by nursing students who were trained to gather information from the participants and deliver a tailored intervention that addressed any of the participants' misconceptions or information needs about SARS. Karan et al. sought to evaluate the national public health communication programme in their survey. [23] A multimedia campaign was conducted that involved press conferences, print and television adverts explaining infection control measures, a dedicated television channel, web site, help lines, and a 'SARS kit' containing a thermometer that was posted to every home. The Singapore response also included fines and imprisonment for individuals who did not comply with quarantine, and fines for some unhygienic behaviours. [23] In the outbreak of infective haemorrhagic conjunctivitis, in both Taipei and Keelung cities delivered public service messages and health education in schools, ran a telephone help line and provided the media with information. [22] However, Taipei instigated further steps: On a single day, the Taipei mayor addressed the press, a letter from the department of health was given to children to give to their parents and SMS text messages with information and infection control advice were sent to all 2.2 million Taipei citizens with mobile phones. [22] The Health Protection Agency (now Public Health England) undertook a communication intervention to inform pupils and parents about an outbreak of meningococcal disease and to arrange mass antibiotic prophylaxis for all pupils and staff. [9] The outbreak became apparent on a Friday afternoon, and the Health Protection Agency (HPA) issued letters to parents and released a press statement for radio on the following Monday. The following day, a briefing was held prior to the mass distribution of antibiotics. [9]

## 3.4.2.1.4 Results

Participants in the school-based intervention by Farahat et al. demonstrated improved knowledge and practice outcomes. [26] Significant positive changes in knowledge about the cause, source, transmission, symptoms, complications and treatment of pandemic influenza were reported. Positive changes related to self-reported behaviours were also noted for respiratory and hand hygiene, infection control, and self-care. Overall, the proportion with satisfactory knowledge increased from 43% before the intervention to 68% afterwards, and the proportion with good practice rose from 57% to 65%. [26] Evaluation of the Thailand multi-media response to the avian influenza involved interviewing participants after the events and asking them about their practices before and after the intervention, and as such it may be prone to recall bias. All four knowledge outcomes were significantly improved (believing that it is safe to touch dead poultry 40% to 14%; that it is safe for children to touch dead poultry 23% to 5%; preparing raw poultry with other food 50% to 37%; safe to eat undercooked chicken or eggs 21% to 6%). [21] Behavioural practices did not improve to the same extent, with only those touching dead poultry with bare hands dropping from 39% to 11%). [21] During the SARS epidemic, the median lag time between developing symptoms and hospitalisation in Beijing reduced during the time period of the outbreak from six days between 5 March and 9 April, to five days between 10 April and 20 April, and two days between 21 April and 15 June.25 Following the tailored telephone intervention, Chan et al. reported improvements in paired before and after analyses for knowledge about two of five points of knowledge about SARS transmission, but no change for the other three. [20] For each question, between four and ten people (out of 122) answered correctly before the intervention, but incorrectly after it. [20] For knowledge about transmission by droplets, for example, 62 people answered correctly before and after the intervention and 28 people answered incorrectly beforehand, but correctly afterwards, 19 answered incorrectly both times and four answered correctly before, but incorrectly afterwards. [20] It was notable that for some outcomes (e.g. for whether animals could transmit

SARS), the vast majority of respondents answered incorrectly before and afterwards. [20] Unpaired analyses of behavioural outcomes also showed changes, but largely in the opposite direction to that expected. Overall, participants less frequently washed hands with soap or after coughing/ sneezing (reduced from 1.3 to 1.7 on a four point rating scale with 1 = very often and 4 = not at all), less frequently covered their mouth when coughing/sneezing (reduced from 1.3 to 1.9), and were less likely to use a surgical mask (1.3 to 2.2). [20] The authors speculated that this might be because the SARS epidemic was abating at that time, and there may have been less concern by the time of the second survey, one week after the first. It is, however, possible that the intervention had undesirable effects. The intervention's content is difficult to appraise because it was non-standardised, being tailored to each individual by the interviewers depending on their apparent knowledge. [20] The evaluation of Singapore's response to SARS compared time points during and after the epidemic. The authors reported that 90% sometimes or always washed their hands regularly during the epidemic, but 80% did so afterwards. [23] The recommended practice of monitoring one's own temperature daily, which can be assumed to have a zero prevalence prior to the public health campaign, was 85% (always or sometimes) during the epidemic and 31% afterwards. [23] In the mass communication programme aimed at combating further spread of acute haemorrhagic conjunctivitis, school absenteeism and surveillance data were assessed. [22] School absenteeism for affected pupils, desirable because it prevented further onward transmission of the virus, increased from 10% before the intervention to 62% afterwards. [22] There was a fall in overall daily incidence from 0.093% to 0.056% following the intervention. The outbreak in Taipei lasted only 13 days, while that in Keelung lasted 34 days. The crude attack rate in Taipei was 2%, and that in Keelung was 14.9%. [22] In qualitative responses to the Health Promotion Agency's response to an outbreak of meningococcal disease in a school, many pupils reported that the official communications had been too slow, because interpersonal communication had spread the news over the preceding days, but that this had been accompanied by misinformation and uncertainty. [9] The report indicates that 74% of school pupils already knew about the meningococcal disease outbreak before information was released by the school and the Health Protection Agency. [9] The Chan et al. uncontrolled before and after study during the SARS epidemic high-lights a problem with uncontrolled studies: protective behaviours became less common during the period of the study, possibly because of a lessen-ing concern about the disease as the outbreak abated. [20] If the study had taken place earlier in the outbreak, it might have detected increases in protective behaviours as concern was rising, and might have attributed the improvement to the intervention.

## 3.4.2.2 COMMUNICATION TO PROMOTE RESPONSE TO NATURAL DISASTERS

### 3.4.2.2.1 Setting

One study relating to the response to natural disasters was identified, 17 relating to the wildfire event in San Diego, California, USA, in 2007 that was also studied by Strawderman et al., [16] described above (Early Warnings).

### 3.4.2.2.2 Participants

Sugerman et al. conducted telephone interviews with 1,802 adults (of 18,687 calls made). [17] Ten percent of calls were conducted in Spanish. The most frequent age range was 35-64 years, the study sample was older than the general population, and 50% of the sample were male. [17]

### 3.4.2.2.3 Description of Interventions

The health messages promoted by the San Diego County Health and Hu-man Services Agency and American Heart and Lung Association during a three week multi-media campaign that used television, radio, newspapers and the Internet were evaluated. [17] They advised residents to stay in-doors, drive with all windows closed, run air conditioners on recirculate, keep home windows closed, use HEPA air filters, only exercise indoors, wet ash before clean-up, use N95 respirators during clean-up, limit activities to what is absolutely necessary, boil tap water before drinking and drink bottled water. [17]

### 3.4.2.2.4 Results

The messages reached 88% of respondents, with television being by far the most common medium (77%) followed by radio (7%). [17] Following the warnings, participants spontaneously recalled being told to stay indoors (68%), to keep windows closed (18%) and only to exercise indoors (11%), but eight other messages were recalled by less than 5%. [17] Fifty-nine percent stayed inside most of the day, 76% kept windows closed, 88% did not participate in outdoor sports, 76% wet ash during cleanup, 16% used home air conditioning, 10% used HEPA air filters and 8% wore a N95 mask. [17] It is possible, however, that residents might have engaged in some of these precautions independently of the media campaign.

### 3.4.2.3 COMMUNICATION TO PROMOTE RESPONSE TO WATER SUPPLY DISASTERS

### 3.4.2.3.1 Setting

Four studies of the response to water supply disasters were found: One in Haiti, [32] one in the UK8 and two in the USA. [15,19] The Haiti study followed major flash floods due to Tropical Storm Jeanne. [32] The study in the UK occurred in the context of major floods in Gloucestershire, England, that caused 140,000 homes to lose their water supply and subsequently be supplied with untreated water. [8] The two USA studies took place in Boston, after the collapse of a major water tunnel that carried water to 2 million individuals and residents were supplied with untreated water. [15,19]

### 3.4.2.3.2 Participants

The Haitian study interviewed 100 families who had received education and a water purification product following a natural disaster. [32] Following the water crisis in Gloucestershire, 159 individuals (of 1,000 invited) who lost water supply were interviewed (40% male). [8] The sample was slightly older on average than the local census (at least partly due to the absence of children from the survey). In Boston, Galarce et al. analysed surveys from 267 people who were affected by the water crisis (48% male; modal age 30-44 years). [15] Participants were recruited from a research database (78%) and purposefully recruited from affected areas (22%). [15] Wang et al. surveyed 525 adults (31% male; modal age 25-34) who were opportunistically recruited from hospital clinics and waiting rooms. [19]

### 3.4.2.3.3 Description of Interventions

In Haiti, community demonstrations were given of how to use PuR®, a proprietary water flocculation and purification treatment, three to six weeks after Tropical Storm Jeanne. [32] The floods compromised and contaminated sources of drinking water. The US Centers for Disease Control and Populations Services International (PSI) had collaborated on the development of this product. PSI and the community leaders promoted, distributed and educated about the use of the water purification treatment. [32] In Gloucestershire, a non-standard, locally produced 'Do Not Drink' notice was delivered to every affected household before untreated water was supplied to households, seven days after they lost all water supply. [8] After a further seven days, a notice changing advice to 'Boil Water' was also delivered. Finally, a 'Water Safe' notice was issued. The local authorities communicated primarily through these notices, but local media also disseminated information. [8] Galarce et al. described the issuing of a boil water notice by the Water Authority and dissemination by the Mayor's office, Boston Public Health Commission, schools, businesses, faith-based organisations, police, newscasters, the Centers for Disease Control and Prevention Health Alert Network, reverse 911 systems, phone calls, the Internet, by vehicles with 'bullhorns' and by other emergency management systems. [15] The extent to which each was used was not described. Wang et al. investigated the same event and issuing of a boil water notice, but did not describe its dissemination. [19]

*3.4.2.3.4 Results*

Thirty-seven of the 100 Haitian families reported treating their drinking water before the floods. Following the flood and intervention, 58 used the product while other families used a variety of other reliable and unreliable methods. [32] Knowledge about how to use the treatment was high: only two opened the packet using their teeth, 83 knew how much water to mix a sachet with, 88 knew how long to mix for, 79 knew how long to let the water stand for and 80 knew to put the flocculated waste in the latrine. [32] Seventy eight answered all questions correctly. Use of the water treatment was not well sustained, however. Only 22 families had PuR®-treated water at the time of the interview, and only a few had used it often during the few weeks between distribution and survey. The authors suggested that this may have been because sample sachets were distributed without households knowing how to access further supplies. [32] In the Gloucestershire water crisis, 89% received advice about the 'do not drink' notice, 71% about the 'boil water' notice and 88% about the 'water safe' notice. [8] However, only 42% used the delivered notice for information during the 'do not drink' stage, 36% used it during the 'boil water' stage and 35% used it when the 'water safe' stage was reached. Local radio was more widely used at all stages. Questioning about respondents' knowledge revealed misunderstandings: Knowledge of the correct action during both the 'do not drink' and 'boil water' stages was low (23% and 27%). Compliance with the advice was not complete, and some people who did avoid drinking tap water continued to use it for brushing teeth and preparing food, which was against the advice. During the 'do not drink' stage, 9% of people drank un-boiled tap water, 16% brushed teeth with it and 21% prepared food with it. Many people used boiled water against advice during the 'do not drink' notice for food preparation (47%), to brush teeth (38%) and to drink (hot, 42%; cold 21%). When the advice was changed to 'boil water', 42% prepared food with, 38% brushed teeth with, and 29% drank un-boiled water. [8] In the Boston water crisis, Galarce et al. found that 12.5% of people drank un-boiled tap water, 78% of respondents followed the advice to flush the cold water tap for 1 minute following the resolution of the water problem, and 59% of respondents flushed the warm tap for 15 minutes. [15] The message successfully reached 89% of the sample on the first day of the crisis. [15] The Wang et al. study reported that only 2.4% of their sample drank un-boiled tap water, and their data indicate that 74% of their sample knew about the crisis on the first day. [19] Their survey reported 47% using bottled and boiled water, 41% using bottled water only and 9.6% using boiled water only. [19] The study of water treatment in Haiti suggested that all households used some water treatment method following the floods, and that the participants were aware of how to use the water treatment appropriately. [32] The study did not explicitly explore what happened when PuR® water treatment was not being used, so it is not clear whether alternative appropriate methods were being used or whether untreated water was also consumed. The intervention to disseminate information in Boston appears to have been on a larger scale than that used in the Gloucestershire crisis. The study following floods in England demonstrated misunderstandings by those affected and only moderate compliance with the recommended actions. [8] The USA studies both showed higher compliance with advice, though it is worth noting that the Boston crisis lasted only 4 days, while that in England lasted up to 17 days for some residents. [8,15]

### 3.4.3 EFFECT OF RISK COMMUNICATION INTERVENTIONS TO IMPROVE DISASTER RECOVERY

#### 3.4.3.1.1 Setting

One study took place following the 11 September 2001 New York terrorist attacks,14 and two studies took place following Hurricane Katrina in New Orleans. [10,11]

#### 3.4.3.1.2 PARTICIPANTS

Media campaigns were conducted with the populations of New York and New Orleans as their intended audience. The monthly calls to the New York helpline, LifeNet, from November 2000 to December 2002 were enumerated. [14] Similarly, calls to the New Orleans Crisis Line were counted (total 29,659 in the study period). [10] In the second New Orleans study, 968 adult African Americans were interviewed during and after the media campaign. [11]

### 3.4.3.1.3 Description of Interventions

In New York, a mass media campaign was conducted using print, television, radio and other media (mainly fliers and billboards) between September 2001 and December 2002 with the aim of informing the city's population of the availability of a help line for mental health problems, which could provide advice and refer callers to medical services where necessary. [14] In the context of this review, calling the help line was regarded as a behavioural outcome. Following Hurricane Katrina, a media campaign ran for 11 weeks in 2006 on four radio stations targeted at African Americans. [10,11] Messages were broadcast five times each weekday on four radio channels. Five different messages with a focus on stress and depression were played. The messages promoted preventive behaviours (normal productive routine, social and physical activity and working to resolve conflicts), and information about an existing telephone help line that provides information and referrals for physician support, counselling and crisis intervention. A comparison group was made by comparing the number of calls to another phone number for the same help line that was not promoted in the campaign.

### 3.4.3.1.4 Results

In New York, major increases in advertising activity appeared to be accompanied by increases in call volume to the help line. [14] Prior to the attacks, between 2,000 and 3,000 calls were made each month. In the month of peak advertising expenditure (September 2002), 9,000 calls were made (though this does coincide with the anniversary of the event). [14] Similarly, in New Orleans, the number of calls to the advertised help line increased from a mean of 100 each day, to 125 during the campaign and 134 each day after the campaign. [10] In the second study of this intervention, no change in combined post-traumatic stress disorder (PTSD) understanding, preventive behaviours (keeping routine, monitoring stress, talking with others, being productive and problem-solving) or screened incidence (indicated by avoidance, losing interest, isolation, losing hope, being jumpy and having difficulty sleeping) was found when comparing surveys taken before and during the campaign. A regression analysis incorporating the date of interview relative to the commencement of the programme showed an increase in PTSD beliefs/understanding and preventive behaviours, but no change in PTSD incidence. [11] These interventions appear to have been effective at promoting the behaviour of phoning a help line for mental health problems following disasters. The campaign in New Orleans may have improved understanding and knowledge. The lack of change of PTSD incidence may be due to ineffectiveness of the intervention or due to a lack of sufficient time or power to detect any change in incidence.

## 3.4.4 RISK OF BIAS IN INCLUDED STUDIES

We used the Cochrane 'risk of bias' tool, which is designed for use with randomised control trials. Where a category was not applicable to the study design, 'Unclear risk' was chosen.

### 3.4.4.1 ALLOCATION (SELECTION BIAS)

Only one study was identified that allocated individuals randomly to one of two interventions. [13] In that study, by Eisenman et al., the allocation method and concealment were described. [13] The Tanes Beat the Quake study used an unstated method of randomisation to allocate group time slots, not individuals. [18,33] It was also not stated whether allocation occurred before or after the time slots had been selected by participants. The randomisation of groups increases the risk of selection bias. Virtually all the other controlled studies compared two different areas, or two groups of areas. Usually this was for practical reasons, and randomisation may not have been possible. For example, Ardalan et al. allocated intervention or control status to 31 villages and later adjusted analyses for possible confounders. [27] The authors chose the allocations, increasing the risk that any differences in outcome between the intervention and control groups are due to something other than the intervention. Blando et al. studied two groups of people who had themselves chosen whether or not to receive the intervention several years earlier, which presents a high risk of selection bias. [12] That study does not aim to be a straightforward evaluation of effectiveness, however, and the study should be interpreted in that light.

## 3.4.4.2 BLINDING (PERFORMANCE BIAS AND DETECTION BIAS)

Blinding participants to the intervention that they are receiving is generally not possible in for the interventions identified in this review, although Eisenman et al. used interviewers who were blinded to intervention status in their randomised trial. [13] No other studies mentioned blinding. Outcome assessment in before and after studies, controlled studies and interrupted time series would benefit from being conducted blind to the time point or intervention.

## 3.4.4.3 INCOMPLETE OUTCOME DATA (ATTRITION BIAS)

The only randomised trial identified in this study had substantial attrition from both groups in the study, particularly from the high-intensity intervention. [13] This could have affected the final results, since a per protocol analysis was presented. Ardalan et al. sought to avoid attrition by taking a further sample of participants for the post-intervention assessment. [27] Many studies only conducted one interview with each participant, during which (if necessary) they asked participants to recall past as well as present knowledge or behaviours. Whilst avoiding attrition, this does increase risk of recall bias. In other studies, attrition was a significant problem. In the SARS intervention by Chan et al., for example, one third of participants were lost to follow-up between two interviews. [20] There was a risk of non-response bias in many of the studies, which was not often addressed. Rundblad et al. and Blando et al. both compared their study groups to the census data for the local population, but even this may not guarantee that people who are recruited are representative of the wider population in other characteristics. [8,12]

## 3.4.4.4 SELECTIVE REPORTING (REPORTING BIAS)

Some of the studies (mainly studies of preparedness) were clearly designed as prospective intervention studies. Numerous other reports sought to evaluate the response to disasters that had already occurred, in which case hypothesis could be formed cognisant of the general outcome of the interventions. Some of these may still have entailed a prospective collection of data. Others, however, could have generated hypotheses after data were already available. This is particularly possible for research into infectious diseases, given the presence of significant surveillance programmes in some countries. For instance, the use of 'lag time' in the SARS epidemic as an outcome, as reported in Pang et al., might carry some risk of being a post hoc analysis. [25]

## 3.5 DISCUSSION

### 3.5.1 SUMMARY OF EVIDENCE

Twenty seven studies of risk communication interventions for the mitigation of, preparedness for, response to, and recovery from disasters were included in this systematic review. The contexts, interventions and outcomes were diverse, and meta-analysis was not appropriate. Some disaster mitigation and preparedness interventions appeared to improve knowledge and behaviour relating to disaster risks. There was little robust evidence of the effectiveness of risk communication for disaster knowledge, behaviour and health outcomes in the response and recovery phases of disasters. One intervention was associated with an undesirable reduction in protective behaviours.

## 3.5.1.1 MITIGATION AND PREPAREDNESS INTERVENTIONS

All four trials were found in this category. All mitigation and preparedness studies reported that the interventions that they reported were effective to some extent. Eastwood et al. reported a high level of intended compliance with public health advice before and after an intervention, but did not make statistical comparisons of the changes. [6] Due to the already high compliance (over 90% for each measure), future studies in such contexts would therefore need to be very large to detect significant improvements. Dumais et al. reported significant improvements in knowledge for schoolchildren about influenza, which was intended only to facilitate further health education. [7] The Roess et al. study of a monkeypox intervention found modest improvement in knowledge outcomes and some behaviours, but did not successfully affect some high risk behaviours. [28] Assessing the longer term effect of the programme is likely to be difficult. Preparedness and mitigation for natural disasters was a relatively well-studied area with several prospective trials. Increased likelihood of behavioural preparedness was shown in controlled studies by Eisenman et al. and Ardalan et al. [13,27] Games were used by two authors to increase knowledge, with apparent success. [18,31,33] The effectiveness of the evacuation warnings is difficult to assess because of the many interacting factors in the situations. The Mauritius and India evacuations had relatively low voluntary compliance, whereas the Reverse 911 communication in the San Diego wildfires apparently provided a strong impetus for people to act. [16,17,29,30]

## 3.5.1.2 RESPONSE INTERVENTIONS

Few of the response interventions were prospectively planned. The prospectively planned studies by Chan et al. and Farahat et al., though taking place in the context of ongoing disasters, were similar in character to the preparedness interventions for infectious diseases. [20,26] Farahat et al. demonstrated improvements in knowledge and behaviour over three months, while Chan et al. reported a negative change for behaviour one week after their intervention. [20,26] Attributing causality in the absence

of a control group and in the context of widespread public and media interest in the topic of concern is difficult, and limits the value of these studies.
All the other studies attempted to evaluate an ongoing or past risk communication response to a disaster. In these contexts, too, there are many factors that affect interpretation, including many other non-communication
interventions that take place concurrently. The studies of the UK and USA
water crises demonstrated that the communications to alert the public to
the need to take action to avoid using contaminated water were successful
in reaching almost all affected, but that in spite of this reach, a significant
minority of people either did not understand the advice given or chose not
to follow it. [8,15,19] In Haiti, despite a high level of knowledge, the water
treatment was apparently not used all the time. [32] The factors that affect
decisions about whether to comply with the advice may differ between
these contexts.

## 3.5.1.3 RECOVERY INTERVENTIONS

Three recovery interventions were found, including two studies of the
post-hurricane Katrina response in New Orleans. [10,11] Use of the mental health help lines in New York and New Orleans increased with promotion. [10,11,14] Serial surveys of the audience in New Orleans suggested
no change in one analysis, and changes in knowledge and behaviour, but
not incidence of PTSD in a different analysis. [10,11]

## 3.5.1.4 DISASTER-SPECIFIC INTERVENTIONS

We grouped the disasters primarily by phase and secondly by disaster type.
It is possible, however, that there are important lessons for disaster types
that transcend phases. We therefore also considered these reports together
by disaster type. There were eleven studies related to natural disasters. [10
,11,13,16,17,18,24,27,29,30,31,33] All five preparedness studies reported
that their interventions (games, interactive discussion groups or teaching)
were effective means of increasing knowledge or preparedness behaviour.
[13,18,24,27,31,33] The only randomised trial identified for this review

provided evidence in favour of a health promotion discussion group approach to general disaster preparedness over the simple provision of written information. [13] In the three early warning studies of natural disasters diverse methods of communication were used. Reverse-911 appeared to be a promising method of communicating with at-risk populations, and people were able to validate their own risk using the internet. [16,29,30] A study of a mass media campaign in response to a natural disaster suggested that some health messages were received and selectively acted on by the target population. [17] Two studies of a recovery intervention to a hurricane suggested that a mass media campaign caused more people to contact a help line and that the media campaign might have increased understanding about post-traumatic stress disorder and might have been associated with increases in some preventive behaviours. [10,11] It is interesting to note that natural disaster preparedness interventions, which authorities might wish to target at a whole population, mainly involved interpersonal communication and seemed quite resource-intensive. During disasters, responses were characterised by the need to communicate quickly, often by all available methods. The ability to directly communicate with people believed to be at risk, such as by the Reverse 911 alert, offers potential advantages over the use of third-party broadcast media, which usually targets a wider audience than those directly at risk.

There were ten studies related to infectious disease outbreaks, epidemics and pandemics. [6,7,9,20,21,22,23,25,26,28] A group education approach was effective in increasing knowledge and improving planned behaviour related to a disease in a village and in two school settings. [7,26,28] In another school setting during an outbreak of meningococcal disease, a qualitative study suggested that formal communication was slower than informal electronic and telephone communication, resulting in incorrect information being shared by school pupils. [9] Studies of telephone education related to infectious disease disasters reported inconsistent results. During a SARS outbreak, one study reported an increase in potentially harmful behaviours, whilst a study of a pandemic influenza intervention suggested increased willingness to comply with protective behaviours. [6,20] Multi-channel communication interventions were used in four other studies of infectious disease disasters. [21,22,23,25] One of these used mass SMS text messages to give infection control advice in one of two settings. [22] It is not possible to draw firm conclusions about the effectiveness because of the study designs, but the results of Yen et al. suggested that the use of mass SMS text messages may have contributed to improved compliance with infection control procedures and faster resolution of the outbreak.

## 3.5.2 LIMITATIONS

### 3.5.2.1 ISSUES RELATING TO STUDY DESIGN

Almost all the studies took place in the context of group interventions. However, no studies took full account for this in their analyses. This is a major problem for many of the studies where interventions were allocated at the group level. Analysing group-level studies at an individual level without accounting for the similarity of individuals within groups results in the study having more power than it should, and causes estimates of effect size to be unduly precise. [34] Most of the studies were controlled or uncontrolled before and after studies and few of these used appropriate paired analyses. Separating the effect of the intervention from outside influences in uncontrolled studies is very difficult, particularly in disaster situations. The suddenness of many disasters that require evacuation means that planning and conducting prospective studies is difficult. Some disaster risk communication interventions are, however, amenable to study by more reliable methods, including individual or cluster randomised trials. In places where disasters occur relatively often, it may be possible to plan prospective comparisons of putatively similarly effective communication methods. Ethical issues must be addressed when planning such studies, but in principle, preparedness studies in which the control group subsequently are offered the intervention, or response studies that compare two putatively similar methods of risk communication (where it is not standard practice to use both together) are likely to be ethically sound.

## 3.5.2.2 ISSUES RELATING TO INTERVENTION DESIGN

We had anticipated that this review would identify and evaluate studies that employed modern communications, including Internet-based social media. However, no studies that met the inclusion criteria tested these methods as an intervention. Conventional web sites were used in some organisational communications. Many complex interventions that occurred in response to disasters used many methods of communication at once and did not describe in detail how each was used. Two-way dialogue between the public and professionals was a feature of many preparedness interventions, but was not a common practice in responses to disasters, which tended to follow the traditional unidirectional model of disaster risk communication.

## 3.5.2.3 ISSUES RELATING TO THE OUTCOMES STUDIED

Due to the diversity of interventions and contexts, the outcomes for most studies differed. Knowledge outcomes were usually assessed in a survey following an information intervention that provided the basis for that knowledge. However, in the context of the early warnings, simply receiving the warning was assumed to be a knowledge outcome. Yet it is likely that simply receiving an early warning of an impending disaster is not the same as knowing and understanding the content of the message. Other outcomes could be valid and might be as important as knowledge and behaviour.

## 3.5.3 POTENTIAL BIASES IN THE REVIEW PROCESS

The use of the term disaster may have influenced the nature of studies included in this review, because events with similar cause but which do not meet the definition of disaster because they caused less severe disruption (possibly even because of a good public health response) will not have been included in this review. Valuable learning may therefore be lost because good practices that prevent an event overwhelming services and causing a disaster might not be found. Other studies may not have associated their research with a disaster, as they may be defined by the cause, and not the effect, of the disaster. In some reports, it was difficult to ascertain whether an event met the definition of disaster, since the local context may not be sufficiently described to indicate whether services were overwhelmed. This is particularly the case with preparedness and mitigation interventions as, for example, prevention efforts for many infectious diseases could be considered disaster mitigation, but may not have been presented as such in the published literature. The distinction between mitigation, preparedness and response to disasters sometimes seemed artificial, since it divided similar interventions that happened to take place before and during disasters (e.g. pandemic influenza)

## 3.6 CONCLUSIONS

### 3.6.1 IMPLICATIONS FOR PRACTICE

Most of the studies included in this review reported improvements in disaster-related knowledge and behaviour. Due to the differences between the studies, it is not possible to conclude that one method of risk communication is superior to others. It is important to note the potential for harm from interventions, such as might have been the case in Chan et al. [20]

### 3.6.2 IMPLICATIONS FOR RESEARCH

The major finding for future research from this study is that there is an absence of high-quality robust trials relating to disaster communication that should be remedied. Modern internet-based interactive social media present opportunities for risk communication, and may facilitate evaluation because it may be possible to invite recipients to complete knowledge or behaviour questionnaires, or even to request position-based information from mobile devices. Randomised trials (individual and cluster) of risk communication may have become more difficult in recent years because of the likelihood of 'contamination' between intervention and control groups due to sharing of information, which means that designing comparisons of information interventions will require careful planning to either prevent, or more likely, incorporate, the interpersonal information sharing that is a defining feature of modern communication methods.

## REFERENCES

1.  United Nations International Strategy for Disaster Reduction. Terminology on disaster risk reduction. 2009
2.  Burnham GM. Chapter 1: Disaster Definitions. In: Burnham GM & Rand EC, editor(s). The Johns Hopkins and Red Cross and Red Crescent Public health guide in emergencies. Second edition. Geneva: International Federation of Red Cross and Red Crescent Societies, 2008.
3.  Haddow KS, Haddow G. Disaster communications in a changing media world. Butterworth-Heinemann, 2008.
4.  Reynolds BS, Seeger MW. Crisis and Emergency Risk Communication. Atlanta. 2012
5.  Glik DC. Risk communication for public health emergencies. Annu Rev Public Health. 2007;28:33-54.
6.  Eastwood K, Durrheim D, Francis JL, d'Espaignet ET, Duncan S, Islam F, Speare R. Knowledge about pandemic influenza and compliance with containment measures among Australians. Bull World Health Organ. 2009 Aug;87(8):588-94.
7.  Dumais N, Hasni A. High school intervention for influenza biology and epidemics/pandemics: impact on conceptual understanding among adolescents. CBE Life Sci Educ. 2009 Spring;8(1):62-71.
8.  Rundblad G, Knapton O, Hunter PR. Communication, perception and behaviour during a natural disaster involving a 'Do Not Drink' and a subsequent 'Boil Water' notice: a postal questionnaire study. BMC Public Health. 2010 Oct 25;10:641.
9.  Taylor-Robinson D, Elders K, Milton B, Thurston H. Students' attitudes to the communications employed during an outbreak of meningococcal disease in a UK school: a qualitative study. J Public Health (Oxf). 2010 Mar;32(1):32-7.
10. Beaudoin CE. Assessment of a media campaign and related crisis help line following Hurricane Katrina. Public Health Rep. 2008 Sep-Oct;123(5):646-51.
11. Beaudoin CE. Evaluating a media campaign that targeted PTSD after Hurricane Katrina. Health Commun. 2009 Sep;24(6):515-23.
12. Blando JD, Robertson C, Bresnitz E. Communicating information in an emergency preparedness pill distribution campaign. Biosecur Bioterror. 2008 Mar;6(1):57-65.
13. Eisenman DP, Glik D, Gonzalez L, Maranon R, Zhou Q, Tseng CH, Asch SM. Improving Latino disaster preparedness using social networks. Am J Prev Med. 2009 Dec;37(6):512-7.

14. Frank RG, Pindyck T, Donahue SA, Pease EA, Foster MJ, Felton CJ, Essock SM. Impact of a media campaign for disaster mental health counseling in post-September 11 New York. Psychiatr Serv. 2006 Sep;57(9):1304-8.

15. Galarce EM, Viswanath K. Crisis communication: an inequalities perspective on the 2010 Boston water crisis. Disaster Med Public Health Prep. 2012 Dec;6(4):349-56.

16. Strawderman L, Salehi A, Babski-Reeves Kari, Thornton-Neaves T, Cosby A. Reverse 911 as a Complementary Evacuation Warning System. Natural Hazards Review. 2012 Feb; 13(1):65-73

17. Sugerman DE, Keir JM, Dee DL, Lipman H, Waterman SH, Ginsberg M, Fishbein DB. Emergency health risk communication during the 2007 San Diego wildfires: comprehension, compliance, and recall. J Health Commun. 2012;17(6):698-712.

18. Tanes Z. Earthquake risk communication with video games: Examining the role of player-game interaction in influencing the gaming experience and outcomes. 2011.

19. Wang CJ, Little AA, Holliman JB, Ng CY, Barrero-Castillero A, Fu CM, Zuckerman B, Bauchner H. Communication of urgent public health messages to urban populations: lessons from the Massachusetts water main break. Disaster Med Public Health Prep. 2011 Oct;5(3):235-41.

20. Chan SS, So WK, Wong DC, Lee AC, Tiwari A. Improving older adults' knowledge and practice of preventive measures through a telephone health education during the SARS epidemic in Hong Kong: a pilot study. Int J Nurs Stud. 2007 Sep;44(7):1120-7.

21. Olsen SJ, Laosiritaworn Y, Pattanasin S, Prapasiri P, Dowell SF. Poultry-handling practices during avian influenza outbreak, Thailand. Emerg Infect Dis. 2005 Oct;11(10):1601-3.

22. Yen MY, Wu TS, Chiu AW, Wong WW, Wang PE, Chan TC, King CC. Taipei's use of a multi-channel mass risk communication program to rapidly reverse an epidemic of highly communicable disease. PLoS One. 2009 Nov 23;4(11):e7962.

23. Karan K, Aileen L, Elaine PYL. Emerging Victorious Against an Outbreak. Integrated Communication Management of SARS in Singapore Media Coverage and Impact of the SARS Campaign in Moving a Nation to be Socially Responsible. J Creativ Comm. 2007 Nov; 2(3), 383-403.

24. Yasunari T, Nozawa M, Nishio R, Yamamoto A, Takami Y. Development and evaluation of 'disaster preparedness' educational programme for pregnant women. Int Nurs Rev. 2011 Sep;58(3):335-40.

25. Pang X, Zhu Z, Xu F, Guo J, Gong X, Liu D, Liu Z, Chin DP, Feikin DR. Evaluation of control measures implemented in the severe acute respiratory syndrome outbreak in Beijing, 2003. JAMA. 2003 Dec 24;290(24):3215-21.

26. Farahat T, Al-Kot M, Al-Fath OA, Noh A, Diab N. Promotion of knowledge, attitude and practice towards swine flu A/H1N1;(An intervention study on secondary school children of Menofia Governorate, Egypt). Menoufia Med J. 2010;23(2):83-94.

27. Ardalan A, Naieni KH, Mahmoodi M, Zanganeh AM, Keshtkar AA, Honarvar MR, Kabir MJ. Flash flood preparedness in Golestan province of Iran: a community intervention trial. Am J Disaster Med. 2010 Jul-Aug;5(4):197-214.

28. Roess AA, Monroe BP, Kinzoni EA, Gallagher S, Ibata SR, Badinga N, Molouania TM, Mabola FS, Mombouli JV, Carroll DS, MacNeil A, Benzekri NA, Moses

C, Damon IK, Reynolds MG. Assessing the effectiveness of a community inter-vention for monkeypox prevention in the Congo basin. PLoS Negl Trop Dis. 2011 Oct;5(10):e1356.

29. Perry SD. Tsunami warning dissemination in Mauritus. J Appl Commun Res. 2007 Nov;35(4):399-417.

30. Sharma U, Patwardhan A, Parthasarathy D. Assessing adaptive capacity to tropical cyclones in the East coast of India: a pilot study of public response to cyclone warn-ing information. Climatic Change. 2009;94:189-209

31. Clerveaux, V, Spence B. The Communication of Disaster Information and Knowl-edge to Children Using Game Technique: The Disaster Awareness Game (DAG). International Journal of Environmental Research. 2009;3(2):209-222

32. Colindres RE, Jain S, Bowen A, Mintz E, Domond P. After the flood: an evalu-ation of in-home drinking water treatment with combined flocculent-disinfectant following Tropical Storm Jeanne -- Gonaives, Haiti, 2004. J Water Health. 2007 Sep;5(3):367-74.

33. Tanes Z, Cho H. Goal setting outcomes: Examining the role of goal interaction in influencing the experience and learning outcomes of video game play for earthquake preparedness. Computers in Human Behavior 2013;29(3):858-69.

34. Clarke M. Commentary: Cluster trials: a few words on why and how to do them. Int J Epidemiol. 2009 Feb;38(1):36-7.

*There are several supplemental files that are not available in this version of the article. To view this additional information, please use the citation on the first page of this chapter.*

# CHAPTER 4

# Near-Real-Time Analysis of Publicly Communicated Disaster Response Information

TREVOR GIRARD, FRIEDEMANN WENZEL, BIJAN KHAZAI, TINA KUNZ-PLAPP, JAMES E. DANIELL, AND SUSAN A. BRINK

## 4.1 INTRODUCTION

Disasters, such as major storm events or earthquakes, trigger an immediate response by the disaster management system of the nation in question. The quality of this response is a large factor in its ability to limit the impacts of the disaster on the local population. Improving the quality of disaster response therefore reduces disaster impacts. Studying past disasters is a valuable exercise to understand what went wrong, identify measures that could have mitigated the issues, and make recommendations to improve future disaster planning and response. The reports that result from this reflective process have a variety of names such as "lessons learned" docu-

*Near-Real-Time Analysis of Publicly Communicated Disaster Response Information. © Girard T, Wenzel F, Khazai B, Kunz-Plapp T, Daniell JE, and Brink SA.* International Journal of Disaster Risk Science *5,3 (2014), doi: 10.1007/s13753-014-0024-3. Licensed under a Creative Commons Attribution License, http://creativecommons.org/licenses/by/4.0/.*

ments (Birkland 2009), "after action" reviews (Comfort 2005; Donahue and Tuohy 2006), and "ex-post" evaluations (Cosgrave et al. 2009; OECD 2010). Due to the focus on disaster response, this article uses the term "post-response" report (Birkland 2009) to refer to documents that evaluate disaster response activities, make recommendations for improvement, and which are issued after the response phase is over.

A recent effort to study natural disasters that goes beyond the typical post-response reports has been started by the Integrated Research on Disaster Risk (IRDR) program, which was established by the International Council for Science (ICSU) in 2010. These activities, called Forensic Disaster Investigations (FORIN), aim to uncover the root causes of disasters through in-depth investigations. The FORIN working group argues that "thoroughly analyzing cases, including both success stories and failures, will help build an understanding of how natural hazards do—or do not— become disasters" (ICSU 2013). In adopting the IRDR FORIN approach to comprehensive understanding of disasters, the Center for Disaster Management and Risk Reduction Technology (CEDIM) adds a time-critical component to the evaluation process. The goal of the CEDIM Forensic Disaster Analysis (FDA) approach is to understand and assess in near-real-time the evolution of the event where information may be scarce or unclear (Wenzel et al. 2012).

CEDIM recently began a pilot study to include the disaster response as a potentially contributing factor to the overall disaster impact and a methodology was developed for this purpose. Thus, the main contribution of this article is the introduction of a methodology for near-real-time analysis of publicly communicated disaster response information. The term "near-real-time analysis" used throughout this article can be defined as the process of collecting the information available within the first 0–5 days of a disaster, analyzing that information, and producing results within approximately one day of the latest information. For example, if a near-real-time analysis was based on the information available on the fifth day after the disaster, the results of that analysis would be available by the sixth day. The aim of the near-real-time methodology is to base analysis on current information and to produce results while the disaster response is still in operation. This methodology represents a first step in analyzing disaster response within days of a disaster. The application of this methodology following a disaster is intended to enhance disaster response and subsequently reduce disaster impacts. The methodology has already been applied to CEDIM FDA activities following tropical cyclone Phailin in India, as well as the Bohol Earthquake and Typhoon Haiyan in the Philippines.

The next section discusses the importance of post-response reports but also identifies a limitation to their ability to enhance a disaster response. Real-time evaluations and other key concepts that have led to the development of our near-real-time methodology will then be discussed in Sect. 3. The near-real-time methodology is introduced in Sect. 4 along with a classification scheme that was created to standardize the information analysis process. This methodology was then tested in near-real-time following disasters that occurred between July and November 2013, using a process we have termed an "information gap analysis," the results of which are discussed in Sect. 5. Finally, three factors are identified in Sect. 6 that will need to be addressed to further strengthen the results of analyses.

## 4.2 CURRENT APPROACH

A common method for analyzing disaster response is to carry out post-response evaluations, often referred to as "lessons learned" or "after action" reports. The main purpose of such reports is to identify what changes should be implemented in order to improve future responses. For example, lessons learned from Hurricane Katrina led US Congress to enact a law in 2006 to restructure the Federal Emergency Management Agency (FEMA) (Starks 2012). Subsequent changes led to improvements in FEMA's response to Hurricane Sandy (Chivers 2012; Starks 2012). Similarly, the post-response report of the 2009 Victorian Bushfires Royal Commission resulted in a AUD 900 million commitment by the Australian Government to implement all but one of the report's recommendations (Sheales 2010). Post-response reports therefore have major potential to influence change in the disaster management system.

A valuable strength of post-response evaluation is that it is based on actual disaster events. The impacts of the disaster can act as proof for pre-existing arguments, such as the often cited need to reinforce school buildings. The events can also bring to light unique issues that were unforeseen during disaster planning, such as the need to alter tsunami warnings in Japan to be more assertive and direct following the Great East Japan Earthquake (Arai 2013).

Post-response reports are typically concerned with operational and tactical matters (Birkland 2009), which require extensive input from those involved in the response. Due to the need for an in-depth understanding of the decisions made and actions, post-response reports can take a long time to produce. Following Hurricane Katrina, Hurricane Sandy, and the 2011 Christchurch Earthquake, official post-response reports were issued 6, 8, and 16 months after each disaster respectively (The White House 2006; FEMA 2013; McLean et al. 2012). Thus, post-response reports do not have the ability to enhance the disaster response being assessed for the obvious reason that they are carried out after the response phase is over. The result, as illustrated in Fig. 1, is that lessons learned can only be applied to future disasters. The time-lag between a disaster and when a post-response evaluation is issued therefore presents an opportunity for other forms of analysis to be carried out.

This article argues that some of the issues raised in post-response reports could be identified within days of a disaster rather than waiting months for a full report to be compiled. The benefit of identifying issues within days of the disaster is that those issues could potentially be corrected during the response phase.

## 4.3 KEY CONCEPTS

In the field of humanitarian relief, the inability of post-response reports to enhance the response under investigation has led to the development of real-time evaluations. The key aspect of real-time humanitarian evaluations is that they are completed while the operation is still underway. The typical time-frame of such reports is to begin field work 4–6 weeks into a mission and complete a report within a month, while the mission is still operational (Jamal and Crisp 2002). This results in findings that are delivered when they may still make a difference to the on-going humanitarian relief phase. The methodology described in Sect. 4 has taken this key aspect of humanitarian real-time evaluations and applied it to analyzing disaster response. Disaster response has a time-frame of days rather than months, requiring an entirely new approach to produce an analysis so quickly.

Furthermore, real-time evaluations in their current form are aimed at enhancing international humanitarian relief projects. International actors are not a major part of the immediate disaster response phase. It is local governments who are the first institutions to oversee a disaster response. If the local system does not have the capacity to manage the response, then the national disaster management system is typically activated. Only in major events does the international community respond through a response that is subject to national government approval and conditions. This order of response underlines the fact that a nation's government controls the immediate disaster response, not the international community. Therefore, carrying out an analysis of the disaster response during the first 0–5 days of the disaster also requires a shift in focus from the international actors to the national government and subsequent disaster management system.

Managing a disaster response involves rapid monitoring and evaluation due to the time-critical environment in which emergency relief efforts take place. This results in the disaster management team making quick decisions and taking rapid actions. The details of this process, the decisions made or actions taken, and the reasons for them are often not made public until well after the disaster, if at all. Yet, as an outsider, aspects of the disaster response can be observed within hours, through news media, social media, and, in particular, time-critical information disseminated by the disaster management system.

The role of information in any disaster response is similar regardless of the location, scale, or type of event. The typical response involves gathering information to understand the impact of the disaster and carrying out actions based on that information to reduce human suffering and protect or restore a variety of systems such as transportation, healthcare, and communications. Production of information following a disaster is therefore crucial to any response. A key concept in this research is that communicating a portion of this information to the public should be a core function of any disaster management system. Information is arguably required by the public during any disaster, regardless of where that disaster occurs. This argument is supported by disaster communication literature. For instance,

Appleby's (2013, p. 9) evaluation of the response to the Great East Japan Earthquake stresses the importance of communicating information to the public and concludes that "information saves lives, that communication itself is a form of aid..." Maxwell (2003) explains that better informed citizens are able to make the correct decisions to protect themselves during disaster situations, which has the added benefit of reducing the strain on government resources. Helsloot and Ruitenberg (2004) go further to argue that the flow of information prior to and during disasters should be directed at the average citizen, because they are major actors in rescue and relief.

The provision of disaster-related information to the public is in the best interest of the response effort because it helps to keep the public safe, reduces the strain on government resources, and enhances public participation in the response. Not only is this disaster-related information vital to the response, but also its very urgent nature makes it ideal to analyze within days of a disaster. The methodology therefore utilizes the information produced by disaster management systems to analyze the disaster response in near-real-time. Consider Fig. 2 which represents the disaster response evaluation cycle if analysis is carried out in near-real-time.

**TABLE 1:** Simulated near-real-time analyses using ReliefWeb

| Disaster | Date of disaster | Country |
| --- | --- | --- |
| Hurricane Katrina | 29 Aug 2005 | USA |
| Cyclone Nargis | 02 May 2008 | Myanmar |
| Pakistan floods | July/Aug 2010 | Pakistan |
| Queensland floods | Dec 2010/Jan 2011 | Australia |
| Christchurch earthquake | 22 Feb 2011 | New Zealand |
| Himalayan earthquake | 18 Sept 2011 | India/Nepal |
| Tropical Storm Washi | 16 Dec 2011 | Philippines |
| Visayas earthquake | 06 Feb 2012 | Philippines |
| Hurricane Sandy | 29 Oct 2012 | USA |
| Yunnan earthquake | 07 Sept 2012 | China |
| Typhoon Bopha | 04 Dec 2012 | Philippines |

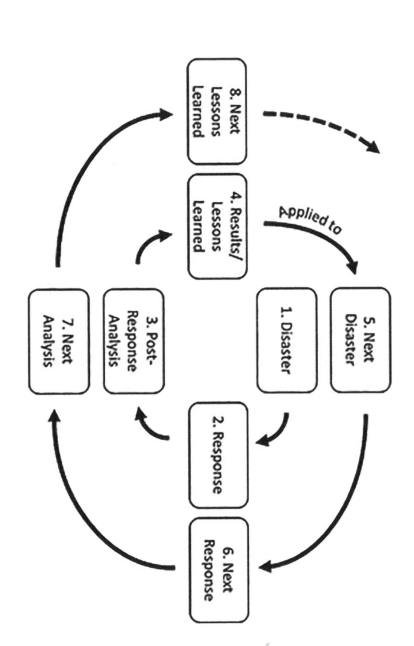

FIGURE 1: Disaster response evaluation cycle: post-response analysis

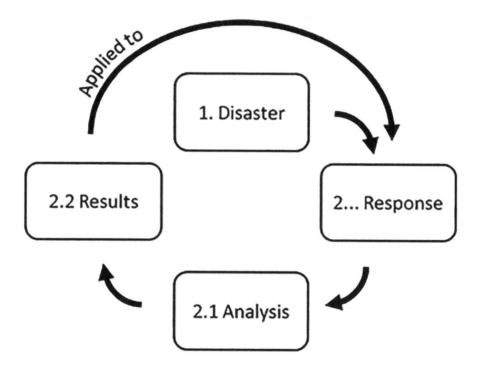

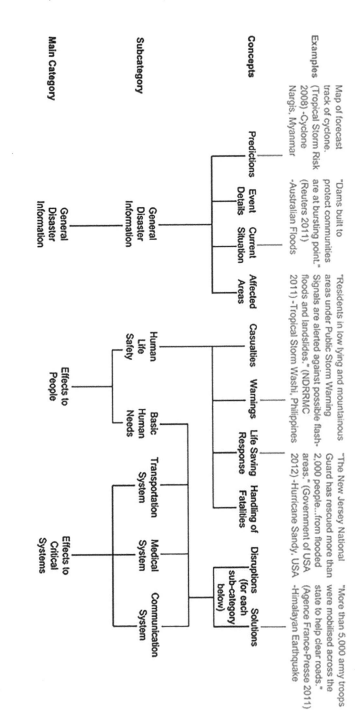

**FIGURE 3:** Classification scheme: critical information needs of the public

When the analysis is completed, while the response is still in operation, it can inform the future direction of that immediate response. In fact, analyses already occur within days following disasters. CEDIM FDA activities involve estimates of potential disaster effects within days of a disaster, such as social and economic impacts and building damage (Wenzel et al. 2013). The insurance industry also conducts catastrophe modelling immediately following many disasters to estimate insured losses. The next section describes the methodology developed to carry out a similar near-real-time analysis of publicly communicated disaster response information.

## 4.4 METHODOLOGY

The analysis is based on information produced by a disaster management system within the first 0–5 days of the response. The data are collected from publicly available sources, with a majority being from ReliefWeb. ReliefWeb is an online service of the United Nations Office for the Coordination of Humanitarian Affairs (UNOCHA) that acts as a clearinghouse for disaster information following an event and collects updates from more than 4,000 sources globally (ReliefWeb 2014). Common forms of disaster updates contained on the website are news and press releases, situation reports, maps, infographics, analyses, appeals, and assessments. During disasters, these updates are posted on ReliefWeb as the information is collected. Since ReliefWeb archives the updates and sorts them by day of release, it allows for the simulation of carrying out a near-real-time analysis of the information following any disaster within ReliefWeb's database. As such, the study began with simulated near-real-time analyses of the 11 disasters identified in Table 1.

### 4.4.1 DEVELOPMENT OF CLASSIFICATION SCHEME

During a disaster situation the public will need to make critical decisions regarding what to do, where to go, how to get there, and so on. While a general assessment of the situation may give the public an indication of the scale of the event, many of the important decisions the public makes during a disaster must be based on specific information. For example, rather than a general description stating that some roads may be flooded, the public needs to know where exactly so they can plan alternative escape routes. In addition to identifying the number of casualties, the public should also know how those casualties occurred so they can better understand the risk to themselves. In order to analyze the extent to which the various information needs are addressed, a classification scheme for the information needs of the public during a disaster was developed.

Development of the classification scheme consisted of three steps: data acquisition, content analysis, and prioritization. Data acquisition consisted of retrieval of all disaster updates available in the ReliefWeb disaster archive for approximately five days after each of the disasters identified in Table 1. Each report was manually broken down into the separate disaster messages it contained. An average of approximately 200 different publicly communicated disaster messages were identified for each of the 11 disasters reviewed. For example, following the Himalayan Earthquake, one message communicated to the public by the Government of India was that "The Darjeeling-Siliguri road has been blocked by 2 landslides, repair work has started and the road is likely to be opened for traffic today itself" (Government of India 2011). Content analysis of all messages retrieved was then carried out to identify general concepts and the relationships between them. Thus, the above message describing blocked roads and road repair work helped develop the concepts transportation system "disruptions" and "solutions." Finally, since the focus is on the information needs of the local population, prioritization consisted of selecting those concepts that were estimated to be most critical to the public in the first days of the response. Figure 3 illustrates how the disaster response messages have helped to develop the concepts, subcategories, and main categories rather than the other way around.

Three main categories have been derived from the concepts observed: general disaster information, effects to people, and effects to critical systems. These details help the public make critical decisions in times of disaster to maintain or improve their or others' well-being. The category "General Disaster Information" describes the general characteristics of the event in either past, present, or predicted future state, and identifies the affected areas without getting into the details of the actual impacts. Examples of general disaster information include magnitude and location of an earthquake or the predicted path of a typhoon. The category "Effects to People" covers human life safety and basic human needs. This information addresses the direct disaster impacts on physical well-being. Items include casualties or potential casualties in the near future, and disruptions to those things that if left without could lead to casualties, such as lack of drinking water, food, shelter, and sanitation. Finally, "Effects to Critical Systems" covers those systems which are important to the immediate well-being of the local population that if left without could also lead to further casualties. Transportation, medical, and communication disruptions therefore signify a potential reduction or elimination of the ability of the local population to maintain or improve their physical well-being. For example, transportation disruptions hamper the ability to leave hazardous areas or access aid, medical disruptions limit the ability to receive emergency care, and communication disruptions restrict the ability to request help.

Once sorted, further content analysis was conducted to categorize the information contained under each concept. The resulting categories are referred to as properties. Three types of properties were observed: basic data, analysis, and root causes. "Basic data" makes up the majority of the information and answers the questions of who, what, where, and when or how long. "Analysis" describes results of inquiry or measurement, such as explaining how disruptions occurred, or identifying levels of needs satisfied or outstanding. "Root causes" identify why aspects of the disaster occurred.

## 4.4.2 BEST OBSERVED PRACTICE REVIEW

Content analysis of all 11 disasters and comparison between them resulted in the establishment of best observed practices for what properties should be associated with each concept and when they can be provided following a disaster. "Best observed practice" refers to the variety of information properties that have been witnessed in practice following the 11 disasters reviewed. This is contrary to best "potential" practice that would need to be based on all disasters as well as systematic research into the information needs of disaster affected communities. Basing the information needs of the public on observed practice confirms that delivery of that information has already been proven feasible. But in order to further develop this classification scheme, future research must consult the expertise of individuals who have been through a disaster situation in order to confirm what information they needed that may not be captured in this classification scheme, which may therefore be extended in the future.

The set of properties for each concept is illustrated in Table 2. The properties answer the questions identified. For example, the properties of the concept "Transportation system disruptions" are: what the disruptions are; where they have occurred; how long they lasted or are expected to last; how they occurred; and why the system was vulnerable in the first place.

The best observed practice review revealed that basic information can be delivered within 1 day (24 h) of a disaster for all categories. Analyses by the disaster management system regarding how impacts occurred were observed within the first 1–2 days but those regarding outstanding needs were often missing in the first five days of the response. If a disaster management system is unable to identify the outstanding needs then it is very difficult to confirm the extent to which the response is meeting the needs of the affected population. Root causes were extremely rare to find in the first five days of the response, which is understandable considering this information does not typically help the immediate response. Nevertheless, the reasons for why the disaster generated the effects it did are critical pieces of information and in-line with the FORIN approach. For example, the low casualties observed in the aftermath of Cyclone Phailin were identified as being the result of a good warning system and excellent coordination between agencies that successfully evacuated almost one million people prior to landfall (Oxfam 2013). This information is very important to disaster-risk-reduction activities, which attempt to learn from both failures and success by understanding the root causes of each. Although this methodology focuses on the first five days of the disaster, including root causes as properties of the applicable concepts ensures the need for this information in the future is identified.

**TABLE 2:** Information needs of public: properties of each concept

| Main categories | Subcategories and concepts | Set of properties/Questions to be answered | | |
| --- | --- | --- | --- | --- |
| | | Basic data | Analysis | Root causes |
| General Disaster Info | General disaster info | What are the characteristics of the event, where will/did they occur, and when? | So what? (Why are these details important?) | How come details result/ed in effects? |
| | a. Predictions, description of event & current situation | | | |
| | b. Affected areas | Who/where is confirmed to be affected, and by what? | — | — |
| Effects to People | Human life safety (and potential threats) | How many casualties, who are they, and where are they located? | How were they injured, killed, or missing? | How come they were vulnerable? |
| | a. Casualties | What are the dangers, where are they expected, and when? | How do the details equal a threat? | How come they are vulnerable? |
| | b. Warnings | | | |
| | c. Life saving response | Who is doing what to combat threats (evacuation, SAR), where, and when? | How will this combat the threat? | — |
| | d. Handling of fatalities | What is being done to deal with fatalities and when? | How do actions meet needs? (outstanding needs) | — |
| | Basic human needs | Who/where is affected, by what, and for how long? | How did they occur? | How come the system was vulnerable? |
| | a. Disruptions | | | |
| | b. Solutions | Who is doing what to meet the basic needs of affected, where and when? | Outstanding needs | — |
| Effects to Critical Systems | Transportation, Medical services, Communications, for each: | What are the disruptions, where, and for how long? | How did they occur? | How come the system was vulnerable? |
| | a. Disruptions | | | |
| | b. Solutions | Who is doing what to meet the associated needs of those affected, where and when? | Outstanding needs | — |

A set of properties is unique to each concept, but is the same for any disaster. Thus, Table 2 is a template that does not change regardless of the disaster being analyzed. Comparing the properties produced in an ongoing disaster with Table 2 results in the identification of questions that remain unanswered, referred to as "information gaps." Two types of information gap analyses have been carried out so far, as discussed in the next section.

**TABLE 3:** Near-real-time analyses

| Disasters | Country | Date | Information sources | Reported in |
|---|---|---|---|---|
| Aceh earthquake | Indonesia | 02 July 2013 | ReliefWeb | N/A |
| Pakistan earthquake | Pakistan | 24 Sept 2013 | Pakistan National Disaster Management Agency, ReliefWeb, and other sources: Al Jazeera news/radio, BBC, CBC, CNN, The Guardian, RTnews | N/A |
| Cyclone Phailin | India | 12 Oct 2013 | ReliefWeb | CEDIM FDA Report no.2 issued 24 Oct 2013 |
| Bohol earthquake | Philippines | 15 Oct 2013 | Earthquake-Report and ReliefWeb | CEDIM FDA Report no.6 issued 02 Nov 2013 |
| Typhoon Haiyan | Philippines | 08 Nov 2013 | National Disaster Risk Reduction and Management Council | CEDIM FDA Report no.2 issued 13 Nov 2013 |

## 4.5 APPLICATION AND RESULTS

The purpose of the methodology is to carry out analyses immediately following actual disaster events. As such, the methodology was applied following five disasters that occurred between July and November 2013, and were incorporated into CEDIM FDA activities, as identified in Table 3.

The publicly communicated disaster response information following each of the five disasters was therefore compared to Table 2, in what we have termed an "information gap analysis." The following discusses the two types of information gap analyses established, as well as a comparison to be carried out upon completion of the first type to improve or clarify the results.

### 4.5.1 MISSING INFORMATION

The first type of information gap analysis compares the properties provided for each concept with those that should be provided according to Table 2. This analysis reveals what key properties are missing for each concept at a selected point in time. Figure 4 illustrates the results of such analysis, carried out 4 days after landfall of Cyclone Phailin in India.

Following landfall, reports uploaded to ReliefWeb by various news and relief agencies, such as Act Alliance, Agence France-Presse, European Commission, Reuters, Sphere India, and Times of India were reviewed to identify key disaster messages. The content of each message was then sorted into the properties of the corresponding concept. For example, Banerji (2013) quoted a government official stating that "...17 deaths were due to people being crushed by falling trees, walls, roofs." This message was sorted under casualties as "basic data" for identifying how many casualties and "analysis" for explaining how the casualties occurred. This process was done for approximately 350 key messages.

Comparing the overall results with the best observed practices identified in Table 2 reveals information gaps that can be further investigated. For example, some concepts, such as "meeting basic human needs" and "meeting transportation needs" are missing analysis of outstanding needs, signifying that the extent to which these actions are meeting the needs of the affected population is unknown. Post disaster needs assessments could therefore be recommended to focus on these concepts. Other fields of inquiry, such as why there was no information concerning medical disruptions or the handling of fatalities, could also be investigated.

The presence of full bars in Fig. 4 does not mean that all information has been provided and that no further details are required. The information in each category will increase with each passing day of the response. The full bars only indicate that each question has been answered; however, the answers may be incomplete or inaccurate leading to the need for further comparative analysis as discussed in Sect. 5.3.

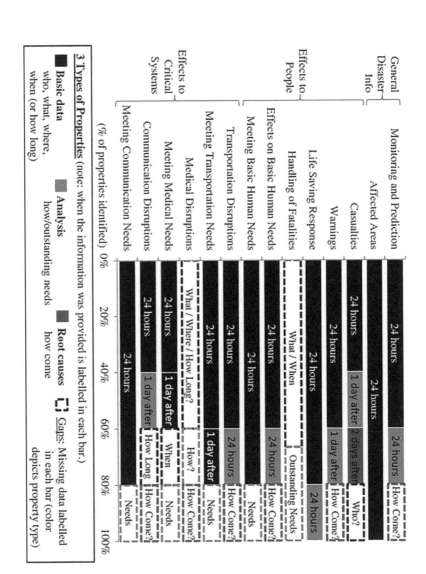

**FIGURE 4:** Information gap analysis: missing information, Cyclone Phailin, 4 days after landfall

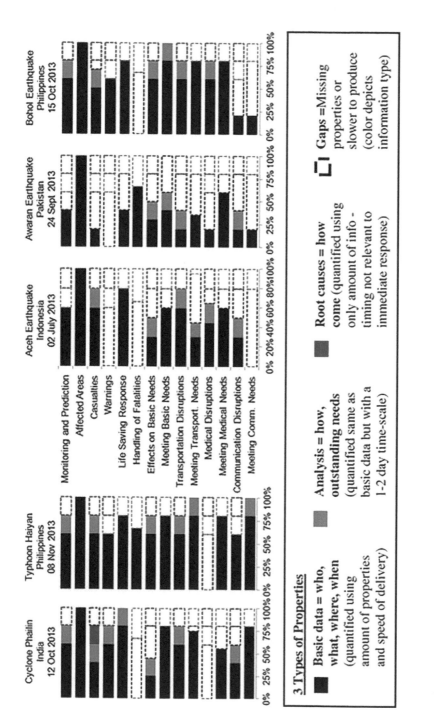

FIGURE 5: Information gap analysis: value of information

### 4.5.2 VALUE OF INFORMATION

As described in Sect. 4, the best observed practice review also revealed how quickly the three types of properties could be identified following a disaster. The second type of information gap analysis therefore calculates the value of the information provided by factoring in the time taken to produce it. Each property is assigned a value of one unit, and if it takes longer to produce than the best observed practices, the value is lowered, decreasing over time. The result is an overall value for each concept that combines the percentage of properties available with the time taken to produce them. This second type of information gap analysis was completed for the five disasters that occurred during the study period, the results of which are illustrated in Fig. 5.

The major benefit of the second type of analysis is that it allows for comparison between disasters and that such comparisons can be made within days following a disaster. Because time is such a major component, analyses of the second type are better suited for disasters with a finite starting point, such as earthquakes, volcanic eruptions, storm events, and flash-floods. Other events, such as widespread prolonged flooding or droughts could be limited to the first type of information gap analysis.

### 4.5.3 COMPARATIVE ANALYSIS

The information gaps illustrated in Fig. 4 identify the questions from Table 2 that are clearly unanswered; hence, the focus is on the information that has not been provided. Further understanding of the information needs of the public can be obtained by carrying out a comparative analysis of the provided information. Two important factors that must be examined are the quality of the information provided and the relevance of the information gaps identified.

Information quality can be analyzed in terms of the level of detail, coverage, and accuracy. The level of detail refers to the amount of questions answered from Table 2 and is therefore revealed through the first type of information gap analysis. The coverage refers to the percentage of actual disaster impacts and subsequently required disaster response activities that are identified. For example, information that focuses on a city may leave out rural areas where disaster impacts have occurred and in which response activities are therefore required. Issues regarding coverage and accuracy of the information can potentially be identified by comparing the information contained under different concepts. The basic human needs and transportation, medical, and communication system subcategories have intentionally been split into "disruptions" and "solutions" for this purpose. For instance, the near-real-time analysis completed three days after the 2013 Pakistan Earthquake compared the information provided under basic human needs "disruptions" and "solutions." Although the information provided under "solutions" discussed provision of relief goods, it appeared they did not match the quantities identified under "disruptions." In particular, a UNOCHA (2013) report issued two days after the earthquake stated that the government had dispatched 7,600 tents. At the same time, it was reported that 21,000 houses had been destroyed (Saifi 2013) and over 100,000 people made homeless (Agence France-Presse 2013). This represents a "coverage" issue, as the solutions do not appear to cover the full extent of the disruptions. Further information would therefore be required to explain how the shelter needs will be satisfied for those who cannot be accommodated by the tents.

Accuracy issues can also potentially be identified if different information sources have conflicting information. For instance, three days after Typhoon Haiyan made landfall in the Philippines the official confirmed death toll was only 255 with 38 missing (NDRRMC 2013); a day earlier a local official estimated the death toll to be 10,000 (Reuters 2013). Based on this discrepancy, the accuracy of both figures could be called into question.

Comparing between concepts can also help to establish the relevance of the missing information. In some cases, information gaps do not need to be filled. For example, if there are no medical disruptions then there is no need to identify medical solutions. Conversely, if there are large areas that have experienced communication system failure, then identifying solutions to communicate with those potentially affected would be very important.

This information gap analysis represents a starting point. The framework of the classification scheme then allows for more in-depth analysis by comparing within and between subcategories. The result is identification of additional information needs to account for coverage or accuracy issues, and a better understanding of how relevant the information gaps are.

## 4.6 DISCUSSION

Figure 5 illustrates the variety in results of the analyses carried out so far, the following section discusses three factors to be considered prior to directly comparing results. Addressing these items for future analyses is planned in order to improve the accuracy of results and strengthen comparisons.

### 4.6.1 DISASTER TYPE

The potential to compare between disaster types, such as storm events on the left of Fig. 5 with earthquakes on the right, needs to be further investigated. Information for storm events begins flowing prior to landfall, particularly for the categories "monitoring and prediction," "warnings," and "life saving response." For example, the predicted path, timing, and wind speed of Cyclone Phailin was provided two days before landfall (Thomson Reuters Foundation 2013), and warnings to fishermen were issued (Act Alliance 2013) and evacuations underway (Sphere India 2013) one day before landfall. In contrast, earthquakes occur suddenly, resulting in reactionary disaster response messages rather than precautionary. The ability to compare between disaster types will be further investigated as part of future research.

### 4.6.2 INFORMATION SOURCE LIMITATIONS

ReliefWeb was the major source of information for the initial 11 disasters analyzed. Most reports on ReliefWeb are in English, with some in French and Spanish, and a very limited amount in Arabic. Information contained in reports of other languages is therefore unknown unless the reports have already been translated. Furthermore, since a primary purpose of Relief-

Web is to inform humanitarian assistance providers (ReliefWeb 2014), there are fewer reports on disasters that do not require international aid. A combination of both of these issues is potentially why only one update specific to Germany was found in relation to the June 2013 flooding. Another issue with ReliefWeb, but also with disaster data in general, is that currently it appears disasters need to be large in scale in order to generate enough publicly available information to assess. For all of the above reasons, other information sources are continuously being investigated.

Different sources of information were therefore used to analyze the five disasters, as identified in Table 3. Analyses for the Aceh Earthquake and Cyclone Phailin used only information found on ReliefWeb, while the Pakistan Earthquake and Bohol Earthquake used additional sources of information. The analysis for Typhoon Haiyan used only information found in the NDRRMC situation reports available on their website. Although the reports appeared to be comprehensive, it was found that other sources provided some critical information that the NDRRMC situation reports were missing. This was revealed by an additional review, which compared an information gap analysis based on only NDRRMC situation reports with one that also included ReliefWeb sources. The analysis was also extended beyond the typical first five days to include the information produced within 12 days after landfall. During this time no basic data was provided in the NDRRMC reports that described the disruptions to the medical system. This information was provided by other agencies, and is included in reports by International Medical Corps, World Health Organisation, United Nations Population Fund, International Organisation for Migration, Agence France-Presse, Médicines Sans Frontièrs, and UNOCHA. Most detailed were the lists of medical disruptions and needs provided by Humanity Road six days after landfall. This finding highlights the importance of reviewing all information sources to achieve an accurate analysis of publicly available information.

### 4.6.3 LOCAL CONTEXT

The near-real-time analysis of the 2013 Pakistan Earthquake used data from the Pakistan National Disaster Management Agency website, Relief-

Web, and a variety of news network websites in an attempt to access all available information. These sources, and those used for all of the analyses so far, have been retrieved via the internet, which represents a global information source; however, the focus of the analysis is on the critical information needs of the local population. This raises two questions, the first of which is: what information on the internet is available to or actually reaches the local population? Local populations may not have internet access or they may only have access to a limited amount of online information. For example, affected populations without working computers may be able to access social networking sites such as Twitter and Facebook with cellular phone applications, but cannot download important situation reports. The second question is: is the affected population receiving local disaster messages that cannot be found on the internet? Local sources are very important information sources for an impacted population, and include formal and informal information providers. Formal sources may include local radio, newspapers, posters, or loudspeaker broadcasts. Informal sources may include neighbors, friends, and family with individuals accessing these sources in person, through phone calls or text messaging. Therefore, examining what information is actually reaching the local population from both the internet and local sources will help to improve the accuracy of future analyses.

## 4.7 CONCLUSIONS

Near-real-time analysis of disaster response is a new field of research. It is complementary to later in-depth post-response analysis and to real-time evaluation as done by international relief agencies. Near-real-time analysis will help to learn from disasters, to appreciate achievements and understand deficiencies in response by local agencies and institutions. As a first step towards these goals, this article has introduced a methodology for conducting a near-real-time analysis of the publicly communicated disaster response information. The establishment of a disaster data classification scheme has supported this analysis and has led to the development of standards in information production following any disaster. Comparison to those standards has resulted in the identification of information gaps, a process termed an "information gap analysis." Two types of analyses were discussed. The first type is intended to reveal the missing information by identifying which typical questions from the public remain unanswered. Further comparative analysis can potentially reveal issues regarding quality of the information provided and relevance of the information gaps identified. The second type of analysis calculates a value for the information provided to facilitate comparison of results between disasters. The intent is that such comparisons can act as a first step in measuring the performance of those responsible for gathering and distributing critical disaster information to the public. Due to the potential for incomplete or inaccurate information in the first 0–5 days of the response the near-real-time analysis methodology may be limited to identifying the deficiencies that are clearly evident. The advantage of the methodology is that those deficiencies are identified quickly, at a time when they can still be corrected.

## REFERENCES

1.  Act Alliance. 2013. Cyclone Phailin: Heavy rains lash Andhra Pradesh. http://www.actalliance.org/resources/alerts_and_situation_reports/Alert41_2013_India_CyclonePhailin.pdf. Accessed 30 Mar 2014.
2.  Agence France-Presse. 2011. Rescuers push into Himalayan quake "ground zero." http://reliefweb.int/report/india/rescuers-push-himalayan-quake-ground-zero. Accessed 30 Mar 2014.
3.  Agence France-Presse. 2013. Pakistan quake survivors face long wait for aid. http://reliefweb.int/report/pakistan/pakistan-quake-survivors-face-long-wait-aid. Accessed 9 July 2014.
4.  Appleby, L. 2013. Connecting the last mile: The role of communications in the Great East Japan Earthquake. Internews Europe. https://www.internews.org/sites/default/files/resources/InternewsEurope_Report_Japan_Connecting the last mile Japan_2013.pdf. Accessed 30 Mar 2014.
5.  Arai, K. 2013. How to transmit disaster information effectively: A linguistic perspective on Japan's tsunami warning evacuation instructions. International Journal of Disaster Risk Science 4(3): 150–158.
6.  Banerji, A. 2013. Killer Indian cyclone wreaks havoc, 1 million evacuated. Agence France-Presse. http://reliefweb.int/report/india/cyclone-phailin-pummels-india-half-million-evacuated. Accessed 30 Mar 2014.
7.  Birkland, T.A. 2009. Disasters, lessons learned, and fantasy documents. Journal of Contingencies and Crisis Management 17(3): 146–156.

8.  Chivers, W. 2012. FEMA from Katrina to Sandy: Lessons learned? Journal of Risk and Crisis Communication. http://www.journalriskcrisis.com/fema-from-katrina-to-sandy-lessons-learned/. Accessed 6 Dec 2013.

9.  Comfort, L.K. 2005. Risk, security, and disaster management. Annual Review of Political Science 8: 335–356.

10. Cosgrave, J., B. Ramalingam, and T. Beck. 2009. Real-time evaluations of humanitarian action: An ALNAP guide – Pilot version. Overseas Development Institute. http://www.alnap.org/resource/5595. Accessed 30 Mar 2014.

11. Donahue, A.K., and R.V. Tuohy. 2006. Lessons we don't learn: A study of the lessons of disasters, why we repeat them, and how we can learn them. Homeland Security Affairs 2(2). http://www.hsaj.org/index.php?fullarticle=2.2.4. Accessed 24 July 2014.

12. FEMA (Federal Emergency Management Agency). 2013. Hurricane Sandy FEMA after-action report. United States Federal Emergency Management Agency. http://www.fema.gov/media-library/assets/documents/33772. Accessed 30 Mar 2014.

13. Government of India. 2011. Earthquake update in Sikkim and elsewhere on 19 Sept, 2011 at 4.00 pm. http://img.static.reliefweb.int/report/india/earthquake-update-sikkim-and-elsewhere-19-sept-2011-400-pm. Accessed 30 Mar 2014.

14. Government of USA. 2012. DOD provides update for hurricane Sandy response. http://reliefweb.int/report/united-states-america/dod-provides-update-hurricane-sandy-response. Accessed 30 Mar 2014.

15. Helsloot, I., and A. Ruitenberg. 2004. Citizen response to disasters: A survey of literature and some practical implications. Journal of Contingencies and Crisis Management 12(3): 98–111.

16. ICSU (International Council for Science). 2013. Disaster risk (IRDR). http://www.icsu.org/what-we-do/interdisciplinary-bodies/irdr/?icsudocid=working-groups. Accessed 10 Dec 2013.

17. Jamal, A., and J. Crisp. 2002. Real-time humanitarian evaluations: Some frequently asked questions. Geneva: United Nations High Commissioner for Refugees Evaluation and Policy Analysis Unit. http://www.unhcr.org/3ce372204.html. Accessed 17 Feb 2014.

18. Maxwell, T.A. 2003. The public need to know: Emergencies, government organizations, and public information. Government Information Quarterly 20(3): 233–258.

19. McLean, I., D. Oughton, S. Ellis, B. Wakelin, and C.B. Rubin. 2012. Review of the civil defence emergency management response to the 22 February Christchurch Earthquake. Ministry of Civil Defence and Emergency Management. http://www.civildefence.govt.nz/assets/Uploads/publications/Review-CDEM-Response-22-February-Christchurch-Earthquake.pdf. Accessed 13 Aug 2014.

20. NDRRMC (National Disaster Risk Reduction and Management Council). 2011. NDRRMC update: Sitrep No.1 re: Preparedness and response to the effects of tropical storm "SENDONG", 16 December 2011. http://reliefweb.int/report/philippines/ndrrmc-update-sitrep-no1-re-preparedness-and-response-effects-tropical-storm. Accessed 30 Mar 2014.

21. NDRRMC (National Disaster Risk Reduction and Management Council). 2013. NDRRMC update: SitRep No. 12 Effects of typhoon "Yolanda" (Haiyan). http://reliefweb.int/report/philippines/ndrrmc-update-sitrep-no12-effects-typhoon-yolanda-haiyan. Accessed 9 July 2014.

22. OECD (Organisation for Economic Co-operation and Development). 2010. Glossary of key terms in evaluation and results based management. OECD. http://www.oecd.org/dac/evaluation/2754804.pdf. Accessed 30 Mar 2014.

23. Oxfam. 2013. Cyclone leaves destruction and homelessness in India – But many lives saved by quick action. http://reliefweb.int/report/india/cyclone-leaves-destruction-and-homelessness-india—-many-lives-saved-quick-action. Accessed 30 Mar 2014.

24. ReliefWeb. 2014. Web site. http://reliefweb.int/about. Accessed 13 Aug 2014.

25. Reuters. 2011. Australia floods inundate Brisbane, 67 missing. http://reliefweb.int/report/australia/australia-floods-inundate-brisbane-67-missing. Accessed 30 Mar 2014.

26. Reuters. 2013. Survivors "walk like zombies" after Philippine typhoon kills estimated 10,000. http://www.trust.org/item/20131110063916-3y9e4/. Accessed 30 Mar 2014.

27. Saifi, S. 2013. Pakistan quake death toll rises to 356. CNN. http://edition.cnn.com/2013/09/26/world/asia/pakistan-earthquake/. Accessed 9 July 2014.

28. Sheales, R. 2010. Victoria unveils response to Black Saturday report. ABC News, August 27. http://www.abc.net.au/news/2010-08-27/victoria-unveils-response-to-black-saturday-report/960660. Accessed 13 Aug 2014.

29. Sphere India. 2013. Sitrep-2: Severe Cyclonic Storm "Phailin". http://reliefweb.int/report/india/sitrep-2-severe-cyclonic-storm-"phailin". Accessed 30 Mar 2014.

30. Starks, T. 2012. Katrina's lessons seen in response to Sandy. CQ Weekly. http://public.cq.com/docs/weeklyreport/weeklyreport-000004197197.html. Accessed 30 Mar 2014.

31. The White House. 2006. The federal response to Hurricane Katrina: Lessons learned. http://permanent.access.gpo.gov/lps67263/katrina-lessons-learned.pdf. Accessed 30 Mar 2014.

32. Thomson Reuters Foundation. 2013. Cyclone Phailin intensifies as it approaches India. http://www.trust.org/item/20131010152401-wtldx/?source=hptop. Accessed 11 Feb 2014.

33. Tropical Storm Risk. 2008. Myanmar: Track and windspeed of severe cyclonic Nargis (as of 01 May 2008). http://reliefweb.int/map/myanmar/myanmar-track-and-windspeed-severe-cyclonic-nargis-01-may-2008. Accessed 30 Mar 2014.

34. UNOCHA (United Nations Office for the Coordination of Humanitarian Affairs). 2013. OCHA Pakistan flash update #3 on Balochistan Earthquake. http://reliefweb.int/report/pakistan/ocha-pakistan-flash-update-3-balochistan-earthquake. Accessed 9 July 2014.

35. Wenzel, F., J.E. Daniell, B. Khazai, and T. Kunz-Plapp. 2012. The CEDIM Forensic Earthquake Analysis Group and the test case of the 2011 Van earthquakes. 15th World Conference on Earthquake Engineering (WCEE) Paper no. 3937, Lisbon, Portugal. http://www.iitk.ac.in/nicee/wcee/article/WCEE2012_3957.pdf. Accessed 20 Nov 2014.

36. Wenzel, F., J. Zschau, M. Kunz, J.E. Daniell, B. Khazai, and T. Kunz-Plapp. 2013. Near-real-time forensic disaster analysis. Proceedings of the 10th International IS-CRAM Conference, Baden–Baden, Germany, May 2013. http://www.iscramlive. org/ISCRAM2013/files/119.pdf. Accessed 20 Nov 2014.

# PART II

# THE INTERNET AND SOCIAL MEDIA

# CHAPTER 5

# The Future of Social Media Use During Emergencies in Australia: Insights from the 2014 Australian and New Zealand Disaster and Emergency Management Conference Social Media Workshop

OLGA ANIKEEVA, MALINDA STEENKAMP, AND PAUL ARBON

## 5.1 INTRODUCTION

People are increasingly using social media during emergency events, such as bushfires, storms and floods (Bird, Ling & Hayes 2012, Cheong & Cheong 2011, CSIRO 2014, American Red Cross 2012, Latonero & Shklovski 2011). Information appears on platforms such as Twitter and Facebook in real time, frequently preceding traditional channels such as television and radio (American Red Cross 2012). Both in Australia and internationally, social media has been widely used to disseminate essential information and updates during emergency events. During the 2010-2011 floods in Queensland, New South Wales and Victoria, Twitter was used by emergency services, politicians, social media volunteers, traditional media reporters and community organisations to disseminate information to the affected communities (Cheong & Cheong 2011). One notable example is the use of Twitter and Facebook by Queensland Police when information and updates about the situation were provided to the community, sometimes as frequently as every few minutes. The platforms were used to control and respond to the spread of rumours and misinformation (Queensland Police 2013). An important advantage was that Queensland Police established their social media presence and strategy before the occurrence of the disaster, which ensured that clear processes for disseminating information and addressing rumours and misleading posts were in place and staff were familiar with the processes. This ensured that Queensland Police maintained their Twitter and Facebook presence throughout the disaster and were able to reach and respond to individuals who did not have access to traditional media channels due to power outages and water damage (Queensland Police 2013). Similarly, Brisbane City Council was able to effectively use social media platforms to disseminate information to their already well-established networks of followers. The Council's dedicated social media resources and commitment to engaging in an open dialog with community members ensured that information was disseminated and evaluated in a timely fashion and questions and concerns were responded to, increasing community confidence (Australian Centre of Excellence for Local Government 2011, Whitelaw & Henson 2014). Community-initiated Facebook groups were also established during this time, which gained an instant following from affected residents and their family and friends. These groups routinely posted information sourced from agencies such as the State Emergency Service and the Bureau of Meteorology to provide a comprehensive collection of updates to followers. Furthermore, group members used the platform to post eyewitness information, questions, requests for help and advice, thus establishing support networks within the affected communities and facilitating community engagement and involvement in providing assistance (Bird, Ling & Hayes 2012).

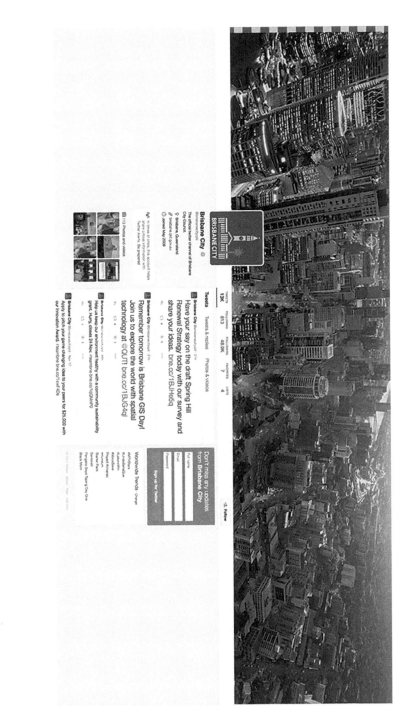

**FIGURE 1:** Brisbane City Council was able to effectively use social media platforms to disseminate information to their already well-established networks of followers.

Internationally, people are increasingly relying on social media during emergency events. A survey conducted by the American Red Cross found that mobile applications and social media are the fourth most popular way for Americans to obtain information during an emergency, following television, radio and online news. Social media is also widely used during emergencies as a source of emotional support and a method of obtaining information and advice about staying safe. Furthermore, Americans are increasingly expecting emergency agencies to monitor social media platforms (three quarters of survey respondents expected a response within three hours of posting a request for help on an organisation's social media page) (American Red Cross 2012). The 2013 attack on Westgate Mall in Nairobi, Kenya illustrates the importance of social media during emergency events. Within moments of the attack, information and photographs were posted to social networks such as Facebook and Twitter, providing details of the location of the attack and the number of casualties (Mohammed 2013). While some early posts contained inaccurate information, such as incorrect locations and nature of the emergency, the community of social media users corrected misleading information, which ensured rapid correction of potentially misleading claims. The use of social media during this event enabled real-time dissemination of updates and warnings, instructing people to stay away from the mall and its surrounding area (Mohammed 2013). The warnings were supported with eyewitness accounts and photographs, which enabled the reliability of incoming information to be assessed by traditional media outlets and other organisations.

The Westgate Mall example illustrates that social media is not only an important tool that can facilitate the dissemination of information by emergency services agencies to communities; it can also alert these organisations to developing disasters and emergency events. Tools exist that enable more efficient analysis of incoming information and provide details on GPS coordinates, number of people affected and the assistance required. An example is the Emergency Situation Awareness tool developed by the CSIRO, which is designed to detect unusual activity on Twitter feeds and alert response agencies when an emergency or disaster is being broadcast and discussed online (Cheong & Cheong 2011). Despite the availability of such technologies, many emergency organisations have been slow to adopt and engage with social media. For this reason, a workshop at the

2014 Australian and New Zealand Disaster and Emergency Management conference provided a forum to discuss the current role of social media in the disaster and emergency sphere.

## 5.2 SOCIAL MEDIA WORKSHOP

The workshop brought together 21 participants from a range of backgrounds, including emergency services, academia and information technology. The main objective of the workshop was to discuss the current state and future development of social media in the emergency management field, highlight current facilitators and barriers to effective use of social media platforms, and suggest improvements and strategies for enabling the use of these technologies by both emergency services personnel and the public. This article outlines the three key themes that were discussed during the workshop.

### 5.2.1 THE CURRENT STATE AND FUTURE OF SOCIAL MEDIA USE IN THE CONTEXT OF EMERGENCIES

Participants overwhelmingly agreed that social media use will become increasingly popular in the near future and the public will expect emergency services and response agencies to have and maintain an active social media presence. A number of participants commented that different social media platforms are likely to attract particular user groups and be more suited for certain purposes. For example, it was agreed that Twitter is best suited for broadcasting frequent updates and is particularly useful for those wanting to use social media to access up-to-date information. On the other hand, Facebook is well-suited to establishing online communities where users can share their own experiences, ask for help and provide assistance where needed. For this reason, participants suggested that emergency organisations would need to establish a presence across all major social media platforms. Participants agreed that it is likely that maintaining a strong social media presence will require dedicated staff and resources, with some suggesting that larger organisations may need to establish social media units or departments. Some participants expressed concern about the potential financial ramifications of employing additional staff and purchasing essential equipment required to maintain an active social media presence.

Participants also commented that the channels the public rely on to obtain information about unfolding emergency events are changing. While television, radio and telephone hotlines were previously the most trusted and widely used means of accessing accurate information, it was suggested that the formation of social media networks will contribute to a shift towards increasing reliance on eyewitness accounts and reports provided by other users. However, some population sub-groups, such as the elderly and unemployed, may be less likely to have access to mobile phone and online communications. Therefore, emergency communications need to be tailored to individual communities and reflect their unique population composition and characteristics (Boon 2014). Participants questioned how the accuracy and reliability of information can be assessed on social media, with some suggesting that new, rapid methods of moderation, validation and verification need to be established and used to limit the amount of misinformation or deliberately misleading reports. A closely related concept was the development and refinement of technologies that enable organisations to efficiently sort through the vast amount of incoming information to extract the key messages and filter out unnecessary 'noise'.

Finally, a number of participants suggested that increased use of social media is likely to contribute to greater community interaction, by enabling community members to comment on, contribute to and provide feedback to emergency services and response agencies about their plans and actions. Social media can contribute to greater feelings of connectedness among residents and their local emergency services and can lead to the establishment of a stronger and more inclusive community voice. However, consideration must be given to the extent to which various community members are likely to participate in discussions. It is likely that some individuals, such as the elderly, those with low English proficiency or low socio-economic status, may be underrepresented in community social media networks and discussions.

- Twitter: suited to broadcasting frequent updates
- Facebook: suited to establishing online communities

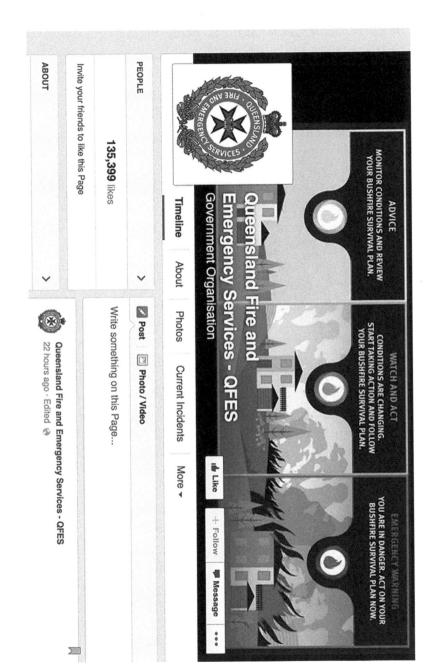

**FIGURE 2:** Posting information on Facebook in real time, frequently preceded traditional channels such as television and radio.

## 5.2.2 CURRENT AND FUTURE POSSIBILITIES AND OPPORTUNITIES FOR SOCIAL MEDIA USE IN THE EMERGENCY CONTEXT

Participants agreed that the expansion of social media use within organisations needs to be supported by a national strategy to guide the development of plans and policies, support long-term objectives and increase organisational commitment. A national social media strategy for organisations may address current resistance to social media use in some settings, which some participants believed may in part be explained by generational differences in attitudes towards social media uptake. Participants stated that it is important to identify and support social media champions within organisations in order to drive change, which may be easier to achieve with a national strategy that encourages social media uptake.

Participants also commented on the opportunity to create a more diverse community of social media users. Many agreed that social media uptake is lower among certain population sub-groups, such as older individuals. Methods of encouraging participation by demonstrating benefits and making the platforms relevant to various population sub-groups need to be developed. One example during the workshop was the expanding use of health technologies, such as blood pressure monitors, that are compatible with smartphone applications and allow users to track changes over time and set goals and reminders. Such targeted technologies are likely to encourage greater use among older individuals. Similar tactics could be employed to demonstrate the utility of social media platforms for this group, such as greater social connectedness and increased participation in community discussions. Importantly, barriers to social media use, such as cost or lack of time need identification and addressing to ensure a diverse population of social media users.

A number of participants commented on the possibilities that stem from increasing use of GPS technology that provide tailored, location-based information to be delivered to target groups. This technology allows organisations to send warnings, alerts and other critical updates to individuals in specific physical locations, thus increasing the information relevance.

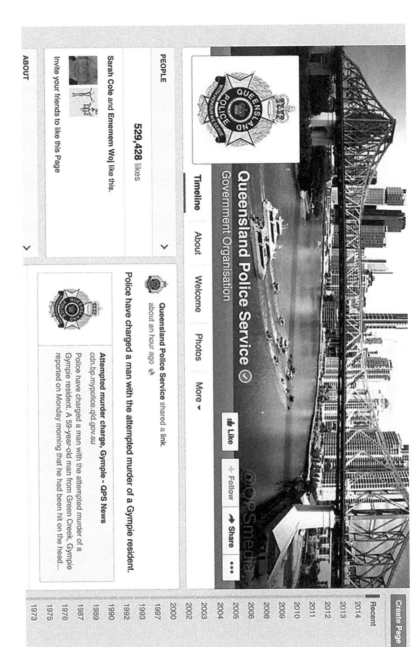

**FIGURE 3:** Queensland Police used their Facebook presence to reach and respond to individuals who did not have access to traditional media channels.

## 5.2.3 CURRENT ENABLERS AND BARRIERS TO EFFECTIVE USE OF SOCIAL MEDIA IN THE EMERGENCY CONTEXT

During the final part of the workshop, participants were asked to identify factors that facilitate or hinder the effective implementation and use of social media by emergency services organisations and the general public. One of the key barriers identified was the lack of dedicated staff and additional resources required to establish and maintain a strong social media presence. Participants commented that the majority of organisations lack dedicated social media staff and the responsibility of maintaining the organisation's social media presence (whether through an organisation's own social media account or by active participation in existing social media networks) is given to those with a special interest in this technology, who then must find time for social media responsibilities around their primary job.

Another potential barrier is the possibility of network failure during emergency or disaster events, particularly in remote areas with poor network coverage. Participants suggested that this barrier may be overcome by developing technologies that enable individual mobile phones to link to each other to ensure coverage is not lost and people are able to access social networks to receive critical updates when they are needed most.

One key advantage of social media platforms discussed was that they tend to be more robust than standard websites and less likely to fail during periods of high traffic, which may occur during emergency events. The capability of social networking platforms to effectively deal with high volume traffic in a cost-effective way means that critical information and updates can potentially be disseminated to large numbers of people and their networks.

Participants also considered the potential consequences of incorrect or deliberately misleading information being broadcast via social media channels. They identified a lack of clarity with respect to who would be held responsible for any consequences arising from such misinformation. In particular, participants felt this might be a deterrent for organisations to maintain a social media presence if they are held responsible for false information posted by others that they fail to rapidly evaluate and remove from their social media profiles. Participants suggested the need for clear policies and guidelines to protect organisations.

It was agreed that dedicated social media training could help organisations to see the merit in establishing and maintaining a social media presence. Participants suggested best-practice local and international examples could be used for training purposes. They believed that this would reduce the amount of trial-and-error that frequently accompanies social media adoption in the absence of dedicated guidance and training, which can act as a deterrent for organisations, particularly those that are under-resourced.

Participants considered that engaging volunteers in social media roles could address the financial and resource barriers to adoption of social media. It was suggested that after receiving initial training and guidance in appropriate social media use, volunteers could play a key role in monitoring social media platforms, posting updates and engaging with the wider community. This approach could potentially have the additional benefit of attracting a greater number of volunteers with a particular interest in social media and community engagement.

## 5.3 CONCLUSION

Social media platforms are powerful two-way tools that can be used to rapidly disseminate information and expose developing emergencies through ongoing monitoring of social media feeds. Despite the advantages and examples of effective use both locally and internationally, many organisations have been reluctant to adopt these technologies and maintain an active social media presence. The workshop highlighted important enablers and barriers to social media use within emergency and response agencies. Clear guidelines, adequate training, engagement of volunteers in social media roles, ongoing support and strategies for dealing with rumours and misinformation are likely to encourage greater uptake of these platforms in the emergency and disaster sphere.

# REFERENCES

1.  Bird D, Ling M & Haynes K 2012, Flooding Facebook - the use of social media during the Queensland and Victorian floods. Australian Journal of Emergency Management, vol. 27, no. 1, pp. 27-33.

2.  Boon H 2014, Investigating rural community communication for flood and bushfire preparedness. Australian Journal of Emergency Management, vol. 29, no. 4, pp. 17-25.

3.  Cheong F & Cheong C 2011, Social media data mining: a social network analysis of tweets during the 2010-2011 Australian floods. PACIS 2011 Proceedings. Paper 46.

4.  CSIRO 2014, Emergency situation awareness tool for social media. At: www.csiro.au/Outcomes/ICT-and-Services/emergency-situation-awareness.aspx.

5.  American Red Cross 2012, More Americans using mobile apps in emergencies. At: www.redcross.org/news/press-release/More-Americans-Using-Mobile-Apps-in-Emergencies.

6.  Latonero M & Shklovski I 2011, Emergency management, Twitter and social media evangelism. International Journal of Information Systems for Crisis Response and Management, 3(4), pp. 1-16.

7.  Queensland Police 2013, Social media case study. At: www.police.qld.gov.au/corporatedocs/reportsPublications/other/Social-Media.htm.

8.  Australian Centre of Excellence for Local Government 2011, Case study on social media use in emergency management. At: www.acelg.org.au/case-study-social-media-use-emergency-management.

9.  Mohammed O 2013, How the Nairobi mall attack unfolded on social media. Global Voices Online. At: http://globalvoicesonline.org/2013/09/23/how-the-nairobi-mall-attack-unfolded-on-social-media/.

10. Whitelaw T & Henson D 2014, All that I'm hearing from you is white noise: social media aggregation in emergency response. Australian Journal of Emergency Management, vol. 29, no. 4, pp. 48-51.

# CHAPTER 6

# Resilient Disaster Network Based on Software Defined Cognitive Wireless Network Technology

GOSHI SATO, NORIKI UCHIDA, AND YOSHITAKA SHIBATA

## 6.1 INTRODUCTION

As advent of recent wireless communication technology, many applications on various fields such as public wireless networks, disaster information networks, or intelligent traffic transportation systems are developed [1–3]. In particular, wireless communication system plays a very important role as disaster use. In fact, in the Great East Japan Earthquake on March 11, 2011, the communication access networks to the Internet in disaster areas were recovered by the 3G mobile communication vehicles and satellite communication system. However, those used networks were introduced individually and operated by each of the mobile phone companies; some mobile phones could not be used on different company's network. The handover function between the different company's networks could not be supported even though one network is very congested and the others have enough available network resources.

In this paper, we introduce a novel cognitive wireless network system which is able to select the best link and route that can provide the best network performance among possible networks by integrating the different type of wireless networks such as 3G, LTE, WiMAX, Wi-Fi, and satellite networks with the different network characteristics such as throughput, RTT, and packet loss rate and periodically monitoring those network states [4, 5]. By exchanging the disaster information through this stratified network, the system can persistently continue to provide communication capability and can automatically perform handover to the other access networks which have enough available network resources by wireless cognitive network functions even if some network node and line failures occur in a part of the network infrastructure. We designed and developed our system as a prototype system based on the SDN technology [6] by integrating 3G, LTE, WiMAX, and satellite network and constructed a testbed disaster network as access network by connecting three different locations in our Iwate prefecture which were seriously damaged by the tsunami from the Great East Japan Earthquake on March 11, 2011.

## 6.2 DISASTER INFORMATION

From the investigation of the previous large natural disasters, the required information varies in time before and after disaster as shown in Figure 1 [7]. Just before the disaster, the forecast and evacuation information are required while, just after the disaster evacuation, resident safety and disaster status information are required where $t_1$ is normal time, $t_2$ is estimated period, $t_x$ is time at disaster, $t_3$ is the period just after the disaster, $t_4$ is stable period, $t_5$ is recovery period, and $t_6$ is recovered time.

Just after disaster happened, the communication network around the disaster area maybe damaged and must be quickly recovered although the required network throughput is small; while being at stable and recovery period, the required throughput will be increased as the time elapsed. Thus, in order to achieve the emergency communication immediately after a disaster, quick recovery of the information network must be made.

**FIGURE 1:** Required disaster information.

Required information varies in time before/after disaster

| Objects | Required information | $t_1$ | $t_2$ | $t_x$ | $t_3$ | $t_4$ | $t_5$ | $t_6$ |
|---|---|---|---|---|---|---|---|---|
| Stricken area resident | Forecast | △ | ○ | | ◎ | ◎ | ○ | △ |
| | Evacuation | | ○ | | ◎ | ○ | ○ | |
| | Resident safety | | | | ◎ | ◎ | ◎ | |
| | Disaster status | | | Disaster | ◎ | ◎ | ○ | |
| | Traffic | | | | ○ | ◎ | ◎ | |
| | Supplied materials | | | | | ◎ | ◎ | |
| | Public service | | | | | ○ | ◎ | |
| | Life line | | | | | ○ | ◎ | |
| | Local government | | | | | ○ | ◎ | |
| Relatives | Resident safety | | | | ◎ | ◎ | ○ | |
| | Disaster status | | | | ◎ | ○ | △ | |
| | Supplied materials | | | | | ○ | ◎ | |

Connection-oriented period

Bandwidth-oriented period

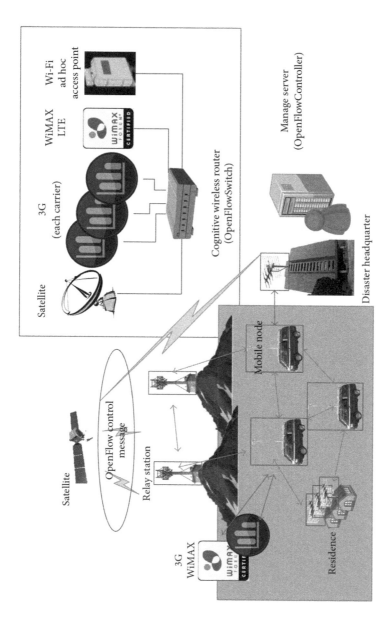

**FIGURE 2:** System configuration.

## 6.3 SYSTEM CONFIGURATION

Figure 2 shows our proposed disaster information network which consisted of wireless cognitive network switches combined with multiple different networks and a cognitive wireless controller. Wired networks can be also used as access networks. The cognitive wireless switches periodically monitor their network states at the several locations and send the monitored network states data to the cognitive wireless controller at the disaster headquarter. All of the received data are accumulated in the cognitive wireless controller and evaluated to select the best access network by weighting those possible access networks. The satellite network is used as a control channel for SDN to exchange the data between the cognitive switches. Each cognitive switch determines the suitable outgoing network for the packets to be send from the incoming network based on the message from the cognitive controller. In order to determine the best performance network, the following techniques perform important roles:

1. network monitoring technology to detect the change of network performance states;
2. optimal selection method to decide the best access network;
3. packet control technology by OpenFlow [8] which changes the link and route to the switch to the best access network.

As monitoring the packet delay, ping tool is used between the observation server and the cognitive wireless switch in a specified time period by averaging the round trip time (TTL) of the proved packets. With packet loss rate monitoring, ping tool is also used by counting the nonreplying packets.

In our system, in order to detect the change of the network states, the wireless cognitive switch has network monitoring function.

The monitored states include the following parameters:

1. link-up/down signal of network link;
2. throughput;

3. RTT between the observation server and each of the wireless cognitive switches;
4. packet loss rate between the observation server and each of the cognitive switches.

With monitoring the network throughput, two methods including passive and active methods are possible [9]. In passive methods, the throughput is calculated by implementing the monitoring function at all of the routers which the packets pass through. In active method, on the other hand, proved packets are transmitted between the end-to-end terminals [10]. In passive method, the monitoring functions have to be installed on all of the routers where packets pass through. This is very difficult because the Internet is huge and managed by different organizations. Therefore, for this reason, in our system, the active method is applied. Furthermore, there are two active methods including available bandwidth measuring methods such as *Iperf* and packet train methods such as *pathChirp* and *PathQuick* [11, 12]. In the available bandwidth measuring method, a large number of packets are inserted, while, in the packet train method, only a limited number of the probe packets are used in a limited period. For this reason, the packet train method is applied in our system.

At monitoring the packet delay, *ping* tool is used between the observation server and the cognitive wireless switch in a specified time period by averaging the round trip time (TTL) of the probe packets. With packet loss rate monitoring, *ping* tool is also used by counting the nonreplying packets.

## 6.4 LINK SELECTION METHOD

### 6.4.1 PROPOSED METHOD OVERVIEW

Our cognitive radio router is equipped with a multiple access network. The system periodically monitors the performance of the wireless network access multiple links and calculates the priority of each access network by extending AHP method based on the parameter values obtained as results of the monitoring. Thus, the system determines the link of an access network based on the priority [13, 14] as shown in Figure 3.

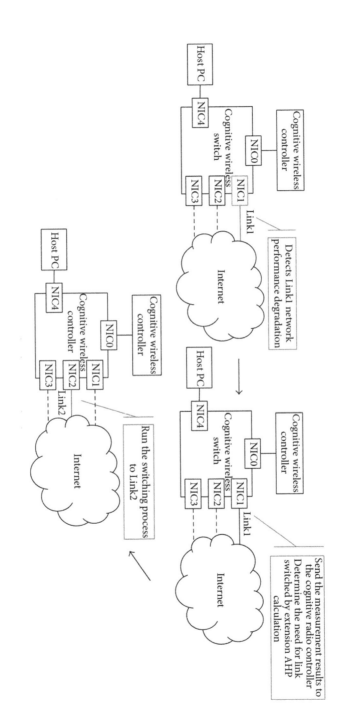

**FIGURE 3:** Link selection method overview.

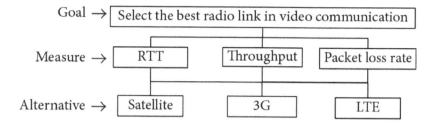

**FIGURE 4:** Examples of AHP hierarchy.

## 6.4.2 AHP METHOD OVERVIEW

In this section, we describe the detail of AHP to be used in the decision-making in the access network switching. AHP is one of the decision-making processes and a more structural approach is used when performing a complicated decision. AHP was proposed in the 1970s by Satty et al. AHP [15] is capable of evaluation of alternatives and quantification of elements by performing the structure of the decision problem. The calculation process is performed in the order of "hierarchy of the problem," "pair comparative evaluation for criteria," "pair comparative evaluation of alternatives," and "the calculation of the total value."

Figure 4 is an example of a layered hierarchy by AHP and is a case of selecting the optimal wireless link between adjacent nodes. In order to solve the problem caused by AHP, it is necessary to stratify the problem first. In this study, we set a goal such as "select the best radio link in video communication" or "select the best radio link of connectivity." Next, in order to select the link that is the most suitable one for a user's request, appropriate network state values (throughput, delay, and packet loss rate) are set. And $p_1$ priority is determined based on the pairwise comparison of the evaluation criteria. On the other hand, $p_2$ priority is determined from the measured value of each alternative.

After that, the hierarchical priorities for evaluation criteria are calculated. As an example, we describe a method of calculating the priority by the measuring network performance. The number of evaluation criteria is defined as n, the weight of each term is defined as "$w_1, w_2, \ldots w_n$," and pair comparison of each element is expressed as $a_{ij} = w_i/w_j$. Furthermore, these pair comparisons can be expressed as A:

$$
A = \begin{bmatrix}
\dfrac{w_1}{w_2} \cdots & \dfrac{w_1}{w_j} \cdots & \dfrac{w_1}{w_n} \\
\vdots & \vdots & \vdots \\
\dfrac{w_i}{w_2} \cdots & \dfrac{w_i}{w_j} \cdots & \dfrac{w_i}{w_n} \\
\vdots & \vdots & \vdots \\
\dfrac{w_n}{w_1} \cdots & \dfrac{w_n}{w_j} \cdots & \dfrac{w_n}{w_n}
\end{bmatrix}
$$

$$
= \begin{bmatrix}
a_{11} \cdots & a_{1j} \cdots & a_{1n} \\
\vdots & \vdots & \vdots \\
a_{i1} \cdots & a_{ij} \cdots & a_{in} \\
\vdots & \vdots & \vdots \\
a_{n1} \cdots & a_{nj} \cdots & a_{nn}
\end{bmatrix}
\tag{1}
$$

$A_{norm}$ normal matrix can be expressed as follows:

$$
A_{norm} = \begin{bmatrix}
b_{11} \cdots & b_{1j} \cdots & b_{1n} \\
\vdots & \vdots & \vdots \\
b_{i1} \cdots & b_{ij} \cdots & b_{in} \\
\vdots & \vdots & \vdots \\
b_{n1} \cdots & b_{nj} \cdots & b_{nn}
\end{bmatrix}
\tag{2}
$$

where

$$
b_{ij} = \frac{a_{ij}}{\sum_{k=1}^{n} a_{kj}}
$$

In addition, each priority $P_i$ of evaluation criteria is calculated by the following equation:

$$p_i = \frac{\sum_{l=1}^{n} b_{il}}{n}$$

(4)

Weight $w_n$ of each evaluation criterion with the range 1–9 is used to compute priority $P_i$ and pairwise comparison matrix $a_{ij}$. Table of evaluation criteria for each purpose is shown in Table 1.

**TABLE 1:** Pairwise comparison matrix of evaluation.

|                  | PER | RTT | Throughput |
|------------------|-----|-----|------------|
| Goal 1 (video)   |     |     |            |
| PER              | 1   | 3   | 1/2        |
| RTT              | 1/3 | 1   | 1/5        |
| Throughput       | 2   | 5   | 1          |
| Goal 2 (VoIP)    |     |     |            |
| PER              | 1   | 1/2 | 3          |
| RTT              | 2   | 1   | 5          |
| Throughput       | 1/3 | 1/5 | 1          |
| Goal 3 (text)    |     |     |            |
| PER              | 1   | 5   | 5          |
| RTT              | 1/5 | 1   | 1          |
| Throughput       | 1/5 | 1   | 1          |

Therefore, priorities $P_1 \sim P_3$ of evaluation criteria for each goal are shown in Table 2.

Next, alternatively, priority is calculated for each alternative with the weight. In this paper, the priority calculation of alternative considers a change in the wireless network. Therefore, after calculating the weight $w_n$ using the measured values of the network state, this weight is applied to calculate the priority of each alternative.

Then, the total value is calculated using the priority of each alternative with the evaluation criteria. Total value is determined by the sum of the products of the priority of alternatives and weights of the evaluation criteria. Finally, the maximum total value of alternatives is selected for optimal wireless access network.

**TABLE 2:** Result of evaluation priority.

| Propose | PER | RTT | Throughput |
|---|---|---|---|
| Goal 1 (video) | 0.3092 | 0.1096 | 0.5813 |
| Goal 2 (VoIP) | 0.3092 | 0.5813 | 0.1096 |
| Goal 3 (text) | 0.7143 | 0.1429 | 0.1429 |

### 6.4.3 EXTENDED AHP METHOD

In this study, we introduce an extension of AHP to determine the wireless access network by the cognitive radio device. To respond to the network state changes caused by the movement or external factors of network environment, the measured value of the network states is used for the calculation of the weights of alternatives. The weight of each alternative is defined as $S_i$. $u_i$ is defined as the upper limit of each alternative. $l_i$ is defined as the lower limit. Further, $n_i$ is defined as the moving average of the measurement period and is determined by the weight 5 for PER (packet error rate) and RTT (round trip time).

On the other hand, the scale of the alternatives is different as shown in 6, and the upper limit of the throughput is defined as $u_{max}$. Furthermore, in order to smooth the fluctuation by the measuring, the moving average of the measured values is defined as "$n_i = 0.6x_i + 0.3x_i + 0.3x_{i-1} + 0.1x_{I-2}$" (where $x_i$ is defined as a network measurement value of i second time):

$$S_i = \begin{cases} \left[1 - \dfrac{n_i - l_i}{u_i - l_i}\right] \times 10; & l_i < n_i < u_i \\ 1; & n_i \geq u_i \\ 9; & n_i \leq l \end{cases} \tag{5}$$

$$S_i = \left[\frac{n_i - l_i}{u_{max} - l_i}\right] \times 10, \quad u_{max} = \max(u_i)$$

$$(6)$$

As an example of the throughput of LTE network where the moving average of measurement $n_i$ is 5.2 Mbps, the lower limit $l_i$ is 0 Mbps, and the maximum value in the measurement history $u_{max}$ is 24 Mbps; then the weight $S_{iLTE}$ is calculated as

$$S_{i_{LTE}} = \left[\frac{5.2 - 0}{24 - 0}\right] \times 10 \approx 0.45$$

$$(7)$$

Table 3 is shown as an example of a pairwise comparison matrix for video communication and Table 4 shows its priority alternatives.

**TABLE 3:** Pairwise comparison matrix example of alternative.

|            | Satellite | LTE | 3G  |
|------------|-----------|-----|-----|
| PER        |           |     |     |
| Satellite  | 1         | 1/2 | 1/2 |
| LTE        | 2         | 1   | 1   |
| 3G         | 2         | 1   | 1   |
| RTT        |           |     |     |
| Satellite  | 1         | 1/5 | 1/3 |
| LTE        | 5         | 1   | 2   |
| 3G         | 3         | 1/2 | 1   |
| Throughput |           |     |     |
| Satellite  | 1         | 1/6 | 1/2 |
| LTE        | 6         | 1   | 3   |
| 3G         | 2         | 1/3 | 1   |

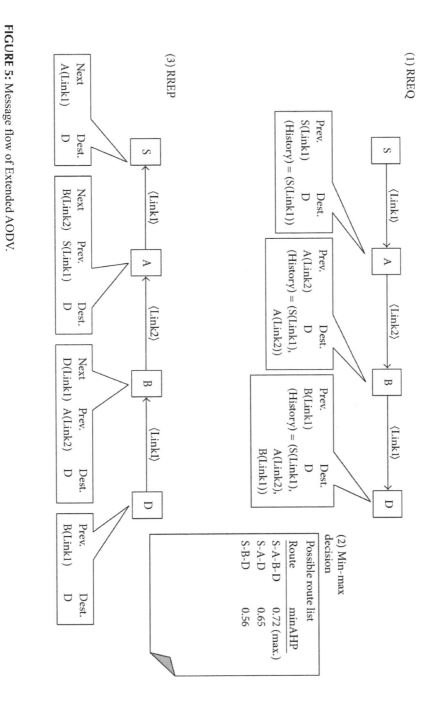

**FIGURE 5:** Message flow of Extended AODV.

**TABLE 4:** Priority of alternative.

| | PER | RTT | Throughput |
|---|---|---|---|
| Satellite | 0.2 | 0.1096 | 0.1137 |
| LTE | 0.4 | 0.5813 | 0.6647 |
| 3G | 0.4 | 0.3091 | 0.2216 |
| Propose | | | |
| Goal 1 (video) | 0.2346 | 0.0819 | 0.4480 |

Therefore, the overall result is shown in Table 5 by calculating the sum of the products of the priority of each alternative of Table 4 on the priority of the evaluation criteria in Table 2.

**TABLE 5:** Overall result.

| Goal 1 (video) | PER | RTT | Throughput | Combined value |
|---|---|---|---|---|
| Satellite | 0.0618 | 0.0121 | 0.0661 | 0.1399 |
| LTE | 0.1237 | 0.0637 | 0.3864 | 0.5737 |
| 3G | 0.1237 | 0.0339 | 0.1288 | 0.2863 |

Finally, if the purpose is video communication, the priority is set to LTE > 3G > satellite. Therefore, LTE is determined as the optimal wireless link. Thus, it is possible to continue to select an optimal access network by periodically calculating a moving average value of the network status.

## 6.4.4 ROUTE SELECTION

This system introduces "Extended AODV [16] which adopted extended AHP in AODV (Ad Hoc On-Demand Distance Vector) which is one of the conventional ad hoc network routing protocols." By Extended AODV, this system supports a change of neighboring communication environment re-actively and realizes the construction of the network where QoS control is possible. The routing in Extended AODV is implemented based on the following algorithm. Specifically, an agent investigates all "the AHP calculation result between nodes existing between candidate routes" and finally really uses the highest route of the bottleneck score between the routes.

In the conventional AODV protocol [17], a route of the number of the smallest hops is chosen, but this may not be necessarily the most suitable root. In Extended AODV, each node adds the calculation result of the priority of each wireless link by the extended AHP to RREQ and RREP and finally makes the most suitable route choice by the min-max method. The destination node finally sends out RREP packet from the reception side towards an origin of transmission and notifies you of the route decision.

The message flow of Extended AODV is shown in Figure 5. When data are sent to address node D by transmission former node S, at first it is delivered a broadcast to the RREQ packet like the normal AODV method by node S. Adjacent broadcast node A adds a postscript to adjacent node ID in front, the used most suitable wireless link ID, the value of the priority by the extended AHP in a route history of RREQ.

Then, in broadcast node A, broadcloth casts an adjacent node as RREQ packet equally, and similar processing is carried out in adjacent node B. Processing is repeated until RREQ packet finally arrives at objective transmission node D. When RREQ packet reaches transmission node, the transmission node waits for the arrival of the RREQ packet at constant time and destination node making the list of the candidate routes with route information and the priority information by the AHP chooses the most suitable route using the following min-max method from a candidate route list.

1. Destination node compares the AHP information in each candidate route.
2. The smallest AHP level is extracted by every candidate route.
3. The minimum every candidate route is compared, and a route that has the maximum in the inside is chosen as the most suitable route.

And, along a route chosen by this min-max method, node D replies to the transmission in RREP packet. The broadcast node replies while referring to an adjacent transmission node made at the time of the RREQ packet transmission, and each broadcast node in this way knows the adjacent transmission, the reception node in this occasion.

## 6.5 PACKET CONTROL BY OPENFLOW

In this system, in order to flow the packets to the selected access network, OpenFlow as one of the SDN frameworks is used. In OpenFlow, Open-FlowController receives various messages from OpenFlowSwitches and executes the events corresponding to the message by event driven method [18]. In our system, the following events are used.

1.  *Switch_Ready.* This event is called when the link between Open-FlowController and OpenFlowSwitch has been established.
2.  *Feature_Reply.* This event is called when the OpenFlowController received a reply from OpenFlowSwitch corresponding to the *Feature_Request* message.
3.  *Access_Change.* This event is called when the current access network is needed to be changed due to network states change. Using the control channel, the *FlowMod* command in OpenFlow protocol is issued to the related OpenFlowSwitches.

By combining those events, the flows of the data packets can be controlled. The message flows between OpenFlowSwitch and OpenFlowController are shown in Figure 6.

First, OpenFlowSwitch issues *Switch_Ready* message to OpenFlow-Controller to inform that the OpenFlowSwitch joins to the access network. Then, the OpenFlowController detects this new join from the OpenFlow-Switch and sends the request message to reply to the message with the OpenFlowSwitch itself, such as the switch ID, the number of admissible access networks, and the MAC addresses of equipped NICs. The Open-FlowSwitch completes the initialization process by notifying this information to OpenFlowController. The initialized OpenFlowSwitches start monitoring network states and those monitored data are sent to the Open-FlowController. This process is repeated for all of the related OpenFlow-Switches.

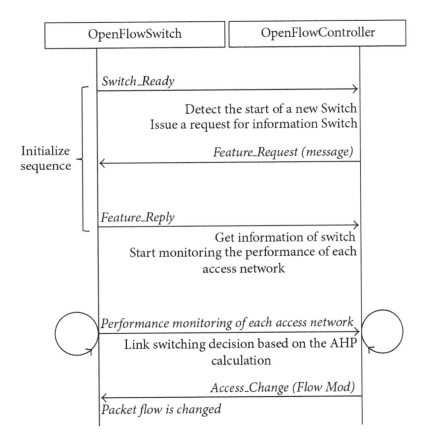

**FIGURE 6:** OpenFlow message flow.

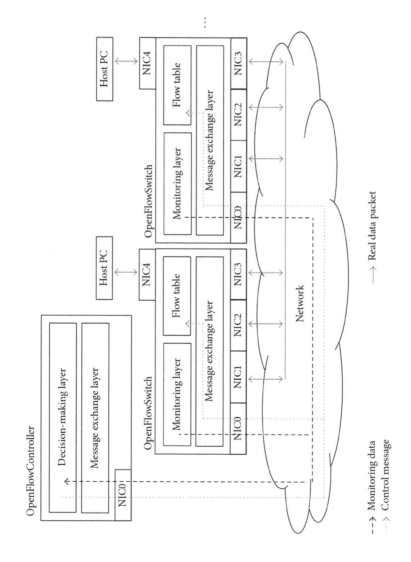

**FIGURE 7:** System architecture.

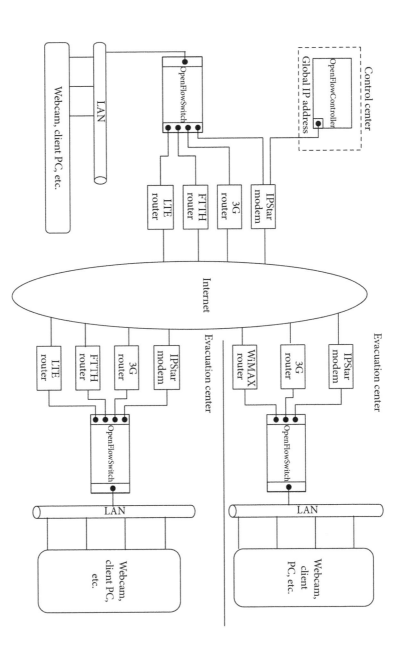

**FIGURE 8:** Prototype system.

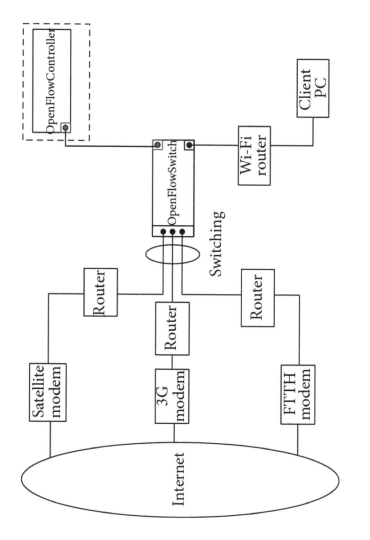

**FIGURE 9:** Performance evaluation environment.

**FIGURE 10:** Performance evaluation devices.

The OpenFlowController can decide whether or not to change the current access network to the selected access network by issuing the *Flow_ Mod* message to the corresponding OpenFlowSwitch.

## 6.6 SYSTEM ARCHITECTURE

The proposed system consisted of an OpenFlowController and multiple OpenFlowSwitches as shown in Figure 7. Furthermore, the OpenFlow-Switch consisted of three components including message exchange layer, monitoring layer, and flow table [19, 20].

The message exchange layer performs exchanging the monitored data and the control messages to the OpenFlowController. OpenFlow message is executed on software on OpenFlowSwitch. The monitoring layer monitors the network state of own OpenFlowSwitch.

The flow table is located in a stack of OpenFlowSwitch. The flow of the packet is defined by a command from OpenFlowController. The Open-FlowController consisted of two components including message exchanging layer and decision-making layer. The message exchanging layer performs exchanging control messages and receiving monitoring data from the OpenFlowSwitch. Exchanging OpenFlow message is executed on a framework on OpenFlowController.

In the decision-making layer, the priority process of the access network is carried out using the extended AHP method. The determined result is notified to all of the related OpenFlowSwitches. By this operation, the flow table of each OpenFlowSwitch is updated.

## 6.7 PROTOTYPE SYSTEM

### 6.7.1 DEVICE CONSTRUCTION

We describe the two main devices of the present prototype system including OpenFlowController and OpenFlowSwitch. OpenFlowController is implemented by Trema [21] which runs on Linux OS based PC. OpenFlowSwitch is implemented by OpenVSwitch [22] which runs on the Linux based PC. In addition, OpenFlowSwitch is connected to various wireless access networks through the NIC/USB connectors [23].

### 6.7.2 SYSTEM CONSTRUCTION

We describe a prototype system to evaluate the proposed method. This prototype system is constructed for the purpose of demonstration and evaluation of dynamic access network switching function to ensure the communication between physically distant locations in an emergency. Therefore, we build a prototype system at three locations including inland site, northern coastal site, and southern coast site of Iwate prefecture which were seriously damaged by the Great East Japan Earthquake on March 11, 2011, as shown in Figure 8.

In each site, we set the OpenFlowSwitch equipped with a variety of wireless access devices for prototype system. Wireless access networks to be used in the present prototype system are as follows:

1.  satellite;
2.  3G/LTE;
3.  WiMAX;
4.  FTTH.

It is necessary to prepare the OpenFlow channel to control each Open-FlowSwitch using OpenFlow protocol. Therefore, the OpenFlowSwitch performs network configuration function to allow TCP connection to OpenFlowController which is disposed on the main site in advance. Furthermore, in order to always open OpenFlow channel, we use the satellite communication network channel for control link. Each OpenFlowSwitch provides a LAN port to control all of the packets by the OpenFlow.

## 6.8 PERFORMANCE EVALUATION

In order to verify usefulness and effects of our proposed system, the performance evaluation of switching link network connectivity was evaluated in the experimental environment as shown in Figures 9 and 10. In the actual disaster situations, physical connection problems occur such as the physical destruction of network equipment, lack of power, and breaking of the cable. Therefore, before making a decision based on the network performance, it is necessary to recognize the availability of each link. In this prototype system, the availability of each link is recognized by monitoring the link state of each NIC. Link state of each NIC is determined by status member belonging to the message object which is retrieved by Feature_Reply event of OpenFlow. If the value of the status member is 0, the link of NIC is available. On the other hand, if value of the status member is 1, the link of the NIC is not available. In that case, the system switches to another available link of NIC immediately.

First we measured the time required to switch from one wireless access network link to another link of the prototype system and then measured the changes of the end-to-end throughput and packet loss performance. For the first case, we measured the switching performance when switching packet flow by OpenFlow protocol. In order to measure the exact switching performance, the delay of OpenFlow channel has to be close to zero. Therefore, OpenFlowController is directly connected to the OpenFlowSwitch by Ethernet. Since OpenFlowSwitch is operated by the very simple mechanism, it cannot obtain the event of rewriting completion of the flow timing and the flow-mod timing. For this reason, the switching performance measurement program is needed to be implemented on the OpenFlowController.

As the measurement procedure of switching time, first, OpenFlow-Controller starts the timer at the transmission timing of "Flow Mod message." At the same time, OpenFlowController sends a "Barrier Request message." Then, OpenFlowController stops the timer upon receiving the "Barrier Reply message" from OpenFlowSwitch. Thus, it is possible to measure the switching time. We implemented the switching time measurement program, ran 100 times switching every 10 seconds in the evaluation, and measured the maximum/minimum/average switching time at that time. The results are shown in Table 6.

**TABLE 6:** Switching process time.

|  | Maximum | Minimum | Average |
| --- | --- | --- | --- |
| Switching time | 196 ms | 67 ms | 80 ms |

The average switching time 80 ms is short enough to switch the link among possible access networks without significant packet loss. However, the maximum value was significantly out of normal distribution because the window manager is running on OpenFlowSwitch in order to perform a visual demonstration. That is, a processing time is increased by the control of the process such as interrupts at the OS level. It is considered that, in order for the operations to be more stable, it is necessary to introduce a dedicated OpenFlowSwitch machine not PC based or reduce the background process as much as possible.

Next we evaluated the end-to-end throughput and packet loss as network performance based on the disaster occurrence scenario. The scenario is as follows. Initially all three access networks including satellite network with average 1.29 Mbps throughput, 3G/LTE network with average

7.20 Mbps, and FTTH with average 25.01 Mbps are alive and the FTTH link is selected. Then a disaster occurred after 20 sec and both the FTTH and 3G/LTE network stopped due to power supply failure. Then link of the FTTH network is automatically switched to the satellite network. After 40 sec elapses, 3G/LTE network is recovered and the network link is automatically switched from satellite to 3G/LTE network. Finally, 60 sec elapses, the FTTH is recovered, and the network link is automatically switched from 3G/LTE to the FTTH. We measured the end-to-end network throughput and packet loss using *Iperf*.

The result of end-to-end throughput and packet loss is shown in Figure 11. After 20 sec from the starting time, the end-to-end throughput suddenly decreased from average 25 Mbps throughput to average 1.29 Mbps by satellite link. After 40 sec, the network link was switched to 3G/LTE network with average 7.1 Mbps. Finally, the 3G/LTE link was switched to the FTTH link with the original 25 Mbps. The packet loss at the switching times of 20 sec, 40 sec, and 60 sec was only under 5%. Thus, even though the disaster occurred and all of the networks were failed, the satellite network could be always alive and maintained the communication link to the Internet and realized resilient disaster network.

## 6.9 CONCLUSION AND FUTURE WORK

In this study, we have implemented a cognitive radio system using the SDN technology. Cognitive wireless device is equipped with LTE and WiMAX, 3G mobile telephone network, and a satellite communication network. We have created a prototype system by placing the three based in cognitive radio devices. Furthermore, we constructed a testbed environment to evaluate the performance and functionality of the system. Eventually we could verify the usefulness and effects of our proposed system.

In the future, we will implement immediately the expansion of AHP module which is the proposed method and network performance monitoring module. Then, by improving from manual to automatic switching process and evaluating the proposed method, we always activate a prototype system in three locations. By using continuous improvement, we will build a practicable system.

## REFERENCES

5.  Y. Shibata, D. Nakamura, N. Uchida, and K. Takahata, "Residents oriented disaster information network," in Proceedings of the Symposium on Applications and the Internet Workshops (SAINT '03), pp. 317–322, January 2003.

6.  D. Sakamoto, K. Hashimoto, K. Takahata, et al., "Performance evaluation of evacuation information network system based on wireless wide area network," in Proceedings of the DPS, pp. 100–112, November 2000, (Japanese).

7.  K. Ito, K. Tsuda, N. Uchida, and Y. Shibata, "Wireless networked omni-directional video distribution system based on delay tolerant network," in Proceedings of the 7th International Conference on Complex, Intelligent, and Software Intensive Systems (CISIS '13), July 2013.

8.  J. Mitola III and G. Q. Maguire Jr., "Cognitive radio: making software radios more personal," IEEE Personal Communications, vol. 6, no. 4, pp. 13–18, 1999.

9.  N. Uchida, K. Takahata, X. Zhang, and Y. Shibata, "Min-max based AHP method for route selection in cognitive wireless network," in Proceedings of the 13th International Conference on Network-Based Information Systems (NBiS '10), pp. 22–27, September 2010.

10. Open Networking Foundation, SDN, https://www.opennetworking.org/.

11. D. Nakamura, N. Uchida, H. Asahi, K. Takahata, K. Hashimoto, and Y. Shibata, "Wide area disaster information network and its resource management system," in Proceedings of the 17th International Conference on Advanced Information Networking and Applications (AINA '03), pp. 146–149, March 2003.

12. OpenFlow, https://www.opennetworking.org/sdn-resources/openflow.

13. A. A. Ali, F. Michaut, and L. Francis, "End-to-end available bandwidth measurement tools: a comparative evaluation of performances," in Proceedings of the IPS-MoMe IEEE/ACM International Workshop on Internet Performance, Simulation, Monitoring and Measurement, Salzburg, Austria, February 2006.

14. A. Gerber, J. Pang, O. Spatscheck, and S. Venkataraman, "Speed testing without speed tests: estimating achievable download speed from passive measurements," in Proceedings of the 10th Internet Measurement Conference (IMC '10), pp. 424–430, November 2010.

15. V. J. Ribeiro, R. H. Riedi, and R. G. Baraniuk, "pathChirp: efficient available Bandwidth estimation for network paths," in Proceedings of the Passive and Active Monitoring Workshop (PAM '03), San Diego, Calif, USA, July-August 2003.

16. T. Oshiba and K. Nakajima, "Quick end-to-end available bandwidth estimation for QoS of real-time multimedia communication," in Proceedings of the IEEE Symposium on Computers and Communications (ISCC '10), pp. 162–167, Riccione, Italy, June 2010.

17. A. Awajan, K. Al-Begain, and P. Thomas, "Quality of service routing for real-time applications using the analytical hierarchy process," in Proceedings of the 10th International Conference on Computer Modeling and Simulation (UKSIM '08), pp. 70–75, Cambridge, UK, 2008.

18. T. Ahmed, K. Kyamakya, and M. Ludwig, "Design and implementation of a context-aware decision algorithm for heterogeneous networks," in Proceedings of the ACM

Symposium on Applied Computing (SAC '06), pp. 1134–1138, Dijon, France, April 2006.

19. T. L. Saaty, "How to make a decision: the analytic hierarchy process," European Journal of Operational Research, vol. 48, no. 1, pp. 9–26, 1990.

20. N. Uchida, G. Sato, Y. Shibata, et al., "Selective routing protocol for cognitive wireless networks based on user's policy," in Proceedings of the 12th International Workshop on Multimedia Network Systems and Applications (MNSA '10), pp. 112–117, June 2010.

21. C. Perkins, E. Belding-Royer, and S. Das, "Ad hoc On-Demand Distance Vector (AODV) routing," Tech. Rep. RFC3561, IETF, 2003.

22. S. Kinoshita, T. Watanabe, J. Yamato, H. Goto, and H. Sone, "Implementation and evaluation of an OpenFlow-based access control system for wireless LAN roaming," in Proceedings of the 36th Annual IEEE International Computer Software and Applications Conference Workshops, pp. 82–87, July 2012.

23. K. Hashimoto and Y. Shibata, "Design of a middleware system for flexible intercommunication environment," in Proceedings of the 17th International Conference on Advanced Information Networking and Applications (AINA '03), pp. 59–64, March 2003.

24. C. W. Pyo and M. Hasegawa, "Minimum weight routing based on a common link control radio for cognitive wireless ad hoc networks," in Proceedings of the International Conference on Wireless Communications and Mobile Computing (IWCM C '07), pp. 399–404, Honolulu, Hawaii, USA, 2007.

25. http://www.trema.info/.

26. OpenVSwitch, http://openvswitch.org/.

27. "USB 3.0 Gigabit LAN Adapter," UE-1000T-G3, PLANEX, http://www.planex.net/product/adapter/ue-1000t-g3.htm.

# CHAPTER 7

# Web 2.0 and Internet Social Networking: A New tool for Disaster Management? Lessons from Taiwan

CHENG-MIN HUANG, EDWARD CHAN, AND ADNAN A. HYDER

## 7.1 BACKGROUND

Disaster response has always been a challenge during and after major disasters due to the impact of disaster itself, the number of organizations and individuals participating in the response[1] and the lack of rapid social networking to support immediate community response. Disaster, regardless of etiology, exceeds the ability of the local community to cope with the event and requires specialized resources from outside the area impacted[2-4]. In a large-scale destructive event, one of the greatest challenges to public health workers and rescuing teams is to have stable and accessible emergency communication systems[5,6]. However, little researches currently exist regarding the use of communication platforms and internet social networks for emergency response.

Emergency response during disasters is often complicated because communication becomes unavailable. The Chi-Chi earthquake in Taiwan and Hurricane Katrina in US have proven that current telephone, radio and television-based emergency response systems are not capable of meeting all of the community-wide information sharing and communication needs of residents and responders during major disasters[7,8]. After 9/11, Preece and Shneiderman et al proposed the concept of community response grids[9] which would allow authorities, residents, and responders to share information, communicate and coordinate activities via internet and mobile communication devices in response to a major disaster. Information technologies has the potential to provide higher capacity and effective communication mechanisms that can reach citizens and government officials simultaneously[10].

## 7.1.1 CONCEPTS AND DEFINITION

Internet social networking (ISN) or online social networking is the use of web based technologies to provide a virtual forum for internet users however diverse and afar to communicate and share ideas and information [11,12]. The term "Web 2.0" has been popularized since the Web 2.0 conference in 2004 hosted by O'Reilly Media and MediaLive[13]. The appearance of Web 2.0, and the availability of broadband networks have significantly enhanced the capabilities of the internet. Web 2.0 was described as "Web as Platform,"—entrepreneurs, software developers, and end users have transformed the internet into a highly interactive medium accessible through microcomputers, smart devices like cell phones, PDAs, and mp3 players. Examples of Web 2.0 tools include search engines (e.g. Google and Bing), encyclopedias (e.g. Wikipedia), videos and photos sharing (e.g. Youtube and Flickr), blogs and social networking websites (e.g. Facebook, Twitter, and Plurk).

Microblogging (e.g. Twitter and Plurk sites) is a social networking tool defined as "a form of blogging for users to send brief text updates (usually less than 200 characters) or micromedia such as photos or audio clips to be viewed by anyone or a specific group which can be chosen by the user [14]." Microbloggers post the message to subscribers, and they in turn can forward the information to others. Microblogging has created a two-way communication platform where dissemination of information is timely and vast [15]. Research has suggested that microblogging has power and potential in a scientific context for exchanging ideas, interests and information for a specific community[16-18].

In Taiwan, the most popular social network microblogging tools are Plurk and Twitter. The amount of global Plurk users coming from Taiwan has increased dramatically from 18.6% in April 2009 to 34.9% in July 2009[19]. Facebook, another popular networking site with 300 million users worldwide, added more than 88,000 new users in Taiwan alone in just one week in July 2009[20]. These new social networking sites, once thought of as fresh online toys for the young, are effective social and public health tools as was demonstrated during typhoon Morakot and its aftermath in August 2009.

This paper is aimed at describing the implications of internet social networking among large web-users during major disasters in order to establish an integrated internet-based emergency response system. Microblogging/Blogging and social networking sites are distributed, decentralized technologies. These sites have empowered the public to share experience and information during emergency and disaster response activities. The following case study provides a lesson for policy makers to consider in introducing technology to enable civil society to dialogue with the official government when facing major disasters.

## 7.2 DISCUSSION

### 7.2.1 CASE STUDY: APPLICATIONS OF SOCIAL NETWORKING IN TAIWAIN MORAKOT TYPHOON DISASTER

During August 8th to 10th 2009, typhoon Morakot, a medium scale tropical cyclone, wrought catastrophic damage in Taiwan, affecting a large portion of Southern Taiwan and leaving over 600 people dead, 76 missing and 24,950 people displaced[21]. Typhoon Morakot ruined more bridges and roads than the disastrous earthquake of September 21, 1999[22,23]. The accumulated rainfalls in parts of southern Taiwan reached 2866 mm, breaking the Central Bureau of Weather's historic record[24]. This storm was the deadliest typhoon to impact Taiwan in the last 50 years and even now the economic loss is difficult to estimate.

The night of August 8th, typhoon Morakot caused historical record levels of rainfall in Southern Taiwan. Web users began reporting the real-time situation on the forum PTT http://pttemergency.pixnet.net/blog , one of the most popular internet social networks in Taiwan. PTT is a bulletin board system with more than 1.2 million registered users and an average 10,000 users online simultaneously. On August 9th, an unofficial Morakot Online Disaster Report Center was established by a group of internet users from the Association of Digital Culture Taiwan http://typhoon.adct.org.tw/ . They advised fellow internet users living near areas battered by the storms to gather information, such as sustained damage or assistance needed on popular social networking websites including Twitter http://twitter.com/ TaiwanFloods  or Plurk http://www.plurk.com/floods . This website was then integrated into local governments' communication systems on August 10 and updated from the official disaster response center. Some users hosted Google maps on which residents who were waiting for rescuing could overlay information such as their current location and, the latest situation of damage caused by severe rainfall and landslide http://www. google.com.tw/intl/zh-TW/landing/morakot/ . Plurk and Twitter users also sent messages to help rescuers acquire accurate position for their family and friends who live in affected areas.

In the initial stage of this typhoon disaster, major response operations were not coordinated efficiently. During the most crucial first few hours after the catastrophe, the Central Response Center underestimated the early scope and gravity of the disaster due to the lack of information and communication from affected areas. Official government communication early in the crisis failed, causing people to turn to websites run by non-governmental organizations, local media and individuals for information. For instance, when traditional emergency reporting systems in Tainan County were overloaded, people instead reported the first aid need directly on the Tainan Commissioner's Plurk. By using microblogging to compile data, local emergency medical system workers had successfully rescued 14 trapped people by the second day of typhoon Morakot[20].

In addition to these examples, Web 2.0 social networking also serves as a platform in resource gathering, logistics allocation and the distribution of relief supplies. Volunteering was another activity promoted through social networking services observed during typhoon Morakot. The social networking services were used to spread the news on volunteering opportunities and to match the users and volunteers to the time and location of need http://morakot.yam.com/ .

## 7.2.2 THE APPLICATION OF ISN ON DISASTER MANAGEMENT

The goals/tasks of disaster management conducted by public health workers include:

1. Preventing unnecessary morbidity, mortality and economic loss resulting directly from a disaster. 2. Mitigating morbidity, mortality and economic loss due to the mismanagement of disaster relief efforts[25]. Therefore, the first priority is to understand the nature of disasters, and through this understanding, we identify the public health problems. Thus, collection, interpretation and dissemination of accurate and timely data from affected areas become necessary during and after the major disasters.

For public health workers and emergency responders, one of the most significant benefits of ISN is the speed to construct a network of professionals around practical, realistic common interests and objectives rather than around traditional bureaucratic structures. The non-hierarchical two-way communication system provided by most Web 2.0 social networks also empowers public users to participate in policy discussions with feedback to influence policy making.

The capacity of current emergency telephone and official communication system in Taiwan was drastically insufficient during the Morakot disaster. For example, the government was unaware of hundreds of survivors in mountainous areas of Kaohsiung county until informed by the news media. The primary reason that the information systems failed is not simply due to the difficult environment that the disaster created or its own internal limitations but rather, inadequate organizational capacity associated with a lack of support and oversight. The 911 emergency telephone system is not designed for disasters which resulted in difficulty in prioritizing or triaging the thousands of incoming calls. A good emergency communication system should be trustworthy, scalable, dependable, and reliable. When people are faced with uncertainty and lacking full knowledge of the risk, they will look to trusted sources of information for guidance[26].

Community response grids and microblogging can help reduce the gaps between residents and professional emergency rescuers in providing direct information during emergencies and understanding the severity and breadth of major disasters[9]. The technologies provide an online environment for information sharing and tracking. Used properly, microblogging can be a valuable component in an overall communication strategy. It is important to note that Twitter and other similar tools run on two-way communication which helps victims and professional emergency responders build relationships and share timely and important information directly with those in immediate need.

## 7.2.3 CHALLENGES TO THE APPLICATION AND USE OF ISN TOOLS

There are limitations and potential mishap of using ISN as a tool for disaster response[27]. First, in general, remote and less developed areas have more challenges in accessing the internet. It is also a reality that the less affluent and the less educated people have less access to information technology. Unfortunately, those residents are usually the most vulnerable. Second, there is the inherent potential problem underlying technologies themselves. Internet, Web 2.0, cabling, routers, networking, electricity grid etc all rely on good functional infrastructure to be effective, but disasters usually destroy infrastructure and interrupt the services. Third, how do we authenticate, validate, and ensure the accuracy of the messages in times of crisis and chaos? With free flow of information, it is very difficult to census and monitor social networking sites. Fourth, we should consider the scalability of those social networking sites. If they are not capable of handling the workload, they would only have a negative impact on efficiency and information sharing. Fifth, research has shown that social networking sites are not secured and private and personal information can be leaked to others[28]. Sixth, internet social networking alone is not a silver bullet in disaster preparations and relief. We must be prudent to integrate all appropriate technologies. During the disaster, lives were saved through the use of Geographic Information System (Google Map) and information was related to the rescue teams through the use of social networking. http://www.google.com.tw/intl/zh-TW/landing/morakot/ . If the systems are implemented correctly, the government should consider integrating internet-based disaster response systems into emergency communication strategies as internet is becoming more widely used for information of all types.

A critical limitation of the approach is the fact that the application of ISN in crisis management around the world is still far from being realized. In low- and middle income-countries, the most significant obstacle impeding widespread internet usage is the widening gap between people with no access and unlimited access to ICT. Illiteracy, limited education, poverty, lack of local language websites and basic computer skills are some of the major factors that restrict the use of ICT by the general population[29]. Perception around age appropriate use may also hinder willingness to use ISN because Web 2.0 tools are often considered to be a recreational activity for young people. Using existing resources to develop a flexible ISN platform tailored to user's socioeconomic status and educational level would be ideal. Other challenges to the use of ISN in disaster management include concerns of technological, social and financial sustainability[30]. There is an increasing need for political support in order to provide an ISN framework to develop a disaster response system at different levels of government. The system's capacity to collect and use information will require human resources in order to truly strengthen humanitarian responses. We suggest that local government in districts and cities be empowered to develop and provide such a system.

We still know very little about how to measure the real impact of ISN and web 2.0 tools in emergency-related activity. So far, there have been very few analyses and no clear methodology exists for such an evaluation. While there is great interest in this topic, few measures of effectiveness have been developed. Nonetheless, we expect to see improvements in early warning of disaster response as a result of increasing ISN use.

## 7.3 SUMMARY

The example of typhoon Morakot in Taiwan had shown that the internet-based Web 2.0 platform, mobile communication technologies and social networking could alter interactions between government and communities they serve for positive benefit during disasters. During the period of typhoon Morakot, government agencies were far behind of news organizations and NGOs in understanding the extent of the damage and identifying where refugees were trapped after the storm. An internet-based emergency response system would have allowed people to use mobile telecommunications devices or wireless computers to report such occurrences to the government to facilitate search and rescue. By using telecommunications technology such as Web 2.0, microblogging and other ISN technologies governments could revolutionize infrastructure to help individual and communities respond to and recover from disasters. Ultimately, it can lead to policy decisions to develop and foster the use of internet-based emergency response systems. This can bring significant benefits to governments, communities, responders and residents faced with threats of natural disasters. By harnessing the power and presence of internet technology and of social networks, we can change the way in which responders and residents are able to share information about and deal with crises.

## REFERENCES

1.  Waeckerle JF: Disaster planning and response. N Engl J Med 1991, 324(12):815-821.
2.  Noji E: The public health consequence of disasters. New York: Oxford University Press; 1997.
3.  Rutherford WH, de Boer J: The definition and classification of disasters. Injury 1983, 15(1):10-12.
4.  de Boer J: Definition and classification of disasters: introduction of a disaster severity scale. J Emerg Med 1990, 8(5):591-595.
5.  Stephenson R, Anderson PS: Disasters and the information technology revolution.

6. Disasters 1997, 21(4):305-334.
7. Spence PR, Lachlan K, Burke JM, Seeger MW: Media use and information needs of the disabled during a natural disaster. J Health Care Poor Underserved 2007, 18(2):394-404.
8. Chan YF, Alagappan K, Gandhi A, Donovan C, Tewari M, Zaets SB: Disaster management following the Chi-Chi earthquake in Taiwan. Prehosp Disaster Med 2006, 21(3):196-202.
9. Jaeger PT, Fleischmann KR, Preece J, Shneiderman B, Wu PF, Qu Y: Community Response Grids: Using information technology to help communities respond to bioterror emergencies. Biosecurity and Bioterrorism-Biodefense Strategy Practice and Science 2007, 5(4):335-345.
10. Jaeger PT, Shneiderman B, Kenneth RF, Preece J, Qu Y, Wu PF: Community response grids: E-government, social networks, and effective emergency management. Telecommunications Policy 2007, 31(10-11):592-604.
11. Shneiderman B, Preece J: Public health - 911.gov. Science 2007, 315(5814):944-944.
12. What is Social Networking? [http://www.whatissocialnetworking.com/]
13. Boyd DM, Ellison NB: Social network sites: Definition, history, and scholarship. Journal of Computer-Mediated Communication 2007., 13(1)
14. O'Reilly T: What is Web 2.0? [http://oreilly.com/web2/archive/what-is-web-20.html] 2005.
15. [http://en.wikipedia.org/wiki/Microblogging]
16. Rigby B: Mobilizing generation 2.0: a practical guide to using Web 2.0 technologies to recruit, organize, and engage youth. 1st edition. San Francisco: Jossey-Bass; 2008.
17. Martin Ebner MS: Microblogging - more than fun? Procceding of IADIS Mobile Learning Conference 2008. Algarve, Portugal 2008.
18. Skiba DJ, Barton AJ: Using social software to transform informatics education. Stud Health Technol Inform 2009, 146:608-612.
19. Boulos MN, Maramba I, Wheeler S: Wikis, blogs and podcasts: a new generation of Web-based tools for virtual collaborative clinical practice and education. BMC Med Educ 2006, 6:41.
20. Alexa Internet I[http://www.alexa.com/siteinfo/plurk.com] 2010.
21. Chiang B: The Might of Online Communities. CommonWealth 2009.
22. Commission NDPaP: Summary of Reconstruction Report. [http://88flood.www.gov.tw/eng/Reconstruction_reports.php#idx1] 2009.
23. staff TCPn: Morakot ruins more bridges than the great earthquake of 1999. The China Post Taipei 2009.
24. Directorate General of Highways MoTaC: [http://www.thb.gov.tw/tm/PrjMlk/Mrke-Book.aspx] Havoc Wrecked by Typhoon Morakot and Responsive Measures Taken. 2009.
25. Central Bureau of Weather T: Climate statistics. 2009.
26. Mathew D: Information technology and public health management of disasters--a model for South Asian countries. Prehosp Disaster Med 2005, 20(1):54-60.
27. Earle TC, Cvetkovich G: Social trust: toward a cosmopolitan society. Westport, Conn.: Praeger; 1995.

28. Brownstein JS, Freifeld CC, Madoff LC: Digital disease detection--harnessing the Web for public health surveillance. N Engl J Med 2009, 360(21):2153-2155.
29. Krishnamurthy B, Wills CE: On the leakage of personally identifiable information via online social networks. In Proceedings of the 2nd ACM workshop on Online social networks. Barcelona, Spain: ACM; 2009.
30. Pan American Health Organization: Information technology in the health sector of Latin America and the Caribbean: challenges and opportunities for the inernational technical cooperation. Washington, D. C.: Pan American Health Organization Essential Drugs and Technology Program; 2001.
31. McDonnell SM, Perry HN, McLaughlin B, McCurdy B, Parrish RG: Information for disasters, information disasters, and disastrous information. Prehosp Disaster Med 2007, 22(5):406-413.

# PART III

# MOBILE PHONES AND OTHER TECHNOLOGY

# CHAPTER 8

# Global Health and Natural Disaster Alerts: Preparing Mobile Phones to Endure the Unthinkable

WLADIMIR J. ALONSO, CYNTHIA SCHUCK-PAIM, AND GHASSEM R. ASRAR

## 8.1 REPORT

We just celebrated the 40th anniversary of the first call made from a mobile phone (BBC 2013). Since then, an extraordinary technological revolution has been unleashed, enabling three-quarters of the world population (and much of the developing world) to have access to this powerful communication device at all times (The World Bank 2012). Nowadays, more people in the world have access to mobiles than to basic sanitation. Almost everywhere, individuals are in constant contact with peers, family, business partners, service providers and an ever growing number of information sources. The rippling effects brought about by these ubiquitous communication opportunities on the living standards of populations include the creation of job opportunities, the promotion of political transparency, the early containment of epidemic outbreaks, the early warning of hazards and the possibility to scale up global health systems (The World Bank 2012; The Economist 2009a; The Economist 2009b; Quadir 2005; Lester & Karanja 2008; BBC Media Action 2012; The Economist 2007).

Mobile phones have also played an increasingly positive role as disaster relief tools. Since the year 2000, natural disasters and extreme weather events have caused over one million deaths and directly affected more than 2 billion people (Guha-Sapir et al. 2013). In addition to mass injury and death, common features of such disasters include damage to infrastructure, difficult access to basic goods, overburden of emergency and medical services and frequent isolation of victims. Although we currently count on sophisticated forecast and response systems (such as early assessment of hurricane paths or of the likelihood of a new disease spreading), new vulnerabilities are also present due to the increasing complexity of infrastructures and rapid expansion of megacities (especially in regions that are geologically and/or meteorologically vulnerable), interdependency of technologies and their massive use by growing populations (Kenett & Portugali 2012). In such contexts, the use of mobile phones can be critical, particularly in light of the likely collapse of terrestrial telecommunication infrastructures following a disaster (Patricelli et al. 2009; Townsend & Moss 2005).

However, several challenges still constrain the greater potential that mobile phones offer as effective mitigation tools in the aftermath of disasters and in other emergencies. For example, during earthquakes, hurricanes, floods, pandemics and other severe disease outbreaks, economic, societal and personal infrastructures are severely affected and governmental capabilities become quickly saturated due to the sheer demand for assistance. Although in such cases timely communication, information gathering and coordination are crucial to assist those in need, the availability, proper functioning and supporting infrastructure of mobile technologies is still fraught with fragilities and limitations that prevent them from being fully effective (Patricelli et al. 2009; Townsend & Moss 2005; West & Valentini 2013; Guo & Su 2012; Effros et al. 2010; The Telegraph 2011; Napolitano 2009; Xia 2011; Palen & Liu 2007; Yang et al. 2009; Zook et al. 2010). Here we discuss ways forward to overcome these limitations, proposing the incorporation of features to increase their resilience and effectiveness as mitigation tools at relatively low cost. Some of the measures proposed are not tied to daunting technological demands, but simply require unlocking capabilities already available, and affordably. Although our focus is mainly on natural disasters and global health crises, the solutions we identify are also useful to manage a wide range of emergencies that routinely affect millions of people around the world, especially in vulnerable and highly populated regions.

## 8.1.1 THE POTENTIAL OF MOBILE PHONES AS EFFECTIVE AID TOOLS

We consider two major mobile phone categories: cell phones and smartphones. In addition to voice communication and text messaging capabilities, cell phones can include features such as digital cameras and radio receivers. Smartphones share these features, but have also become powerful computing machines that can handle complex tasks and accommodate a wider array of human-centric sensor devices (Srivastava et al. 2012). Those capabilities are increasingly explored through the development of software applications across a vast array of themes, including those useful for emergency preparedness and response (West & Valentini 2013). However, cell phones are cheaper, have more energy autonomy, and are still the device of choice among developing nations and regions, and more vulnerable populations (like the elderly), so they should not be overlooked for planning and preparedness purposes. Moreover, while some smartphone apps are also useful off-line, they still require access to a data network to be installed or run, hindering their usefulness when data transfer is not possible. Other communication devices such as tablets, computers and land-lines share several of the capabilities mentioned. However, the ubiquity of mobile phones at all times makes them uniquely suited as a critical resource for assistance in unexpected and disruptive scenarios, hence we will focus mainly on these devices.

We first briefly consider major fronts where current capacities and improvements in mobile phones can harness the power of rapidly developing technologies to serve society, especially in the fields of human health, environment and humanitarian assistance, alerts and emergencies.

## 8.1.1.1 DISTRESS CALLS AND ESTABLISHING FIRST LINE OF CONTACT

Mobile phones already represent the main means to establish the first line of contact to ask (or offer) help, and to obtain information through which help can be offered and achieved, and about the situation of relatives and friends. This is, by far, the most important and useful service that mobile devices offer under dire scenarios. Accordingly, most of the suggestions we will discuss are aimed to secure such capabilities under a wide range of stressing conditions.

## 8.1.1.2 RECEIVING CRITICAL INFORMATION

When other means of communication (TV, radio, computers) are not accessible (e.g., out of reach or impaired), mobile devices can be the only source of information on evacuation plans and procedures, on the availability of shelters and other facilities, services and resources, weather forecasts, survival recommendations and other arguably life saving information.

## 8.1.1.3 DISSEMINATING DATA AND INFORMATION TO AID AGENCIES

During earthquakes, hurricanes, floods, pandemics and other severe disease outbreaks, economic, societal and personal infrastructures are severely affected and governmental capabilities become quickly saturated due to the sheer demand for assistance. In such contexts timely communication, information gathering and coordination are crucial to assist those in need. Mobile phones can provide information and coordination of help to victims and vulnerable individuals, enable rapid data collection (Lurie et al. 2013) and even track in real-time population movements in the context of relief efforts (Bengtsson et al. 2011).

### 8.1.1.4 OTHER APPLICATIONS

Other potential uses may range from those of psychological nature (as they can comfort and even entertain victims, helping lower panic and distress levels) to support of on-site data gathering and parallel computing processing just to name a few. For example, crowd sourcing to collect critically important information about a given situation or on a sustained basis to develop long-term records about environmental, demographic and health factors is also being considered by a wide range of organizations at the national and international levels.

These applications are intended to serve only as examples of practical and innovative ways that mobile devices can be used in service to society, and should not be viewed as an exhaustive list. In the next section we identify some of the current fragilities of mobile devices that limit their use for such conditions and applications, and propose the use of existing and emerging technologies to make them more resilient and useful in the future.

## 8.1.2 EXISTING FRAGILITIES AND PROPOSED SOLUTIONS

Critical capabilities are needed to ensure that mobile phones can serve at least the most essential roles previously discussed. Among obvious features, physical durability, energy autonomy, and network availability are most essential. But other features such as redundancy of frequency channels for communication are also important to turn these devices into effective aid tools in emergencies. We highlight current capabilities and limitations, and propose solutions based on existing and emerging technologies.

### 8.1.3 OFF-LINE OPERABILITY

Both communications and access to remotely stored information are interrupted when the network structure of mobile operators is damaged. In such cases, off-line features can provide assistance.

One such important off-line feature has unnecessarily vanished, or is deactivated, from many modern mobile phones: the radio receptor. Although news, music and information can now be streamed directly from data networks through smartphone apps, direct access to radio stations should not be considered redundant. Data-streaming requires that several antennae and terrestrial structures provided by mobile operators function properly, whereas the signal from each radio station is broadcasted independently. Only one radio station suffices for the mobile user to make use of it. Radio stations have been shown to be important in crises (Xia 2011; Covello & Hyer 2007; Baze 2012; National Association Broadcasters (NAB) 2013), and when combined with social media (if accessible) their impact can be largely amplified (BBC Media Action 2012). The National Association of Broadcasters states that the top 10 phones in the marketplace already include radio chips that are simply not activated (Murray 2010). Given the ease of reactivating radio receptors into mobile devices, their inclusion or activation in all future devices would be highly advisable. Moreover, because the costs of keeping an already existing feature would be likely very low, educating consumers about its effectiveness in emergency and disruptive scenarios could also contribute to a greater market penetration of these devices.

Another off-line feature that can be of great value in a disaster is geolocation capability. GPS access signals directly from satellites, hence does not necessarily depend on internet and data services. However, maps currently in use often access data in real time from on-line sources, rendering the information provided by the GPS nearly useless if map data cannot be downloaded. Users should thus always have a back-up map of their homes or destination and surroundings. Some smartphone apps that can work offline that do not rely on or require a data network to run can be also useful (West & Valentini 2013).

## 8.1.4 ENERGY AUTONOMY

The short battery life of most smartphones (Neild 2013) is a major limitation in emergency situations. Electrical grids can be severely damaged following a disaster, and although a few hours of autonomy may suffice for emitting the first distress calls, most emergencies last much longer. In life-threatening circumstances (such as when victims are under the rubble) the interruption of service can be fatal or cause major damage (Daily Mail Reporter 2011).

Cell phones often have more autonomy, usually several days, as they lack the power-hungry screens and processors of smartphones. Indeed, they have already proven useful during power outages or breakdowns in developing countries (Bengtsson et al. 2011), and are a suggested back-up means of communication even for smartphone users (Stout & Neild 2013). While this may be wise advice, it is unlikely that most smartphone users will constantly carry two devices.

In addition to improving energy autonomy, creative methods of charging mobile phones should be considered. Solar cells, physical motion chargers, micro-fuel cells and external batteries can be purchased separately to provide greater autonomy. Interestingly, solar cells based on nano- and thin-film technologies that are embedded in or integrated in mobile phones are promising technologies. For example, solar powered phones were distributed in the aftermath of the catastrophic earthquake in the Chinese province of Sichuan during efforts to recover mobile communication (Guo & Su 2012; Yang et al. 2009). Some of those solutions could be integrated into future phones.

## 8.1.5 ALTERNATIVE CHANNELS OF COMMUNICATION

Where fiber optic cables and electricity are still operational (no doubt an optimistic scenario in a major catastrophe) the Internet or other packet-switched networks could still be used (Murray 2010). But if mobile phone networks are down or overloaded, alternative channels of communication that are independent of external infrastructure (towers, cables) should be considered. One example is the critical role played by amateur and FRS/ GMRS radios (Baze 2012). Ad-hoc networks by which each mobile phone in range functions as a relay point for other mobile devices also represent a promising technological avenue (Effros et al. 2010; Australian Broadcast Corporation ABC 2010). Another possibility is the integration of two-way radio channels into mobile devices, opening opportunities for close range communication (Zhou et al. 2012). There are also existing satellite phones which do not depend on the terrestrial infrastructure (Baze 2012). Indeed, those were the only devices that could be operated by medical relief teams in the aftermath of the Great East Japan Earthquake in 2011 (Fuse 2011). The ability to access space-based telecommunication networks directly, and affordably, from mobile phones would greatly increase resilience to disasters.

## 8.1.6 PHYSICAL DURABILITY

Durability and ruggedness is not a common feature of most mobile phones. A quick glance at footages of natural disasters suggests that most currently available devices would likely become inoperable under the physical stress imposed during such events. In what is perhaps the early rise of a welcoming trend, some devices are under development with sturdier features such as shock resistance and water proofing (CNET 2013). The technology to improve the ruggedness of mobile phones, for example by using carbon fiber materials, is already available, and manufacturing costs do not seem to be a major barrier.

## 8.1.7 DISTRESS MODE

Individuals who need to let others know about their whereabouts could greatly benefit from the activation of a distress mode in their devices. While saving as much energy as possible (e.g. by turning off non-essential features), a distress mode could regularly send pulse signals, which could be composed of a sound, a flash, and a radio signal containing data with personal information of medical relevance and individual location. This feature could be based on existing Personal Locator Beacons, SPOT Personal Trackers and the Iridium satellite system (Baze 2012) and could be built based on Digital Distress Identifiers that are already used by medically impaired costumers and as personal emergency alerts in accidents, as well as personal, community, state and regional emergencies. Even if victims fell unconscious, this feature (which could be built-in to enable its activation manually, by a voice command or even remotely by another device using a secure protocol) would increase the possibilities of a successful rescue.

### 8.1.8 NETWORK RESILIENCE

Although mobile phone networks are relatively resilient to external shocks, disasters can affect power supply, destroy towers, and cause complete loss of functionality (Townsend & Moss 2005; West & Valentini 2013; Bengtsson et al. 2011; Bengtsson et al. 2011; Baze 2012). During the superstorm Sandy in 2012, which took place in one of the most developed and prepared places on Earth, mobile phone networks were frequently down (Allen 2012; The Economist 2012). Network data links should therefore be not only more resistant to damage, but also redundant, diversified and able to activate back-up systems when antennas and cables are damaged (Patricelli et al. 2009; Xia 2011; Fuse 2011). There is not much that consumers or manufacturers can do in this regard (other than promote redundancy by allowing mobile phones to use more than one network provider in the same device). Ultimately, the resilience of the communications network is a matter of national security. It is thus up to governments to detect fragilities in the system and overcome them by appropriate investments and implementation of a legal framework through which this can be achieved.

## 8.2 CONCLUSION

Most people live their entire existence without direct experience of major collective disasters. This shapes our perceptions as consumers and the features we seek in the products we purchase, which in turn guide the development and design of those products. But major public emergencies do happen and are in fact frequent worldwide (Lurie et al. 2013). Although mobile communication devices have already proven to be extraordinary aid tools in these situations (The Economist 2009a; BBC Media Action 2012; The Economist 2007; West & Valentini 2013; The Telegraph 2011; Chen 2010), much more can be done to minimize their fragilities and increase their effectiveness. We believe that such concerns should be taken into account by consumers, policy makers, designers and manufacturing companies.

The features that make a mobile phone commercially attractive to daily use are not necessarily incompatible with those that make it useful in case of emergencies. For example, the improvement of battery life and physical resistance are not only critical in collective emergencies, they may also eliminate daily nuisances. This may be particularly important in developing and low income settings, where over 80% of the world population lives. In such cases, features such as robustness and battery life are expected to be even more crucial (e.g., if access to electricity is costly or unreliable). For example, a study among Bangladeshi students found that battery life was more important in purchasing decisions than the presence of a camera, color display, sound performance, memory capacity, style and even price (Siddique et al. 2013).

Other features, including the introduction of distress radar emission signals or walk-talk capabilities, could nevertheless increase costs. In such cases, consumers can be informed on the potential uses of such features, so they can create the demand for the market to fulfill.

The emerging field of Mobile Health (m-Health) focuses predominantly on software and application development, but largely takes hardware specifications for granted. But improvement of key features can make a difference in critical contexts, as even simple voice or text communication is not possible when devices—or their supporting infrastructure—are impaired. Important features can be incorporated by policy or by educating consumers (hence manufacturing companies) on the specifications that can be helpful in emergency conditions. With few exceptions (such as ensuring that all devices can receive radio signals), we favor the market-based approach, as regulatory measures quite often can dampen competition and innovation, and may hamper what is perhaps the most useful feature of mobile phones in a disaster: their ubiquity and vast penetration.

Companies and individuals who made the mobile revolution possible are the embodiment of how technological innovation and creativity can speed up the achievement of well-being for billons of individuals. In fact, the widespread use of the technological wonders represented by mobile phones may prove to be one of the greatest allies in the management of natural disasters, public health emergencies and humanitarian crises. Part of this extraordinary potential has already been achieved in currently available devices. However, even more would be possible if we can ensure robust communication for all those trapped in all too common "unthinkable" situations.

# REFERENCES

1.  Allen E: First an Electricity Blackout and now Cell Phone Coverage is Down as Users in Manhattan Battle Signal Failures. Mail Online; 2012. accessed Nov 4, 2013 at http://www.dailymail.co.uk/news/article-2225217/Superstorm-Sandy-New-York-CELL-PHONE-coverage-users-battle-signal-failures.html
2.  Australian Broadcast Corporation ABC: Mobile invention could be desert lifeline. ABC; 2010. accessed Nov 4, 2013 at http://www.abc.net.au/science/articles/2010/07/12/2951206.htm#.Ucxwlz7wKrh
3.  Baze A: Personal Emergency Communications: Staying in Touch Post-Disaster: Technology, Gear and Planning. Max Publications; 2012.
4.  BBC: Mobile phone hits 40th birthday. BBC; 2013. accessed Nov 4, 2013 at http://www.bbc.co.uk/news/technology-22013228
5.  BBC Media Action: Still left in the dark? How people in emergencies use communication to survive – and how humanitarian agencies can help. BBC Media Action; 2012. accessed Nov 4, 2013 at http://downloads.bbc.co.uk/mediaaction/policybriefing/bbc_media_action_still_left_in_the_dark_policy_briefing.pdf
6.  Bengtsson L, Lu X, Thorson A, Garfield R, von Schreeb J: Improved response to disasters and outbreaks by tracking population movements with mobile phone network data: a post-earthquake geospatial study in Haiti. PLoS Med 2011, 8:e1001083. 10.1371/journal.pmed.1001083316887321918643
7.  Chen BX: Man Buried in Haiti Rubble Uses Iphone to Treat Wounds. Wired.com Gadget Lab; 2010. accessed Nov 4, 2013 at http://www.wired.com/gadgetlab/2010/01/haiti-survivor-iphone/
8.  CNET: Rugged phones posts on CNET. CNET; 2013. accessed Nov 4, 2013 at http://news.cnet.com/83005_3–0.html?keyword=rugged+phones

9.  Covello VT, Hyer RN: Effective Media Communication During Public Health Emergencies. A WHO Handbook. World Health Organization, Geneva; 2007. accessed Nov 4 at http://www.who.int/csr/resources/publications/WHO%20MEDIA%20 HANDBOOK.pdf?ua=1

10. Daily Mail Reporter: "I"m not going to give up': Woman's last message to rescuers from beneath Christchurch earthquake rubble before her mobile phone battery runs out. Mail Online; 2011. accessed Nov 4, 2013 at http://www.dailymail.co.uk/news/ article-1359354/New-Zealand-earthquake-A-mothers-message-beneath-Christ-church-rubble.html

11. Effros M, Goldsmith A, Médard M: The rise of instant wireless networks. Sci Am 2010, 302:72–77.

12. Fuse A: Medical relief activities conducted by Nippon medical school in the acute phase of the great east Japan earthquake. J Nippon Med Sch 2011, 78:397–400. 10.1272/jnms.78.39722197875

13. Guha-Sapir D, Santos I, Borde A: The Economic Impacts of Natural Disasters. Oxford University Press, Oxford; New York; 2013.

14. Guo Y, Su XM: Mobile device-based reporting system for Sichuan earthquake-affected areas infectious disease reporting in China. Biomed Environ Sci 2012, 25:724–729. 23228844

15. Kenett DY, Portugali J: Population movement under extreme events. PNAS 2012, 109:11472–11473. 10.1073/pnas.120930610934068492778423

16. Lester R, Karanja S: Mobile phones: exceptional tools for HIV/AIDS, health, and crisis management. Lancet Inf Dis 2008, 8:738–739. 10.1016/S1473-3099(08)70265-2

17. Lurie N, Manolio T, Patterson AP, Collins F, Frieden T: Research as a part of public health emergency response. N England J Med 2013, 368:1251–1255. 10.1056/ NEJMsb1209510

18. Murray MJ: Communicating during a disaster. Anesth Analg 2010, 110:657–658. 10.1213/ANE.0b013e3181cf12bd20185642

19. Napolitano D: Getting the Message. Occup Health Safety 2009, 78:28–29.

20. National Association Broadcasters (NAB): Equipping mobile phones with broadcast radio capability for emergency preparedness. NAB; 2013. accessed Nov 4, 2013 at http://www.nab.org/advocacy/issue.asp?id=2354&issueid=1082

21. Neild B: Smartphone Power StrugglesWill we Ever Have Battery-Free Mobiles?. CNN; 2013. accessed Nov 4, 2013 at http://www.cnn.com/2013/02/27/tech/battery-free-mobile-phones/index.html

22. Palen L, Liu SB: Conference on Human Factors in Computing Systems. In Proceedings of the SIGCHI, New York, NY; 2007:727–736.

23. Patricelli F, Beakley JE, Carnevale A, Tarabochia M, Von Lubitz DKJE: Disaster management and mitigation: the telecommunications infrastructure. Disasters 2009, 33:23–37. 10.1111/j.1467-7717.2008.01060.x18513313

24. Quadir I: Mobiles Fight Poverty Video on TED.com. 2005. accessed Nov 4, 2013 at http://www.ted.com/talks/iqbal_quadir_says_mobiles_fight_poverty.html

25. Siddique ZR, Jamil AA, Ali B: Product features affecting buying decision for mobile phone handset: a study on tertiary students segment in Bangladesh. Eur J Bus Manag 2013, 5:139–146.

26. Srivastava M, Abdelzaher T, Szymanski B: Human-centric sensing. Philos Transact A Math Phys Eng Sci 2012, 370:176–197. 10.1098/rsta.2011.0244

27. Stout KL, Neild B: Launch of Nokia's $20 Phone Begs Question: Is one Mobile Enough?. CNN; 2013. accessed Nov 4, 2013 at http://www.cnn.com/2013/02/25/tech/nokia-budget-phone-elop/index.html

28. The Economist: Dealing with disasters: Flood, famine and mobile phones. The Economist; 2007. Accessed Nov 4, 2013 at http://www.economist.com/node/9546242

29. The Economist: Eureka moments. 2009. accessed Nov 4, 2013 at http://www.economist.com/node/14483872

30. The Economist: Mobile marvels. 2009. accessed Nov 4, 2013 at http://www.economist.com/node/14483896

31. The Economist: Success and failure after the storm. The Economist; 2012. accessed Nov 4, 2013 at http://www.economist.com/blogs/schumpeter/2012/11/sandy

32. The Telegraph: Turkey earthquake: Four pulled alive from rubble after victim calls for help on mobileTelegraph.co.uk. 2011. Accessed Nov 4, 2013 at http://www.telegraph.co.uk/news/worldnews/europe/turkey/8846337/Turkey-earthquake-Four-pulled-alive-from-rubble-after-victim-calls-for-help-on-mobile.html

33. The World Bank: Information and Communications for Development 2012. Maximizing Mobile. The World Bank, Washington, DC; 2012. accessed Nov 4, 2013 at http://www.worldbank.org/ict/IC4D2012

34. URLTownsend AM, Moss ML: Telecommunication infrastructure in disasters: preparing cities for crisis communication. 2005. accessed Nov 4, 2013 at http://www.nyu.edu/ccpr/pubs/NYU-DisasterCommunications1-Final.pdf

35. West DM, Valentini E: How Mobile Devices are Transforming Disaster Relief and Public Safety. Brookings Institution, Washington DC; 2013. accessed Nov 4, 2013 at http://www.brookings.edu/research/papers/2013/07/16-mobile-technology-disaster-relief-west

36. Xia Y: Mobile Communication. In Dimensions of Social Policy. Edited by: Katz J. NJ: Transaction Publishers; 2011:87–102.

37. Yang C, Yang J, Luo X, Gong P: Use of mobile phones in an emergency reporting system for infectious disease surveillance after the Sichuan earthquake in China. Bull World Health Org 2009, 87:619–623. 10.2471/BLT.08.060905273326419705013

38. Zhou A, Shi L, Mao Y, Tang J, Zeng Y: Diffusion of new technology, health services and information after a crisis: a focus group study of the Sichuan "5.12" earthquake. Int J Health Plann Manage 2012. doi:10.1002/hpm.2137

39. Zook M, Graham M, Shelton T, Gorman S: Volunteered geographic information and crowdsourcing disaster relief: a case study of the Haitian earthquake. World Medical Health Pol 2010, 2:7–33.

# What It Takes to Get Passed On: Message Content, Style, and Structure as Predictors of Retransmission in the Boston Marathon Bombing Response

JEANNETTE SUTTON, C. BEN GIBSON, EMMA S. SPIRO, CEDAR LEAGUE, SEAN M. FITZHUGH, AND CARTER T. BUTTS

## 9.1 INTRODUCTION

Over the past decade, public-facing agencies and crisis communicators have shifted their formal communication strategies to accommodate new communication channels and messaging technologies. The widespread use of short messaging services on mobile devices [1] coupled with the emergence and growth of microblogging services and status updates on social networking sites [2] have resulted in new mechanisms to reach the public at risk [3, 4], broadcasting information in real time to increase public safety under conditions of imminent threat. As such, emergency messaging strategies have moved from audible sirens overhead to mobile "sirens" in the pockets of the everyday smartphone user. Little is known, however, about public receptivity to short messages under conditions of threat, nor how these messages are shared and redistributed during a crisis event.

Research on the behavioral effects resulting from short messages designed to inform the public about imminent threat and ongoing crisis has only recently begun. In their analysis of social media posts during a crisis event, Sutton et al. [5] (p. 612) introduced the concept of "terse messaging" to explain the processes that occur in environments that restrict message features as well as interactivity among message senders and receivers. The researchers define terse messages as "brief messages that are easily shared and quickly propagated, [having] the potential to reach online users in real time, disseminating information at critical points of a hazard event." Drawing from existing empirical research on warning messages, their work has led to the development of a framework for examining the "terse communication regime," i.e. settings in which: (1) communication takes place via short messages; (2) there is minimal opportunity for clarification of messages by the recipient; (3) there is minimal opportunity for elicitation of additional information from the sender by the recipient; and (4) there is minimal opportunity for sending of additional, follow-up messages by the sender within any given exchange. Importantly, terse regime communication has been found to occur both offline and online in emergency contexts (for examples of the former from the pre-Internet era, see e.g. [6–8]), and has distinct characteristics stemming from the constraints it imposes on information flow. Previously, Sutton et al. [9] conducted an exploratory study on short messages during a natural hazard event, identifying communication patterns occurring among the public in response to messages originated by public officials and disseminated via Twitter during a period of imminent threat. In this work they found that characteristics of short (terse) messages most strongly associated with message passing by the public did not conform in their entirety to content and style features consistent with normative guidelines (see [10]) for longer messages, such as those disseminated via broadcast channels such as television or radio. These prior studies by Sutton and colleagues set a foundation for the study of short messages redistributed under conditions of imminent threat, specifically natural hazard events. In this paper we extend the terse communication framework to the investigation of a new hazard type: terrorism.

The empirical focus of this paper is the public retransmission of terse messages that originate from official sources in response to a terrorist event. Message retransmission is a central aspect of information diffusion, with much work to date investigating its general incidence (see e.g. [11]) dependent on topic [12], sentiment [13], or receiver characteristics [14, 15]. (Throughout this paper, we will use the term "diffusion" to refer generically to the flow of information into and through a target population, "dissemination" to refer to the act of sending information to others, and "retransmission" to refer to the act of passing on messages to others that one has received from some third party. Retransmission is thus one form of dissemination, as is the posting of original messages.) Our specific emphasis in this paper is on the connection between retransmission activity and the local context of initial transmission and/or features of the messages themselves. We argue that retransmission of a given message is a clear and visible sign that the message is actively attended to by members of the public during the period of imminent threat, and hence a behavioral indicator of message salience. Message passing is also a demonstration that certain messages are perceived by the public to have some intrinsic value (being, at the very least, seen as worth sharing with others). Here we examine multiple features of messages—including their content, style, and structure—in order to identify those features that are most consistently associated with message retransmission under imminent threat conditions. We choose to focus on message retransmission rather than passive attention relationships (e.g. who Follows whom) because this provides a more direct indicator of attention to terse messages during the threat period. By examining how message retransmission varies as a function of message properties, we are able to directly examine the factors that are predictive of message amplification.

This paper provides the first examination of retransmission of terse messages from official sources in response to a domestic terrorist attack, the Boston Marathon Bombing in 2013. Using data from 31 official Twitter accounts that were actively posting during the five day period of the Boston Marathon bombing and manhunt, we examine the features of terse messages that are associated with their retransmission. We focus on message content, style, and structure, as well as the networked relationships of message senders to answer the question: what are the characteristics of a terse message sent under conditions of imminent threat that predict their retransmission among members of the public?

This paper is organized as follows: we begin by providing background on disaster warnings, terse communication, and the importance of message amplification via retransmission in the context of a terrorist event. Utilizing case study research methods, we then describe our research context, data collection and analysis activities. We end with a discussion of our results and suggest directions for further inquiry, connecting research findings with implications for crisis communicators.

## 9.2 BACKGROUND

### 9.2.1 WARNING MESSAGES FOR HAZARD EVENTS

Warning messages are routinely issued by public officials in response to an imminent threat at critical time points in the hazard response process. These messages are intended to instruct the population or group at risk on necessary protective actions to make themselves safe. Warning research has largely drawn from theories of collective behavior [16] and emergent norms [17] to explain the social processes that individuals undertake following the receipt of a warning message. Warnings are interpreted and understood through social interaction and sense-making activity, which is strongly influenced by the message itself. From this foundation has grown an extensive history of research on alerts and warnings for disaster events [10] focusing on the effects of messaging channels [18], sources [19, 20], content [21, 22], and hazard type [23] on behavioral intent and behavioral actions in response to a warning message. Individuals engage in a complex process of decision making (see [19]) prior to taking protective action, that is affected by a variety of personal, social, and situational factors.

From the research record, warning scholars have concluded that the content and style of official messages are the strongest determinants motivating appropriate and timely public protective action [10]. For example, content found in effective warning messages includes the message source [19, 24], the timing at which the warning is issued and the time to complete the protective action [21, 23], the hazard type and impact on the population at risk [25], and guidance describing the protective actions that should be taken to reduce harm to life and property [22, 23]. Effective message content should also be delivered in a style that utilizes clear and specific, unambiguous language, that is accurate and consistent both internally and across messages [10]. In cases where warning messages are constrained due to the dissemination channel being used, content and style characteristics may differ; we turn to this next.

## 9.2.2 TERSE COMMUNICATION

Until recently, studies of effective warning messages have focused almost entirely on relatively "long" messages (i.e. [10, 19, 26]), that is messages that are delivered over broadcast channels and are only mildly restricted in their content and character length. These warning messages, when sent via the Common Alerting Protocol, can include up to 1380 characters of text (see [27]) With the advent of social media and other short messaging channels, however, alerts and warnings have become "terse" as they have been adapted to the constraints of online and mobile device messaging.

Terse messages are brief, easily shared messages that are constrained either by medium (such as the channel by which they are relayed) or the sending context and timescale (such as periods of imminent threat when time is limited, requiring quick exchanges of information and limiting interactions). In this context, terseness is not equated with the conventional meaning of rude communicative acts, but instead is understood as quickly relayed bursts of content, necessarily constrained due to extraneous factors. Social media, such as Twitter, which is limited to 140 characters of text, is just one channel by which a terse message can be relayed. Others include SMS messages (limited to 160 characters) and Wireless Emergency Alerts (limited to 90 characters). Twitter, however, is important channel for message dissemination because it includes opportunities for networked message amplification, or retransmission, among online communicators under conditions of threat.

While terse messages distributed over Twitter during a warning period may contain some of the content elements identified as being crucial to an effective warning as described above, character limitations restrict the likelihood that all of the effective messaging elements will be included in a single message. For instance, Sutton et al. [9] examined terse messages sent in the warning period of a wildfire event to understand the impact of Twitter's limitations on message length (and hence amount of content shared in a single message) on message style and content. They found distinct patterns in message content and style generated by official sources under conditions of imminent threat, affecting message retransmission among the public at risk. The message content and style of terse messages sent under conditions of a terrorist attack are the focus of this research.

## 9.2.3 TERRORISM COMMUNICATION

The context of terrorism differs from natural hazard events due to the intent, event forewarning, and outcome of increased societal fear. Terrorist activity has been described as intentional, violent acts, targeted toward unarmed, non-combatant persons unable to defend themselves [28]. Because it is experienced by victims as "uncontrollable" [29], it results in fear response from the public who have a need for sense-making [30] and emotional support [31]. Although it is not a new phenomenon [32], recent events such as 9/11, the anthrax attacks in 2001, and the increasing visible use of improvised explosive devices (IEDs) have made public communication a top priority for crisis responders (see The 9/11 Commission Report). Internationally, IEDs are widely recognized as being a weapon of choice among those engaged in terrorist attacks; they are frequently used by terrorists throughout the world [33]. However, IEDs have been less utilized in the United States: before the 2013 Boston Marathon bombing there were relatively few high-profile instances of such attacks (e.g. the Atlanta Olympic Park Bombing in 1996 and the Oklahoma City Bombing in 1995), although there have been more numerous cases of smaller attacks aimed at abortion providers [34]. As a result, local civic leaders have had few opportunities to issue warnings or instructions about direct threats to public safety and security posed by terrorists via IEDs [35]. Even relative to other types of terrorist attacks, the hidden, latent, uncontrollable, and seemingly capricious nature of the IED threat makes it load heavily on the factors identified by [36] as particularly likely to produce fear and a subjective sense of "risk" in the public at large, creating both a demand for action and a strong affective component to event related communication.

Recent studies on public uses of Twitter in the aftermath of terrorist incidents have revealed broad and widespread public attention online [37] that may be useful for officials developing situational awareness during the event [38–40]. Our research centers on the public retransmission of terse messages originated by public officials in order to extend the theoretical framework on terse message retransmission to conditions of terrorist attack.

## 9.2.4 SERIAL RETRANSMISSION OF TERSE MESSAGES

Serial retransmission occurs when the recipient of a message passes this message on to another party (who may, in turn, pass the message to yet others). A major focus of early studies into rumoring behavior, serial retransmission is an important factor in the initial diffusion of information regarding disruptive events both because of its speed (competitive with broadcast media even in the pre-Internet age [41, 42] and because of its wide reach [7, 43]. For response organizations seeking to reach as many persons as possible within a target population, retransmission of formal communications is essential: extensive retransmission allows messages to reach a much wider audience than could be directly contacted, especially within a short span of time. Moreover, extensive retransmission of messages within a population increases the number of times that a given individual is exposed to each message. Such repeated exposure can increase confidence in message veracity [44, 45], which can enhance both compliance and additional message passing [46]. As a number of researchers have noted (e.g., [47–49]), exposure to messages from multiple distinct sources is often necessary to provoke both behavioral change and further message passing, making "saturation" of the target population by informally retransmitted copies or high-fidelity variants of formal communications an important goal for response organizations. To reach a broad audience with critical information during an unfolding hazard event, response organizations thus face the challenge of producing messages that not only communicate effectively to their initial recipients, but that also have a high probability of being retransmitted by those recipients to others in the target population.

The above raises the question of what features are predictive of terse message retransmission in a hazards context. Various approaches to the study of retransmission of terse messages on Twitter in a general (i.e., non-hazard) context have been attempted to date, including Bayesian techniques [50], conditional random fields [51], and classification of the properties of successfully retransmitted messages [52, 53]. Prior work in the disaster context per se has centered on sender and message content features [48, 54]. Research on terse message retransmission during periods of imminent threat (when effective communications are especially important for loss reduction) has shown that content, style, and structural factors affect retransmission rates [9, 55]. For instance, messages containing content describing the impact of the ongoing or imminent hazard, employing a well-defined hashtag used consistently throughout the event, and using imperative and instructional language received substantially more retweets, on average, than those that do not [9]. Furthermore, the features of individual accounts, most specifically, their Follower numbers, are important contributors to predicted message exposure and retransmission rates [9]. This prior work suggests a number of features that could be expected to be predictive of terse message retransmission in the terrorism case; at the same time, the terrorism context differs both in terms of protective action guidance and hazard type from these previously studied events (e.g., wildfires, storms, etc.), and it is therefore non-obvious which if any of these factors will generalize to the former setting. Recent work by [56] examines retransmission for a targeted sample of 256 tweets sent by the general public associated with specific rumors arising during the Boston bombing, finding positive effects on retransmission for the Follower counts of the most influential posters and for hashtag usage. This work suggests that Follower count and tweet structure effects may generalize to the terrorism case (at least for messages originating within the general public), but leaves open the role of other factors—and of whether those effects continue to operate in the same manner for messages disseminated by official entities. The remainder of this paper thus seeks to address the following basic question: what are the content, style, and structural characteristics of terse messages, disseminated by emergency management organizations under conditions of imminent threat, that predict their retransmission among the public during a terrorist event?

## 9.3 METHODS

Utilizing a case study approach [57], we investigate the dynamics of terse message retransmission over a defined period of time for a specific event. The case study approach is suitable for answering research questions such as why and how things are done [58]. Case studies are also important as building blocks for subsequent meta-analytic studies. We are primarily interested in answering questions related to salient features of formal warning messages, including their content, style, and structural features, and how this affects message retransmission by the public. The primary data used for this study are publicly available messages posted to Twitter by official response agencies during the period of threat of the Boston Marathon bombing and manhunt. To address our research questions, we conduct thematic content analysis and statistical analyses on the set of 698 messages produced by 31 official accounts over the five day period and model their predicted retransmission rates by members of the public. In this section we provide a description of the terrorist event and public safety response, then turn to a detailed discussion of our online data collection methods, data coding, and analysis.

### 9.3.1 THE BOSTON MARATHON BOMBING AND MANHUNT

On Monday morning, April 15, 2013 two improvised explosive devices were detonated near the finish line of the Boston Marathon, killing three spectators and injuring more than 200 people. During the week that followed, memorials were held (April 17, 2013), two suspects were identified (April 18, 2013), and a shootout occurred resulting in the death of the first suspect as well as a MIT campus police officer (April 18, 2013). The events lead to shelter in place orders and more than a million people across the city of Boston and contiguous areas were placed on lockdown for close to 24 hours while a massive search was undertaken. The manhunt resulted in the capture of the second bombing suspect in the late hours of the day on Friday, April 19, 2013.

Over the course of the week, social media sites, Twitter in particular, gained significant attention due to their utilization by both the general public and government officials. Popular media sites posted articles about social media use by local public officials [59]. The reports noted the benefits and drawbacks of such community engagement; members of the public tweeted police chatter [60] and banded together in attempts to identify suspects from images captured at the scene of the event [61]. In addition to popular media accounts of the heightened use of Twitter, previous research also supports this convergence of attention online [62]. Key Twitter accounts held by local public officials experienced dramatic surges in attention as they provided real time updates from the scene of the bombing and additional messages throughout the week. Boston Police gained 273,000 new Followers, Massachusetts State Police picked up nearly 26,000 Followers and the Mayor of Boston, Tom Menino, experienced an increase of nearly 17,000 Followers [55].

## 9.3.2 DATA COLLECTION

In this research, terse message retransmission is analyzed by investigating aspects of messages posted via the microblogging service, Twitter. Twitter represents one online venue for social interaction and information exchange in disasters for members of the public and public officials alike. Twitter is a social media platform that enables individuals to post terse (140 character) messages in real time. The platform facilitates information exchange through a set of publish/subscribe relationships, called Following relations. Public content on the platform is searchable allowing users to seek out information and other users of interest. Moreover, the platform itself enables retransmission of content with a single action; retweets, as they are called, allow users to rapidly retransmit information to the public sphere as well as their own personal network in real-time. These features make Twitter an ideal data source through which to examine terse messaging and message amplification in social networks.

Our data collection processes replicate those used previously [62] in order to develop a cross-hazard comparison between cases. For this event, we identified 31 Twitter accounts representing the population of public officials at the local, state, and Federal level who were serving in a public safety capacity prior to the marathon and actively tweeted over the course of the five day period. The set of accounts satisfying these criteria were identified through two processes. First, we searched through our set of user accounts that were already in our data collection system and were within the geographical boundaries of the Boston region, the state of Massachusetts, or represented Federal agencies having a role in terrorism and disaster response. Secondly, we manually sifted through the Twitter "Friend" lists of local official organizations (i.e., organizations that are Followed by the accounts we selected) to identify additional accounts that may not routinely tweet, but could play a role in relaying public information, and we looked for any account that was mentioned or retweeted in posted content from the official accounts. We did not choose to include local media as part of our targeted accounts because our interest lay in the messages posted by public officials, as part of their formal communication strategy during a terrorist incident. In total the set of targeted accounts represents 17 local public officials or organizations, 10 state actors, and four federal entities.

For each account, we retrieve the posting behavior history, along with actor level attributes, using the Twitter API. Twitter's API allows us to obtain up to 3,200 of the most recent messages posted by the user of interest to the public timeline and the timestamp for each post. Data was queried daily over the five day period of the unfolding event to ensure no messages were missed, resulting in a complete dataset of official messages posted to Twitter. We removed any retweets from this set as they are not original content produced by these users. For each message we also obtained a count of the number of times that each message was retweeted (by the time of last data collection). Actor or user-level attributes collected include the number of Friends and Followers of that account at the time of collection, the self-reported location of the user, the account creation date, the timezone of the account, and the number of statuses posted over the lifetime of the account. For the subsequent analysis, we consider the set of 698 messages posted by our targeted accounts, from April 15, 2013 2:49pm (the day and time of the bombing) until 11:59pm on April 19, 2013 (after the manhunt was concluded).

### 9.3.3 CONTENT CODING

Data analysis in this work centers on an examination of the features of terse messages disseminated by officials over the course of the five day period of threat, beginning on the day of the bombing and throughout the manhunt, concluding when the suspects were captured. We conduct a thematic content coding, based upon effective message content and style elements described above, to identify variables that may predict message amplification via public retransmission. Variables include content themes, message style, and network features of posted accounts.

Coding strategies for primary thematic content analysis and message style characteristics replicate those previously conducted by Sutton et al. [62], for cross-hazard comparative purposes. In this case, two researchers manually coded the entire set of official tweets for the observation period, utilizing a deductive content coding strategy that drew from codes that were developed during previous research activities on terse messaging via Twitter during a wildfire event [62]. Both coders were blinded to the retweet count information before and during the coding process, and content codes were hence determined independently of the outcome of interest. To begin, the coders independently scanned all tweets to determine that the original coding categories fit with the Boston event data. They also met to discuss any emerging themes. Next, the set of tweets was split-recoded by both coders, with one half being blind recoded by each researcher and then exchanged and checked for intercoder agreement. Coders agreed on theme codes in approximately 98% of cases. Disagreements were resolved by consensus, following discussion of problematic cases by the coders. Coders ultimately identified 10 primary themes (plus two additional categories; one for tweets that were not on-topic, i.e. pertaining to the Boston event, and one for tweets that did not fit into any category). Primary themes range from evacuation guidance and sheltering in place to hazard information (such as listings of phone numbers and resources). A full list of content themes can be found in Table 1.

**TABLE 1:** Content analysis coding categories for messages from Boston Marathon Bombing.

| Thematic content | Definition and example tweet |
| --- | --- |
| Advisory | Messages containing advisory information such as requesting that people clear the area of the bombing and the actions to take while the city is on lockdown |
| | *#MediaAlert: WARNING: Do Not Compromise Officer Safety by Broadcasting Tactical Positions of Homes Being Searched* |
| Closures/openings | Messages containing information on closures/openings of events, facilities, or roads |
| | *ATTENTION: The #MBTA is SUSPENDED on ALL modes until FURTHER NOTICE* |
| Corrections | Messages containing corrections to previously posted information |
| | *We now know @bstonmarathons is a scam. We should know better and apologize for perpetuating the exploitation of the bombing. #embarrassed.* |
| Evacuations/ shelter in place | Messages that provide specific guidance about how to protect oneself in disaster, in this case, sheltering in place |
| | *ATTENTION: City-wide shelter in place advised. Armed and dangerous person(s) still at large. Police actively pursuing every lead.* |
| Hazard impact | Messages containing descriptions of the hazard itself such as location, containment, etc., and descriptions of the hazard impact such as number of injuries |
| | *176 people went to area hospitals #tweetfromthebeat* |
| Information | Messages containing updates, available resources, and images of the suspects |
| | *@healthyboston has some tips for helping children cope with yesterday's events http://t.co/TgykZFNYSS #bostonmrathon* |
| Help/directed communication | Messages directly responding to a member of the public's requests for assistance or information |
| | *@Kend129 1–93 is open* |
| Thank you/ appreciation | Messages that include statements of thanks and appreciation |
| | *@RedCross: Thanks to generosity of volunteer blood donors there is currently enough blood on the shelves to meed demand. #BostonMarathon* |
| Volunteer/donate/help | Messages that suggest ways to volunteer or donate to the disaster response efforts |
| | *AG's Office Offers Tips to Giving Wisely after Marathon Tragedy http://t.co.bC96Ysl4Ex @bostonmarathon #mapoli* |
| Emotion/judgement/evaluative | Messages containing emotive statements about the event, the response, and the recovery efforts |
| | *Yesterday was a very sad day for our city. Thank you to all first responders & spectators for quick thinking & heroic acts. #bostonmarathon* |
| Unsure/not on topic | Messages that are not directly related to the Boston Marathon Event response or could not be determined to be related |
| | *@tedslater we have asked facilities to check the HVAC thanks for letting us know.* |

Following methods used in previous research in this area [62], two researchers also manually coded each tweet for aspects of message style. Style aspects, which emphasize how content is relayed or displayed to affect message specificity or clarity [10] include the following: (1) how each sentence in the tweet functions within the English language as either declarative, imperative, interrogative, or exclamatory; and (2) whether a tweet includes a word or phrase in ALL CAPS we distinguish between capitalizations used as either a category signifier or to emphasize a portion of the tweet.

In addition, we used automated techniques to code for conversational microstructure elements within the tweet (i.e. conventional aspects of Twitter-based syntax that lend to message retransmission or engagement) [62]. These include whether the tweet was directed at or responding to another Twitter user (begins with @name), contained a mention of another user, contained a hashtag keyword, and referenced further information available online in the form of links to URLs (usually shortened by using bit.ly or another short URL service).

For both thematic content and style features, messages were coded in a non-mutually exclusive manner; in other words, a single tweet could contain several types of content as well as multiple sentence features or other stylistic aspects.

## 9.3.4 MEASURING AND MODELING MESSAGE RETRANSMISSION

A central observation of our and prior work (as cited above) is that not all messages are equally likely to be passed on by others; we thus seek to identify the factors that enhance or inhibit message transmission, by means of statistical analyses. Our analyses are in turn based on a basic model of the retransmission process, which may be summarized as follows. Consider an original message, broadcast from a targeted account to the public stream. The message has particular style and content features (as described above), each of which may serve to enhance or suppress the probability that a given message recipient will pass it onward. Likewise, the probability that a recipient will retransmit the message may be positively or negatively affected by characteristics of the sender (e.g., the type or prominence of the associated organization) and/or by the context in which the message was sent (e.g., the number of individuals following the sending organization at the time of transmission, or whether the message was simultaneously posted by multiple organizations as part of a deliberate amplification strategy). Finally, there may be additional, idiosyncratic factors relating to unmeasured and/or unpredictable aspects of the communication setting that also impact retransmission probability. In the context of this study, we note that the number of persons at least peripherally exposed to any given message is generally quite large, and that the probability of message passing by any given individual is generally quite small; given any fixed retransmission probability, we thus expect the number of times a given message is passed on (the retweet count) to be approximately Poisson distributed. Note, however, that the presence of idiosyncratic (i.e., random) factors implies that the retransmission probability for a message with the same observable characteristics will fluctuate from one occasion to another; a natural model for this variation is the gamma distribution, leading to a final retweet count distribution which is negative binomial given the observed message, sender, and contextual features.

Under the above model, the effects of message, sender, and contextual features on the expected retweet count can be estimated by negative binomial regression. As an additional test on the assumptions underlying the above process model, we also compared our results to regression models based on Poisson and geometric distributions. The former model corresponds to a process like the above, but without idiosyncratic variation in retweet probability; the latter model corresponds to a sequential process in which messages are passed serially with some given probability from one user to another, until the "passing chain" fails (at which point no further retransmission occurs). Neither the Poisson nor the geometric model were favored over the negative binomial model using the corrected Akaike Information Criterion (AICc), a standard model selection index. The negative binomial model, with an AICc of 7876, had a substantially lower score than the Poisson model (817655) and the geometric model (8027). In addition, we favored the negative binomial model specification over Poisson due to overdispersion of the dependent variable. We tested for this using Cameron and Trivedi's Test for Overdispersion [63], the null hypothesis being that the variance of the dependent variable is equal to the mean. The z-score for this test was 5.434 with a p-value $< 1e-7$, suggesting that a Poisson model (which assumes a mean equal to the variance) was not appropriate. This suggests that neither alternative process provides a better account of the observed data. Finally, inspection of the data also indicated that most retransmission occurred as a single step, rather than via long chains of sequential message passing, in line with our above theoretical model. We thus note that our choice of analytic procedure is not merely one of convenience, but is founded on a specific model of the communication process that was found to outperform theoretically plausible alternatives.

Given the above, our analysis proceeds by modeling the log of the expected number of retweets for each original message as a linear function of message, and context covariates (as described below). Because sender effects (i.e., differential propensities for messages to be retransmitted as a function of sender) can come from many strongly correlated attributes (e.g., total number of statuses, local/state/federal status, government sector, number of reciprocated ties "Friends," perceived prominence and reliability, etc.), not all of which can be measured, we include fixed effects for each sender as additional terms in the model; this controls for sender-level heterogeneity. Coefficients representing the strength of each effect are then estimated by negative binomial regression, with best-fitting models selected by AICc.

## 9.4 RESULTS

### 9.4.1 MODELING MESSAGE RETRANSMISSION

As discussed in the methods section above, we built a model of message retransmission to assess the relative influence of content and style elements, as well as message exposure, on the number of times a message is retweeted among the public. We use the R statistical computing platform [64] to fit a negative binomial regression model for these data. As noted above, the negative binomial family allows us to account for observed overdispersion in the retweet rates relative to either a Poisson or geometric family, and is consistent with a process in which there are many sources of heterogeneity in the retweet process (only some of which can be captured via observed covariates).

**TABLE 2:** GLM negative binomial model using source, style and theme variables predicting number of per-tweet retweets during the Boston Marathon Bombing.

|  |  | Estimate | exp(β) | Std. error | z value | Pr (>|z|) |
|---|---|---|---|---|---|---|
|  | (Intercept) | −18.18*** | 0.00 | 2.63 | −6.91 | 0.00 |
| Source |  |  |  |  |  |  |
|  | Source fixed effects[a] log (Followers) | 2.50*** | 12.21 | 0.30 | 8.33 | 0.00 |
| Tweet style |  |  |  |  |  |  |
|  | Directed tweet | −2.42*** | 0.09 | 0.22 | −10.79 | 0.00 |
|  | Flagged third party | −0.60*** | 0.55 | 0.15 | −3.97 | 0.00 |
|  | Incl. URL | −0.44*** | 0.64 | 0.12 | −3/61 | 0.00 |
| Theme |  |  |  |  |  |  |
|  | Advisory | 0.70*** | 2.02 | 0.15 | 4.78 | 0.00 |
|  | Closures/openings | −0.53*** | 0.59 | 0.18 | −3.02 | 0.00 |
|  | Evacuation/shelter | −0.50*** | 0.60 | 0.23 | −2.23 | 0.03 |
|  | Hazard impact | 1.17*** | 3.21 | 0.27 | 4.36 | 0.00 |
|  | Thank you | −0.75*** | 0.47 | 0.23 | −3.29 | 0.00 |
|  | Emotion/evaluative | 1.29*** | 3.62 | 0.20 | 6.40 | 0.00 |
| Use of ALL CAPS |  |  |  |  |  |  |
|  | EMPHASIS | 0.42 | 1.52 | 0.23 | 1.82 | 0.07 |
|  | SIGNIFIER | 0.61* | 1.85 | 0.25 | 2.48 | 0.01 |

[a]*Note: Although not shown here, source accounts (excluding "Alert Boston" for a baseline) are included as dummy variables to directly estimate fixed effects. Table 3 shows these effects. Dispersion parameter: 2.07 (Theta = 0.56). Null deviance: 9398 on 697 degrees of freedom. Residual deviance: 7802 on 664 degrees of freedom. AICc: 7876. *p < 0.05, ***p < 0.001*

Table 2 shows the result of the model selection process. Each of the primary content theme codes, stylistic features such as the use of capitalization or sentence type, structural elements such as directed messages and links, and account characteristics (e.g the number of Followers of the account posting the message) are considered as potential predictors in our model. In the table below we show the top model based on the small-sample-size adjusted Akaike Information Criterion (AICc), a model selection index that considers both goodness-of-fit to the observed data and model parsimony (in particular, the risk of overfitting). This criterion is minimized for the best fit model (i.e., lower AICc values indicate models that fit better given the number of parameters they employ). We note that inclusion of additional model terms did not result in qualitatively different results.

For the top model, we show the regression coefficient estimates for each variable in Table 2, along with the standard error estimate, z-score, and p-value. The residual deviance of the model is 7802 on 664 degrees of freedom, a substantial improvement over the null deviance of 9398 on 697 degrees of freedom. Included variables were also cross-checked with repeated applications of the model selection process while holding out a random subset (10%) of the data; the final variables in the reported model were included in the final models in the replicated data sets at least 95% of the time (out of 1000 replications), suggesting that the results of the AICc selection process are fairly robust. Each of the content elements included in the model has been discussed in detail in previous sections. We also include the logged number of incoming Followers of the sending account at the time each original message was posted; the Follower count is an aspect of network structure that we predict to be associated with increasing message exposure, and hence increased retweet rates. As shown in Table 2, incoming ties do indeed have a positive effect on the number of retweets per message (with a doubling in the number of Followers increasing the expected number of retweets by a factor of approximately 5.66). As noted above, we account for unobserved heterogeneity between source accounts that may affect the dependent variable via sender-level fixed effects. The reference organization here is the 'AlertBoston' account. (One account, 'NWSBoston,' showed too little posting activity during the period for its conditional mean to be reliably estimated, as reflected in the large standard error for its fixed effect within Table 3. We retain it here for completeness.) The negative binomial coefficients are interpreted as affecting the expected log count of the number of retweets. For example, a message containing emotion, judgment, or evaluative content increases the expected log count of the number of retweets by 1.29, i.e. increasing the expected retweet rate by 2.62 times compared to a tweet that does not contain emotion, judgment, or evaluative content (all else held constant). To aid in interpretation of these effects (especially in the context of multiple predictors), we find it helpful to consider the predicted retweet count for various predictors interest, reported in percentages. To simplify interpretation, we describe effect sizes here in terms of the number of additional retweets that would be gained or lost relative to the baseline upon adding or removing a message feature. Thus, a feature that multiplies the expected retweet rate by a factor of 1.5 is described as adding 50% more retweets, while a feature that multiplies the rate by a factor of 0.75 is described as resulting in 25% fewer retweets. Effect sizes stated in terms of multipliers may be found in Table 2. We discuss some of these variables presently as they correspond to the primary question: what makes a difference in the behavioral outcome of retweeting; message thematic content, style features, or network exposure (Follower count)?

First, we address the extent to which thematic message content affects the predicted number of retweets in our observed data. These effects are summarized graphically in Fig 1. We find that messages containing hazard impact, advisory, or emotive/evaluative thematic content are the strongest predictors of message retransmission. Messages that contain content on hazard impact are predicted to result in, on average, 221% more (i.e., additional) retweets than those tweets not on that topic (all else held constant). Those that contain advisory information, instructing people on what actions to take, are predicted to result in approximately 102% more retweets. Those that contain emotive/evaluative content, including tweets that provided encouragement or restored confidence, result in 262% more predicted retweets. By contrast, messages containing content on closures or openings, including transportation system information, are predicted to have about 41% fewer retweets, all else held constant. In addition, Tweets that include content about thanks and gratitude are predicted to have 53% fewer retweets than others.

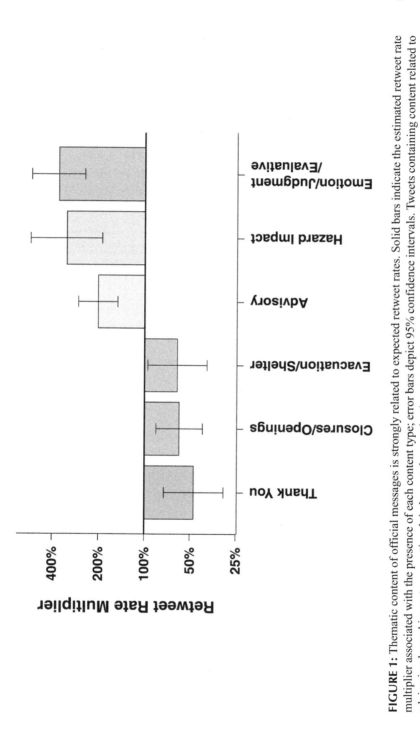

**FIGURE 1:** Thematic content of official messages is strongly related to expected retweet rates. Solid bars indicate the estimated retweet rate multiplier associated with the presence of each content type; error bars depict 95% confidence intervals. Tweets containing content related to advisories, hazard impact, or emotional, judgmental, or evaluative statements were on average retweeted at 2–3.5 times the rate of messages without such content. "Thank you" messages, by contrast, were retweeted at just under 50% the base rate.

**TABLE 3:** GLM negative binomial fixed effects predicting number of per-tweet retweets during the Boston Marathon Bombing.

| | Estimate | exp(β) | Std. error | z value | Pr(>\|z\|) |
|---|---|---|---|---|---|
| (Intercept) | −18.18*** | 0.00 | 2.63 | −6.91 | 0.00 |
| BOSTON_EMS | −0.61 | 0.54 | 0.35 | −1.77 | 0.08 |
| BostonFire | −3.07*** | 0.05 | 0.69 | −4.42 | 0.00 |
| BostonLogan | −0.72 | 0.49 | 0.58 | −1.24 | 0.21 |
| BostonParksDept | 1.17 | 3.24 | 0.68 | 1.74 | 0.08 |
| Boston_Police | −4.64 | 0.01 | 1.04 | −4.45 | 0.00 |
| CherylFiandaca | −0.18 | 0.83 | 0.38 | −0.49 | 0.63 |
| DHSgov | −9.10*** | 0.00 | 1.93 | −4.72 | 0.00 |
| FBIPressOffice | −8.87*** | 0.00 | 1.46 | −6.09 | 0.00 |
| fema | −8.30*** | 0.00 | 1.74 | −4.78 | 0.00 |
| femaregion1 | −2.51* | 0.08 | 1.05 | −2.39 | 0.02 |
| HealthyBoston | −2.43*** | 0.09 | 0.65 | −3.72 | 0.00 |
| MassAGO | −1.49 | 0.23 | 1.39 | −1.07 | 0.29 |
| MassDOT | −2.20 | 0.11 | 0.59 | −3.74 | 0.00 |
| MassEMA | −1.18* | 0.31 | 0.52 | −2.29 | 0.02 |
| MassGovernor | −4.17*** | 0.02 | 0.77 | −5.42 | 0.00 |
| MassGuard | 0.03 | 1.03 | 0.74 | 0.04 | 0.97 |
| MassStatePolice | −2.80*** | 0.06 | 0.67 | −4.18 | 0.00 |
| mayortommenino | −1.77*** | 0.17 | 0.63 | −2.83 | 0.00 |
| mbtaGM | −3.02*** | 0.05 | 0.64 | −4.73 | 0.00 |
| MDARCommish | 2.02 | 7.56 | 1.76 | 1.15 | 0.25 |
| NotifyBoston | −2.21*** | 0.11 | 0.57 | −3.87 | 0.00 |

*Dispersion paramter: 2.07 (Theta = 0.56). Null deviance: 9398 on 697 degrees of freedom. Residual deviance: 7802 on 664 degrees of freedom. AICc: 7876. \*p < 0.05, \*\*\*P < 0.001*

We next consider whether message style or the inclusion of conversational microstructure elements affects the predicted count of retweets in our models. We find that the inclusion of all three microstructure elements, directed messages, a flagged third party, and the inclusion of a link, had a negative effect on predicted retweets. In our model, directed tweets (messages directed to a single individual) have 91% fewer predicted retweets than those that are not directed; tweets with a link, URL, have 36% fewer predicted retweets than those without; tweets that flag a third party are likely to have 45% fewer predicted retweets than others. Tweets using ALL CAPS as a signifier have 85% more predicted retweets as those without; those using ALL CAPS to emphasize a portion of the message, however, were not predicted to have significantly more retweets than those without such emphasis.

Finally, we also address the effect of network structure (specifically, the number of Followers) on predicted retweets. The number of Followers associated with sending accounts at the time of message broadcast is significantly related to the number of retweets (even net of other sender-level characteristics). Messages disseminated from accounts with more Followers have more predicted retweets, all else held constant. For every logged unit increase in the number of Followers, the number of predicted retweets from each tweet increases by 1,121% (Put more intuitively, doubling the Follower count increases the expected number of retweets by a factor of about 5.67.) This is an extremely powerful effect: organizations with many Followers can garner much more attention—and retweets—than those with few Followers. It is also important to bear in mind that this effect implies much more room for change in attention by small and/or local organizations than large, highly visible national ones. This is because proportionately large changes in Follower count are much easier for organizations with few Followers than those with many (an effect also observed by [62] in other hazard events). Low-visibility organizations that increase their Follower counts by a large factor over the course of an unfolding event are predicted to see a dramatic explosion in retweet rates, while established players (e.g. the Federal Emergency Management Agency, FEMA) with many Followers will typically see little change. This has important implications for Public Information Officers or other authorities within low-visibility organizations, who may encounter a sudden shift in attention to their posts that vastly exceeds past experience. We turn to these implications in the section that follows.

## 9.5 DISCUSSION

This research focuses on message retransmission as an indicator of public attention in response to official messages sent during a period of imminent threat. Building on prior work that laid out a research framework for analyzing "terse messages," our analysis centered on the official messages communicated via Twitter in response to a terrorist incident and the five day threat period that continued post bombing event. Our research has shown that terse messages were disseminated and amplified via Twitter in the immediate aftermath and throughout the investigation and manhunt following the Boston Marathon bombing. From these we have identified a set of message features that affect predicted message retransmission among the public, contributing knowledge to the terse communication framework and providing valuable lessons about effective message design for terse communication channels in response to an terrorist event.

The messages generated and disseminated by public officials during the threat period spanned a variety of content areas, most of which were consistent with findings from other recent non-terrorist events [55, 62]. Importantly, two of the three thematic content areas that held salience among the public, as represented by predicted message retransmission, appear to hold consistently regardless of hazard type. Terse messages that include information about hazard impact and public safety advisories hold high importance among the public attending to social media messages under a period of imminent threat. One additional thematic area, messages with "emotive" type of content (content that could also be interpreted as encouraging or resiliency-building) was also found to predict retransmission rates. This differs from prior research in suggesting that a number of factors that may contribute to message salience, including the type of hazardous threat and the geographical scale of the audience attending to messages online in a disaster event.

Terrorist events often occur suddenly and without warning; they expose many to horror, appear to be beyond the control of any one person, threaten life and the lives of family members and friends, and place excessive demands on coping [65]. Research suggests that many of these characteristics are associated with survivors' reporting that they feel some loss of their sense of control, predictability, safety, and trust [66, 67]. Because of the potential for negative psychological effects, public-facing communicators are often advised to disseminate messages that promote social cohesion and resilience [68]. In the aftermath of the bombing and throughout the manhunt, public officials used Twitter as one channel to assure the public that government agencies were responding collaboratively and expeditiously while exhorting the community of Boston that they are "one Boston" and "Boston strong." Many of these restorative messages also demonstrated empathy, acknowledging sadness and respect for the victims of the bombing, while remaining vigilant about the pursuit of the perpetrators. It is possible that the emotive messages disseminated from official accounts served as a type of supportive intervention among the public, something that held high value among observers both near and far.

In contrast, messages that included words of gratitude or thanks were predicted to have lower rates of retweeting. Many of these messages were directed to individual persons or organizations, referencing specific situations in comparison with the emotive messages that were directed to a broader audience and, apparently, designed to uplift the entire community that was simultaneously recovering from the initial attack while remaining vigilant of further terrorist activity.

Messages dedicated to disseminating practical warnings on closures/openings, as well as tips on evacuation/shelter, had lower rates of retweeting. Most of these tweets were posted during the widely publicized manhunt, which was covered in other media forms. Since most people in the region were already locked in their homes, there would be little need to retweet this kind of information. The closures/openings reflect something similar to the evacuation/shelter in place tweets. During the manhunt, everything was shut down, with information distributed over traditional media forms. When the ban was lifted, it was made public through mass media.

It is also clear that over the five day period of imminent threat, the events in Boston attracted attention from a population of online observers drawn from a large geographical area. The scale and location of this audience leads to questions of whether emotive messages (or any other specific thematic area) are passed on by those closest to the threat, or by curious onlookers from across the globe. Future research is needed to investigate the geographical nature of retransmitted messages to address questions about which audiences are retweeting what kinds of content. Such insights will add to knowledge on the networked effects of warning via social media, as one channel for terse communication. It will also contribute knowledge about key nodes that facilitated retransmission of topic-specific message dissemination under conditions of threat.

Consistent with prior research, we also find that message style contributes to predicted message retransmission. Message style is important for increasing clarity and delivering unambiguous, consistent information. These are largely elements that increase understanding and reduce misinterpretation or confusion. In this case, we found that the use of ALL CAPS to signify the subject of the message was a strong predictor of retweets. ALL CAPS within a message may increase the visibility of specific content; the use of signifiers such as UPDATE or MEDIA ADVISORY may reduce ambiguity about the content of the message.

In addition, the inclusion of a weblink remains a barrier to message retransmission. In both cases studied thus far, one a natural hazard event and this, a terrorist event, we have found that a messages that include a URL are less likely to be retweeted among the online public. Twitter users appear to prefer brief messages that are easily transmitted across the network. Messages that include a link, and therefore require additional steps to acquire valuable information, may be perceived as more time consuming (to access and download the link) and resource-intensive (in terms of bandwidth required) in contrast with soundbites delivered in 140 characters or less. Our results indicate that terse messages containing a URL have a negative effect on message retransmission. Terse message retransmission appears to be a selective activity among message receivers. Perhaps those messages that are less complex, requiring few steps to gain the maximum amount of information, are the most relevant to Twitter users during periods of imminent threat. Alternately, messages that include URLs may simply lead users to switch their attention from Twitter to some other site, with the consequence that many never return to retweet the initial message. Future research is needed to investigate users' motivations to pass along a message with or without a URL.

Finally, account features, most specifically Follower numbers, remains a strong predictor of retweet activity, suggesting that increasing connections among Followers is extremely valuable. While message design features remain key components to communicating specific content, message visibility via high Follower numbers is crucial for amplification across a broad spectrum of individuals.

## 9.6 CONCLUSIONS

This study contributes to the growing body of work on allocation of attention and on message retransmission during hazard events. We find that, rather than any single effect dominating the process, retransmission of official Tweets during the Boston bombing response was jointly influenced by message content, style, and sender characteristics. This implies that simplistic models based e.g. only on network properties are unlikely to correctly predict which messages will be amplified in similar settings. On the other hand, relatively simple heuristics incorporating all three feature types may potentially perform well (as suggested by the large effect sizes observed in our fitted model).

Our research suggests that messages that include content on hazard impact and advisory information are likely to be highly salient with an online audience in an unfolding emergency. Furthermore, under conditions of terrorist threat, messages promoting community resiliency appear to have a highly positive effect on public retransmission. Importantly, messages that include a URL will decrease predicted rates of message retransmission. These findings suggest that there is a specific set of messages that can be preliminarily drafted to meet the standards and character limitations of terse messaging formats, prior to an event occurring. As we learn more about appropriate protective actions for terrorist attacks, very specific instructional messages can be created to prevent further casualties and to shore up resiliency to future attacks.

Terse messaging under conditions of imminent threat will require sophisticated planning on behalf of public communicators. As Sellnow and Sellnow state, [69] (p. 124), "the acute phase of a crisis leaves little time for traditional dialogue." It also leaves little time for decision making about how to communicate key messages that will meet the public safety needs of those at risk and address the ongoing issues that arise in response to imminent threat, or time to grow one's Follower numbers to reach more individuals. This research builds upon previous findings, demonstrating consistent patterns of message saliency among the public online while identifying key content areas specific to communicating during a terrorist event; our findings can help to shape message design strategies for crisis communications on terse messaging channels. As more agencies adopt Twitter and other terse messaging platforms such as Short Messaging Services for broadcast alerts in a disaster context, communication strategies must include attention to effective message elements that will appeal to a broad audience capable of amplifying messages through retransmission while simultaneously growing a broad Follower base.

## REFERENCES

1. Duggan M. Cell Phone Activities 2013. Pew Research Center; 2013. Available at: http://pewinternet.org/Reports/2013/Cell-Activities.aspx.
2. Duggan M, Smith A. Social Media Update 2013. Pew Research Center; 2013. Available at: http://pewinternet.org/Reports/2013/Social-Media-Update.aspx.
3. St Denis LA, Palen L, Anderson KM. Mastering Social Media: An Analysis of Jefferson County Communications during the 2013 Colorado Floods. In: Proceedings of the 11th International Conference on Information Systems for Crisis Response and Management (ISCRAM). College Park, Pennsylvania.; 2013.
4. Stephens KK, Ford J. Notification networks of ICTs and Sources in Campus Emergencies. In: In Proceedings of the 11th International Conference on Information Systems for Crisis Response and Management (ISCRAM). College Park, Pennsylvania.; 2014.
5. Sutton J, Spiro ES, Fitzhugh S, Johnson B, Gibson B, Butts CT. Terse Message Amplification in the Boston Bombing Response. In: Hiltz SR, Pfaff MS, Plotnick L, Robinson AC, editors. Proceedings of the 11th International Conference on Information Systems for Crisis Response and Management (ISCRAM). College Park, PA USA; 2014.
6. Danzig ER, Thayer PW, Galanter LR. The Effects of a Threatening Rumor on a Disaster-Stricken Community. Washington D.C.: National Academy of Sciences—National Research Council; 1958. Publication 517.
7. Erickson BH, Nosanchuk T, Mostacci L, Dalrymple CF. The Flow of Crisis Information as a Probe of Work Relations. Canadian Journal of Sociology/Cahiers Canadiens de Sociologie. 1978;p. 71–87. doi: 10.2307/3339794.
8. Scanlon TJ. Post-Disaster Rumor Chains: A Case Study. Mass Emergencies. 1977;2(126):22–27.
9. Sutton J, Spiro E, Butts C, Fitzhugh S, Johnson B, Greczek M. Tweeting the Spill: Online Informal Communications, Social Networks, and Conversational Micro-

structures during the Deepwater Horizon Oilspill. International Journal of Information Systems for Crisis Response and Management. 2013;5(1):58–76. doi: 10.4018/jiscrm.2013010104.

10. Mileti DS, Sorensen JH. Communication of Emergency Public Warnings. Landslides. 1990;1(6). doi: 10.2172/6137387

11. Boyd D, Golder S, Lotan G. Tweet, Tweet, Retweet: Conversational Aspects of Retweeting on Twitter. In: 43rd Hawaii International Conference on System Sciences (HICSS). Kuari, HI, USA: IEEE; 2010. p. 1–10.

12. Naveed N, Gottron T, Kunegis J, Alhadi AC. Bad News Travels Fast: A Content-based Analysis of Interestingness on Twitter. In: Proceedings of the 3rd International Web Science Conference. ACM; 2011. p. 8–15.

13. Asiaee T A, Tepper M, Banerjee A, Sapiro G. If You Are Happy and You Know It... Tweet. In: Proceedings of the 21st ACM International Conference on Information and Knowledge Management. New York, NY, USA: ACM; 2012. p. 1602–1606.

14. Abel F, Gao Q, Houben GJ, Tao K. Analyzing user modeling on Twitter for personalized news recommendations. In: Proceedings of the 19th International Conference on User Modeling, Adaption and Personalization UMAP'11. Berlin, Heidelberg: Springer; 2011. p. 1–12.

15. Xie S, Tang J, Wang T. Resonance Elicits Diffusion: Modeling Subjectivity for Retweeting Behavior Analysis. Cognitive Computation. 2014;p. 1–13. doi: 10.1007/s12559-014-9293-9

16. Blumer H. Collective Behavior. In: Lee AM, editor. Principles of Sociology. New York, NY USA: Barnes & Noble; 1951. p. 166–222.

17. Turner R, Killian L. Collective Behavior. Prentice-Hall; 1987.

18. Sorensen JH. Hazard Warning Systems: Review of 20 Years of Progress. Natural Hazards Review. 2000;1(2):119–125. doi: 10.1061/(ASCE)1527-6988(2000)1:2(119).

19. Lindell MK, Perry RW. Warning Mechanisms in Emergency Response Systems. International Journal of Mass Emergencies and Disasters. 1987;5(2):137–153.

20. Stephens KK, Barrett AK, Mahometa MJ. Organizational Communication in Emergencies: Using Multiple Channels and Sources to Combat Noise and Capture Attention. Human Communication Research. 2013;39(2):230–251. doi: 10.1111/hcre.12002.

21. Mayhorn CB, McLaughlin AC. Warning the World of Extreme Events: a Global Perspective on Risk Communication for Natural and Technological Disaster. Safety Science. 2014;61:43–50. doi: 10.1016/j.ssci.2012.04.014.

22. Mileti DS, Fitzpatrick C. Communication of Public Risk: Its Theory and Its Application. Sociological Practice Review. 1991;2(1):20–28.

23. Drabek TE. Understanding Disaster Warning Responses. The Social Science Journal. 1999;36(3):515–523. doi: 10.1016/S0362-3319(99)00021-X.

24. Mileti DS, Darlington J. Societal Response to Revised Earthquake Probabilities in the San Francisco Bay Area. International Journal of Mass Emergencies and Disasters. 1995;13(2):119–145.

25. Sellnow TL, Sellnow DD, Lane DR, Littlefield RS. The Value of Instructional Communication in Crisis Situations: Restoring Order to Chaos. Risk Analysis. 2012;32(4):633–643. doi: 10.1111/j.1539-6924.2011.01634.x. pmid:21605151

26. Vogt BM, Sorensen JH. Preparing EBS Messages. Oak Ridge, Tennessee.; 1992.

27. Mileti D, Wood M, Bean H, Liu BF, Sutton J, Madden S. Comprehensive Testing of Imminent Threat Public Messages for Mobile Devices. In: FEMA/National Consortium for the Study of Terrorism and Responses to Terrorism; 2012.

28. Banks WC, De Nevers R, Wallerstein MB. Combating Terrorism: Strategies and Approaches. CQ Press; 2007.

29. Sheppard B. Mitigating Terror and Avoidance Behavior Through the Risk Perception Matrix to Augment Resilience. Journal of Homeland Security and Emergency Management. 2011;8(1). Article 26. doi: 10.2202/1547-7355.1840.

30. Griffin-Padgett DR, Allison D. Making a Case for Restorative Rhetoric: Mayor Rudolph Giuliani & Mayor Ray Nagin's Response to Disaster. Communication Monographs. 2010;77(3):376–392. doi: 10.1080/03637751.2010.502536.

31. Kaniasty K, Norris FH. Social Support in the Aftermath of Disasters, Catastrophes, and Acts of Terrorism: Altruistic, Overwhelmed, Uncertain, Antagonistic, and Patriotic Communities. Bioterrorism: Psychological and Public Health Interventions. 2004;p. 200–229.

32. Slovic P. Terrorism as Hazard: A New Species of Trouble. Risk Analysis. 2002;22(3):425–426. doi: 10.1111/0272-4332.00053. pmid:12088221

33. Science N, Council T. Research challenges in combating terrorist use of explosives in the United States. Washington D.C.: Executive Office of the President, National Science and Technology Council, Subcommittee on Domestic Improvised Explosive Devices; 2008.

34. Federation NA. Clinic Violence; 2014. Retrieved from http://www.prochoice.org/about_abortion/violence/index.html.

35. Covello V, Becker S, Palenchar M, Renn O, Sellke P. Effective Risk Communications for the Counter Improvised Explosive Devices Threat: Communication Guidance for Local Leaders Responding to the Threat Posed by IEDs and Terrorism. Burlington, MA: The US Department of Homeland Security, Science and Technology Directorate, Human Factors/Behavioral Sciences Division; 2010.

36. Slovic P. Perception of Risk. Science. 1987;236:280–285. doi: 10.1126/science.3563507. pmid:3563507

37. Cheong M, Lee VC. A Microblogging-Based Approach to Terrorism Informatics: Exploration and Chronicling Civilian Sentiment and Response to Terrorism Events via Twitter. Information Systems Frontiers. 2011;13(1):45–59. doi: 10.1007/s10796-010-9273-x.

38. Oh O, Agrawal M, Rao HR. Information Control and Terrorism: Tracking the Mumbai Terrorist Attack Through Twitter. Information Systems Frontiers. 2011;13(1):33–43. doi: 10.1007/s10796-010-9275-8.

39. Kwon KH, Oh O, Agrawal M, Rao HR. Audience Gatekeeping in the Twitter service: An investigation of tweets about the 2009 Gaza conflict. AIS Transactions on Human-Computer Interaction. 2012;4(4):212–229.

40. Oh O, Agrawal M, Rao HR. Community Intelligence and Social Media Services: a Rumor Theoretic Analysis of Tweets during Social Crises. MIS Quarterly. 2013;37(2):407–426.

41. Bantz CR, Petronio SG, Rarick DL. News Diffusion After the Reagan Shooting. Quarterly Journal of Speech. 1983;69(3):317–327. doi: 10.1080/00335638309383658.

42. Greenberg BS. Diffusion of News of the Kennedy Assassination. Public Opinion Quarterly. 1964;28(2):225–232. doi: 10.1086/267239.

43. Richardson R, Erickson BH, Nosanchuk T. Community Size, Network Structure, and the Flow of Information. Canadian Journal of Sociology/Cahiers canadiens de sociologie. 1979;p. 379–392. doi: 10.2307/3340260

44. Arkes HR, Hackett C, Boehm L. The Generality of the Relation between Familiarity and Judged Validity. Journal of Behavioral Decision Making. 1989;2(2):81–94. doi: 10.1002/bdm.3960020203.

45. Hawkins SA, Hoch SJ, Meyers-Levy J. Low-Involvement Learning: Repetition and Coherence in Familiarity and Belief. Journal of Consumer Psychology. 2001;11(1):1–11. doi: 10.1207/S15327663JCP1101_1.

46. Rosnow RL, Yost JH, Esposito JL. Belief in Rumor and Likelihood of Rumor Transmission. Language & Communication. 1986;6(3):189–194. doi: 10.1016/0271-5309(86)90022-4.

47. Centola D, Macy M. Complex Contagions and the Weakness of Long Ties. American Journal of Sociology. 2007;113(3):702–734. doi: 10.1086/521848

48. Starbird K, Palen L. Pass It On?: Retweeting in Mass Emergency. In: Proceedings on the 7th International Community on Information Systems for Crisis Response and Management (ISCRAM). Seattle, Washington USA; 2010.

49. Suh B, Hong L, Pirolli P, Chi EH. Want to be Retweeted? Large Scale Analytics on Factors Impacting Retweet in Twitter Network. In: Proceedings of the 2010 IEEE Second International Conference on Social Computing (SocialCom). Minneapolis, MN: IEEE; 2010. p. 177–184.

50. Zaman T, Fox EB, Bradlow ET. A Bayesian Approach for Predicting the Popularity of Tweets. Annals of Applied Statistics. 2014;. doi: 10.1214/14-AOAS741.

51. Júnior JPS, Almeida L, Modesto F, Neves T, Weigang L. An Investigation on Repost Activity Prediction for Social Media Events. In: In Web Information Systems Engineering-WISE 2012. Berlin Heidelberg: Springer; 2012. p. 719–725.

52. Peng HK, Zhu J, Piao D, Yan R, Zhang Y. Retweet Modeling Using Conditional Random Fields. In: Data Mining Workshops (ICDMW), 2011 IEEE 11th International Conference on. IEEE; 2011. p. 336–343.

53. Zhu J, Xiong F, Piao D, Liu Y, Zhang Y. Statistically Modeling the Effectiveness of Disaster Information in Social Media. In: Global Humanitarian Technology Conference (GHTC). IEEE; 2011. p. 431–436.

54. Bruns A, Burgess JE. The Use of Twitter Hashtags in the Formation of Ad Hoc Publics. In: In 6th European Consortium for Political Research General Conference. University of Iceland, Reykjavik, Iceland; 2011. p. 25–27.

55. Spiro E, Sutton J, Johnson B, Butts C. Following the Bombing [Online Research Highlight]; 2013. Available at http://heroicproject.org.

56. Lee J, Agrawal M, Rao HR. Message Diffusion Through Social Network Service: The Case of Rumor and Non-Rumor Related Tweets During Boston Bombing 2013. Information Systems Frontiers. 2015;. doi: 10.1007/s10796-015-9568-z.

57. Yin RK. Case Study Research: Design and Methods, 5th Edition. Thousand Oaks, CA: Sage Publications; 2014.

58. Sellnow TL, Ulmer RR, Seeger MW, Littlefield R. Effective Risk Communication: A Message-Centered Approach. New York, NY USA: Springer Science and Business Media, LLC.; 2008.

59. cbsnews com. News C, editor. Boston Marathon: with No Phones, Text and Social Media Help Get Out Updates; 2013. Retrieved from http://www.cbsnews.com/news/boston-marathon-with-no-phones-text-and-social-media-help-get-out-updates/.

60. News NG. Social Media Shapes Boston Bombings Response: Twitter and Facebook Created National Response, May Help Authorities; 2013. Retrieved form http://news.nationalgeographic.com/2013/13/130415-boston-marathon-bombings-terrorism-social-media-twitter-facebook/.

61. cnbc com. News C, editor. Social Media Played Critical Role in Boston Marathon Response; 2013. Retrieved from http://www.cnbc.com/id/100645753.

62. Sutton J, Spiro ES, Johnson B, Fitzhugh S, Gibson B, Butts CT. Warning Tweets: Serial Transmission of Messages During the Warning Phase of a Disaster Event. Information, Communication & Society. 2014;17(6):765–787. doi: 10.1080/1369118X.2013.862561.

63. Cameron AC, Trivedi PK. Regression-Based Tests for Overdispersion in the Poisson Model. Journal of Econometrics. 1990;46(3):347–364. doi: 10.1016/0304-4076(90)90014-K.

64. Team RC. R: A Language and Environment for Statistical Computing. Vienna, Austria.: R Foundation for Statistical Computing; 2014.

65. Sattler DN. Resiliency, Posttraumatic Growth, and Psychological Distress After the Attacks on America. In: In Natural Hazards Research and Applications Information Center, Public Entity Risk Institute, and Institute for Civil Infrastructure Systems, Beyond September 11th: An account of post-disaster research. Special Publication No. 39. Boulder, CO USA: Natural Hazards Research and Applications Information Center, University of Colorado.; 2003. p. 315–332.

66. Baum A. Toxins, Technology, and Natural Disasters. In: Stress and Coping: An Anthology (3d Edt.). New York, NY; 1991. p. 97–139.

67. Updegraff JA, Taylor SE. From Vulnerability to Growth: Positive and Negative Effects of Stressful Life Events. Loss and trauma: General and close relationship perspectives. 2000;25:3–28.

68. Ruggiero A, Vos M. Terrorism Communication: Characteristics and Emerging Perspectives in the Scientific Literature 2002–2011. Journal of Contingencies and Crisis Management. 2013;21(3):153–166. doi: 10.1111/1468-5973.12022.

69. Sellnow T, Sellnow D. The Instructional Dynamic of Risk and Crisis Communication: Distinguishing Instructional Messages from Dialogue. The Review of Communication. 2010;10(2):112–126. doi: 10.1080/15358590903402200.

*There is some supplemental information that is not available in this version of the article. To view this additional information, please use the citation on the first page of this chapter.*

# PART IV

# UNDERSTANDING THE CHALLENGES TO EFFECTIVE COMMUNICATION

# CHAPTER 10

# Leveraging Public Health Nurses for Disaster Risk Communication in Fukushima City: A Qualitative Analysis of Nurses' Written Records of Parenting Counseling and Peer Discussions

AYA GOTO, RIMA E. RUDD, ALDEN Y. LAI, KAZUKI YOSHIDA, YUU SUZUKI, DONALD D. HALSTEAD, HIROMI YOSHIDA-KOMIYA, AND MICHAEL R. REICH

## 10.1 BACKGROUND

Experience from past nuclear accidents shows that poor risk communication increases uncertainty and panic among the public [1], which has
also been observed after the Fukushima nuclear disaster that occurred on
March 11, 2011 following the Great East Japan Earthquake. The central
government of Japan failed to inform the municipal governments of the
occurrence and severity of the incident in a timely manner, leading to cha-
otic migrations among residents, and eventually causing excess mortality

among vulnerable populations such as the institutionalized elderly [2,3]. Mothers of young children are among the most-affected in the Fukushima nuclear incident, as inconsistent information about radiation levels in breast milk posted by two different professional organizations (the Japanese Society of Obstetrics and Gynecology and the Japan Radiological Society) had further created high levels of confusion in terms of maintaining safety for their children [4].

This confusion around risk-related information continued into 2013 [5]. Two years after the disaster, the World Health Organization reported that in the two most affected locations of the Fukushima prefecture, the lifetime risk of thyroid cancer among girls exposed as infants had increased by up to 70%. However, the baseline risk is low and even a large relative increase only represents an absolute increase of as low as 0.005 in terms of life-time cumulated probability of developing the cancer [6]. The concept of risk is difficult to understand, even among health professionals, and its comprehension is even more complicated when a relative risk is high in spite of a low absolute risk [7]. This leads to major challenges for people, especially for families with small children in deciding on how to address the risks they are exposed to. In this case, Fukushima City is located about 70 km from the nuclear power plant, and the estimated additional lifetime risk of thyroid cancer is approximately half of that in the two locations mentioned above [6]. Nevertheless, the population of children under 5 years old in the city had declined by nearly 15% during the two years following the disaster.

Although the importance of empowering local residents via proper risk communication to allow them to make autonomous decisions in post-disaster recovery processes is recognized and recommended in Japan at the national level [2], no guidelines have been developed on how to plan or implement this at the community level. This has led to confusion among public health nurses (PHNs), who in Japan work in a public sector, provide a wide range of community health services, and are often the first point of contact with residents. The Japanese government has recognized the pivotal role they play, as PHNs are tasked with community assessment, health planning, service provision, networking and service evaluation at the municipal level. However, PHNs have voiced concerns about their safety and their insufficient level of knowledge to provide adequate services in the aftermath of the nuclear disaster [8]. In the year before the disaster, researchers from the National Mental Health Center in Japan had already revised the disaster mental health guidelines that were endorsed by mental health professionals. However, an agreement was not reached in defining the roles of PHNs in a disaster setting [9].

To develop proper maternal and child health strategies that can be adopted to support residents facing anxiety about radiation, regular meetings were held in Fukushima City in 2011 between a team of public health researchers from Fukushima Medical University (organized by the first author) and city PHNs in reaction to the disaster [10]. These meetings were expanded in the subsequent year to include three training workshops, aiming to provide PHNs with knowledge on the health effects of radiation exposure and create opportunities for information sharing among peer nurses. In addition, there were collaborations with PHNs to derive additional insight from their routine work. This included the analyses of child health checkup records written by PHNs, with particular attention to information from parenting counseling sessions conducted between PHNs and mothers, as they are one of the most affected population groups in the disaster. Mothers in Japan are required to report their pregnancies to a municipal office, and municipalities are mandated to provide health checkups for 18 and 36 months old children. PHNs are the main service providers of such checkups, as they assess children's physical health while providing mothers with parenting counseling. As this community model of needs assessment and strategy planning by PHNs with technical support from a local university amidst an emergency situation is rare, both in the Fukushima context and scientific literature on disaster recovery, the understanding derived from this model is instrumental in alleviating existing post-disaster challenges in Japan and in future disaster occurrences.

The concerns of disaster-affected residents have to be carefully examined so that communication needs and strategies for improving risk communication in a community setting following a disaster can be appropriately delineated. This study focuses on mothers and PHNs (given their role in the Japanese community health setting) following the nuclear incident in Fukushima. Launching new systematic surveys in a post-disaster situation was not feasible. Concern with not overburdening either community members or professionals, information from existing healthcare services and disaster recovery efforts (i.e., mandated child health checkups and the afore-mentioned community model between the University and city PHNs) were capitalized upon in Fukushima City to undertake this line of academic inquiry.

In this study, a qualitative approach has been adopted to look at existing records of parenting counseling to examine the residents' concerns after the disaster with the nuclear incident, and PHNs' peer discussions to delineate possible strategies that can be taken to alleviate these concerns (see Figure 1). The overarching aim is to elicit insights into steps that can be undertaken for risk communication strategies during disaster recovery efforts. Although health planning processes of PHNs have been investigated by previous research [11], little is known about the challenges they face in a crisis setting. The primary advantage of our study design is the possibility of documenting concerns within the community before and after the disaster, as a significant limitation in disaster studies is often the lack of baseline data [12]. Moreover, using two different sources of qualitative data have allowed us to explore issues from varying perspectives. This research will inform current and future efforts in disaster recovery, especially in terms of facilitating appropriate communication on topics of major concern in situations of disasters and crises.

## 10.2 METHODS

This was a qualitative analysis study utilizing two available data collected at the Fukushima City Health and Welfare Center and applying two analytical methods that are highly practical.

### 10.2.1 DATA COLLECTION

Data was drawn from parenting counseling records and from peer discussions among PHNs.

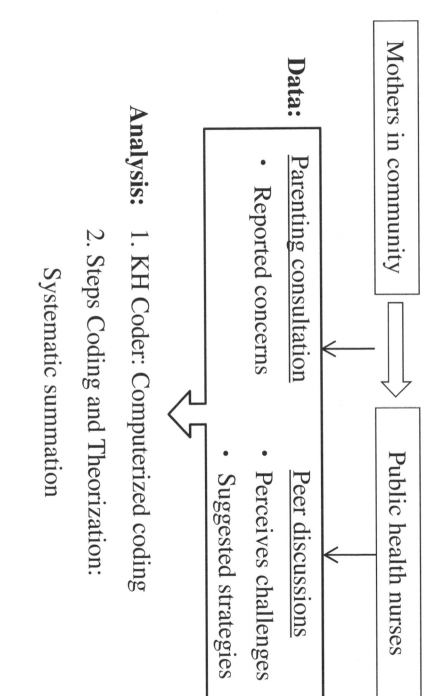

**FIGURE 1:** Framework for data analyses.

## 10.2.1.1 PARENTING COUNSELING RECORDS

Both quantitative and qualitative data on parenting counseling were collected from a series of cross-sectional studies consisting of mothers who attended their children's 18-month health checkups at the Fukushima City Health and Welfare Center between April to May of 2010, 2011 and 2012. In Japan, mothers are required to report their pregnancies to a municipal office, and the municipal offices are in turn mandated to provide child health checkups. The attendance rate of the 18-month health checkups in Fukushima City for these three years was over 90%. It was one month after the disaster (i.e., April 2011) when regular health services including children's health checkups resumed in the city. Based on sample size calculation for analyses of quantitative data (to detect expected associations), the study period was specified to be from April to May. The number of mothers enrolled in the checkups was 156 in 2010, 218 in 2011, and 131 in 2012. For each year, PHNs' records from parenting counseling were scanned from the child health checkup files for the first consecutive 50 attendants and then transcribed into a database. Based on our previous pilot study, it was known that approximately 30% of mothers would voice concerns about effects of radiation in parenting counseling after the disaster [10]. The amount of qualitative data to be derived from each counseling session was also known. Coupling these insights, it was discerned with consensus among the authors involved in data collection that a sample size of 50 records of parenting counseling sessions per year will generate sufficient data for analyses.

## 10.2.1.2 NURSES' PEER DISCUSSIONS

We collected another set of data from PHNs attending three training workshops conducted in July and October 2012, and January 2013. These workshops were co-organized by the Gender-Specific Medicine Center and Department of Public Health of Fukushima Medical University School of Medicine, aiming to provide professional training and information sharing opportunities for PHNs in Fukushima City. The number of attendants was 20, 29 and 25 in each workshop, respectively. There were 39 PHNs working at the Fukushima City Health and Welfare Center at the time of study, and all except those assigned to service provision duties when the workshops took place attended. Each workshop consisted of a one-hour lecture by a university physician, followed by an hour of group discussion. The topics for each lecture were, in order of occurrence, women's health, radiation, and thyroid cancer. In the group discussion, we handed each PHN three note sheets and asked them to write down their reflections after the lectures. All collected note sheets were then systematically transcribed into our database.

## 10.2.2 ANALYSIS PLAN

Both datasets were subjected to identical analysis methods (refer to Figure 1)—transcribed data were first analyzed by text mining using the KH Coder, a software program developed by K. Higuchi at Ritsumeikan University in Japan [13]. This text mining is a computerized process of extracting information from collected information, and has increasingly received attention among researchers as a way to improve the consistency of qualitative analysis, especially during the coding stage [14]. The KH coder has recently been used to analyze medical articles in academic journals and newspapers in Japanese [15]. The program segments sentences, lists frequently used words, and develops a hierarchical analysis diagram showing relationships among words with their corresponding frequencies.

We then focused on the top 20% of the words that were most frequently listed, and reviewed sentences that included these words to examine the full context in which the words were used. By referring to a diagram generated by the KH coder, we then categorized the words into major topics, eliminating common words that appeared in sentences across the different topics after categorization (e.g., "mother" and "think" in the parenting counseling data). We then calculated the proportion of cases that included each topic. A "case" refers to a mother in the parenting counseling data, or a note sheet from the PHNs' workshop data. Since the KH Coder calculates word frequencies without analyzing the full context, some misclassifications were observed and manually eliminated when calculating this proportion of cases in each topic. This analysis procedure was repeated twice by the first author with a one-month interval in between to ensure consistency.

Second, cases related to specific topics of our interest (such as "disaster-related issues" among the parenting counseling data, and "action plans" among the workshop data) were analyzed by Steps Coding and Theorization (SCAT) [16]. SCAT was developed as an accessible qualitative data analysis method by T. Otani from Nagoya University in Japan. This method is appropriate for small-scale qualitative studies with a limited amount of qualitative data including answers to open-ended questions in surveys, and has been used by researchers in the fields of medical education and palliative care [17]. The analysis consists of two steps – first decontextualization to generate themes from sentences, followed by theorization to construct theories summarizing collected information. In the first decontextualization process, we extracted key words from original sentences, rephrased them by using professional terms, created themes, and then labeled each case. In the second recontexualization process, we developed a storyline from the emerging themes. The first and third authors independently performed the SCAT analysis of data extracted from each workshop, and the first author then compared and combined the results, with consensus achieved with the third author subsequently.

Compared with the classic grounded theory for qualitative analysis, which often requires a large amount of text data, the KH coder enhances consistency and reproducibility especially in data coding [14], and SCAT further enables systematic analysis of a small amount of text data [16]. We thus applied KH coder first to extract categories and then SCAT to deepen our interpretation of the categories that are most pertinent to our study's objectives. One of this study's aims is to test the usefulness of these methods in a community health practice setting.

## 10.2.3 ETHICAL CONSIDERATIONS

This study was conducted in collaboration with the Fukushima City Health and Welfare Center. All data were copied anonymously without any identifiers of families and PHNs, and conducted in accordance with Ethical Guidelines for Epidemiological Research issued by the Japanese Ministry of Education, Culture, Sports, Science and Technology, and the Japanese Ministry of Health, Labour and Welfare. Data collection on parenting counseling was submitted to the ethical review boards at the Fukushima Medical University and the city office, and reviews were waived. The data analysis plan of the PHNs' group discussions was submitted to an IRB Review Specialist at the Harvard School of Public Health, but a review was also waived as this was categorized as a quality improvement study.

## 10.3 RESULTS

### 10.3.1 PARENTING COUNSELING

Figure 2 shows trends found in parenting counseling topics categorized using the KH Coder. The proportions of "child lifestyle" and "communication with a child" decreased while those of "child medical issues", "disaster-related issues," "parental concerns," and "support network" increased. The words included in each topic are listed in Table 1.

The cases that included words in the "disaster-related issues" topic— the records of 13 mothers in 2011 and 9 mothers in 2012—were analyzed by SCAT. In 2011, these mothers experienced relocation and changes in daily family routines. Mothers were worried about children's radiation exposure from playing outside, and needed more information about radiation. These changes in daily life and anxiety toward radiation had negative psychological impacts. In 2012, mothers continued to relocate and voiced concerns about letting their children play outside. They started to ask questions about technical issues, including radiation measurement procedures, and raised concerns about differences in risk perception toward radiation with their spouses. PHNs recorded:

*"[I was asked] What does it mean to measure a parent's exposure level? Another city introduced a machine that a child can get into [and be measured directly]."*

*"The mother is worried about radiation and cannot let [child] play outside. [She worries about] her child licking the sand from her hands after falling down. The father says it is alright to play outside for a short time."*

## 10.3.2 NURSES' PEER DISCUSSIONS

In the KH Coder analysis of the workshop data, we created two topics, "action plans" and "learned knowledge." Since most of the notes included words categorized as "learned knowledge," Figure 3 focuses on the proportion of notes including words categorized as "action plans." We found that 18% of notes in the first workshop mentioned action plans, but this figure increased to 47% in the second workshop, and was 43% in the third workshop. Among words related to "action plans" as listed in Table 2, words (used as a noun or verb) that appeared across all three workshops were "inform" and "knowledge."

The cases that included words in the "action plans" topic—the records of 17, 36, and 35 note sheets in three workshops, respectively—were analyzed by SCAT. PHNs identified their role as an information channel, and emphasized the importance of supporting residents to make autonomous decisions based on credible evidence. More specifically, they recommended measuring radiation levels as a useful tool for residents to have a clear understanding of their own environment. PHNs wrote:

*"It is important for mothers to think by themselves based on accurate information. Public health nurses are their close advisors."*

*"By measuring and calculating your own exposure level, anxiety and worries can be reduced."*

*"[Use] radiation dosimeters. Calculate correctly."*

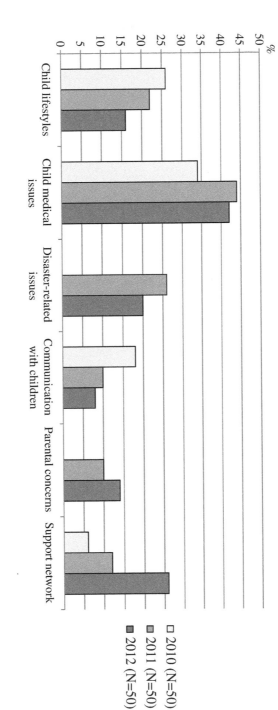

**FIGURE 2:** Proportions of major topics: public health nurses' records of parenting counseling. Number of women (denominator) is 50 in each year.

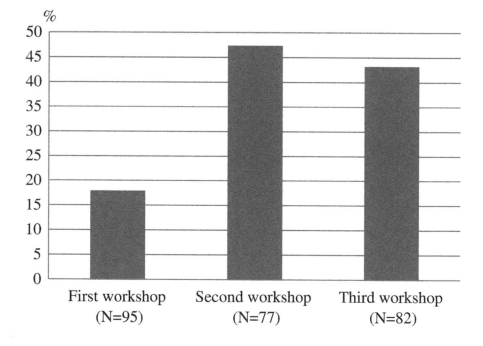

**FIGURE 3:** Proportions of discussion notes including "action plans" words: public health nurses' group discussions in workshops. Denominator is the number of discussion notes in each workshop.

PHNs suggested the need to relay messages in a clearer manner and to have better community-based counseling service that addresses multiple but related concerns regarding parenting in the context of a disaster like Fukushima:

*"Residents demand that we talk to them as the same disaster-affected residents. We must tell them what we think about what we have learned, not just what the government says."*

*"It is important for public health nurses to learn and share knowledge."*

*"[Mothers] need a place where they can ask every little question about their daily lives."*

In particular, there were strong concerns among PHNs that the purpose and results of thyroid cancer screening were difficult to understand, and that clearer, standardized explanations were needed. They further recognized that the matter was not only about improving access to information, but about providing a more careful follow-up system after the screening, taking its psychological impact into account:

*"I understood how to read the screening results, but I am not confident in explaining them to residents."*

*"[Once a thyroid cancer screening is introduced,] we will find cancer cases. It will look like the cancer is increasing. It becomes a problem of how to respond to people's anxiety."*

## 10.4 DISCUSSION

Given the uncertainty caused by inconsistent scientific information around radiation, the analyses of PHNs' interactions with mothers and with their own peers have yielded insight into the challenges and corresponding strategies that PHNs face and can adopt for better communication of risks. This study provides community-based insights on the needs related to health communication and on the ways to improve risk communication following the Fukushima nuclear accident through the perspectives of PHNs, who live and work in, and interact regularly with the local community. This is the first study to delineate such information through a combination of data from PHNs and their interactions with mothers, and is thought to be instrumental to our general knowledge in disaster recovery interventions despite the context to be specific to the Fukushima Nuclear incident.

**TABLE 1:** Words included in major topics: Public health nurses' records of parenting counseling

| Major topics | Words in alphabetical order |
| --- | --- |
| Child lifestyles | Banana, breast milk, crying at night, drink, eat, feed, irregular, meal, milk (two words), morning, nap, night, sleep (two words), vegetable |
| Child medical issues | Apply, bleed, brushing, curved, dry, ear, ear infection, eyes, feet, front teeth, height, immunization, legs, live (vaccine), medicine, nails, occlusion of teeth, pediatrics, prescription, prevention, polio, receive, run, skin, teeth, tooth decay, treat, vaccination, weight, words |
| Disaster-related issues | Daily life, earthquake, evacuation, Fukushima, nuclear, outside, play, radiation |
| Communication with children | Children, cry, dependent, dislike, elder child, hold |
| Parental concerns | Job, mind, overwhelmed, upset |
| Parenting network | Advice, child care, father, grandmother, nursery, parental home |

## 10.4.1 MOTHERS' CONCERNS

Many disaster studies lack baseline data [12]; in contrast, our review of records from routine services of parenting counseling provides this critical baseline, and enabled us to document the changing trends of community concerns before and after the disaster. Many of the post disaster concerns from Fukushima are similar to those documented in other disaster settings [18,19]. The PHNs' records of mothers' reactions after the disaster were similar to those observed after the Chernobyl accident; parental anxiety at a subclinical level is expected according to previous research [18], and the mothers in our study have also raised similar concerns in the year of the Fukushima incident and in the following year. Another observation from the Chernobyl incident was the tendency for mothers to report somatic symptoms of their children despite no abnormalities in medical assessments [19], and our study has likewise observed an increase in consultations on children's medical issues during health checkups in 2011.

**TABLE 2:** Words included in major topics: Public health nurses' group discussions in workshops

| Workshops (Lecture topics) | Words categorized as "action plans" in alphabetical order |
| --- | --- |
| First workshop (Women's health) | Educate, important, inform, knowledge, necessary, promote |
| Second workshop (Radiation) | Calculate, close, confirm, correct, equip, execute, important, inform, information, knowledge, learn, mothers, necessary, play, prevention, public health nurses, understand |
| Third workshop (Thyroid cancer) | Adults, anxiety, children, correct, difficult, equip, explain, future, health, important, inform, information, issue, knowledge, manage, necessary, purpose, radiation, results, risk, safe, situation, think, worry |

Concerns about their children's health further escalated, as evident from statements by mothers attending consultations in 2012 to question PHNs about technical information related to radiation and thyroid screening. Additional knowledge on radiation and its related health risks in PHNs is clearly warranted. Another finding from our study was how these mothers were also voicing conflicts of risk perceptions with their spouses. This resonates with findings from a recent study looking into risk communication after the Fukushima incident, which has shown a distinct higher proportion of mothers in Fukushima to have stronger levels of anxiety as opposed to fathers [20]. It is well known that risk perception differs between sexes, and perceived risk is generally higher among women than men [21]. In lieu of our findings, the strengthening of parenting support programs organized by the city currently is further recommended to address mothers' persistent concerns on risk, and potential conflicts arising from differing risk perceptions within the family. This follows the Inter-

Agency Standing Committee guidelines recommending strengthening of existing resources and capacities as one of core principles in mental health support in a disaster setting [22].

## 10.4.2 EMPOWERING MOTHERS

PHNs, when considering mothers' distinctive concerns, perceived themselves as information channels in the community and recognized the importance of empowering residents with advice so as to allow them to make well-informed decisions. The nurses proposed the provision and use of radiation dosimeters as an empowerment tool, and an expansion of the current scope of consultations to provide residents more opportunities to ask questions pertaining to daily life. The radiation dosimeters became widely sold commercially after the disaster, at a cost of about 30 USD. The availability and usage of radiation dosimeters is an important component for the regain of a sense of control of one's surroundings, as demonstrated by an initiative supported by the European Commission ten years after the Chernobyl accident to successfully improve mothers' sense of control by recommending the measuring of radiation levels in their living environments, and discussing protective measures that can be taken at home [23,24]. PHNs in Fukushima can therefore learn from these experiences and adopt similar activities in their local communities much earlier than the case of Chernobyl so as to better empower mothers and facilitate communication in radiation-related risks. Indeed, in line with recommendations by these post-Chernobyl studies [23,24], Fukushima City has already initiated experience-based learning sessions in which participating residents learn to measure and interpret their own radiation exposure level.

## 10.4.3 IMPROVING NURSES' HEALTH LITERACY SKILLS

The PHNs also recognized their responsibilities and the need to improve their communication skills to better transfer scientific knowledge and information to the community. Previous research in health literacy has indicated that any information provided through parenting support and other city activities should be comprehensible to mothers and their family members [25]. Such access to information would allow residents to make informed lifestyle decisions. This might also relieve unnecessary distress in mothers and within the family. In times of crisis, high quality communication between lay people and healthcare workers is critical both in the relaying of clear and credible information and the engagement of intended audiences [26]. The National Action Plan to Improve Health Literacy has therefore been initiated in the US in 2010, with the goal of developing and disseminating health information that is accurate, accessible, and actionable [27]. Henceforth, increasing awareness of health literacy, a concept only introduced in Japan in the late 1990s [28], is an important step to further bolster quality communication between PHNs and community residents. Although no studies have been published on this front, Fukushima City and Fukushima Medical University are currently organizing and evaluating health literacy workshops for the PHNs.

## 10.4.4 EXPANDING CITY HEALTH SERVICES

Going beyond the individual capacity-building of residents and PHNs, the nurses have also, in their peer discussions, suggested an organizational upgrading of the provision of city health services to improve their communication with the community. Specific suggestions included expanding the frequency of community-based counseling services, and standardizing the provision of information (highlighting the need for systematic information especially with regards to thyroid cancer screening). The importance of improving communication between the community and the local government office, in which PHNs work, is supported by a previous study [29]. In their examination of determinants of people's trust toward government and non-government organizations, they found that an important factor to facilitate government-community relations was the degree of "openness" of an organization attained via the bidirectional communication. In general, a challenge among PHNs working in Japan's hierarchical local government system is the difficulty of initiating new activities that have not been endorsed by the upper levels of the government [30]. The disaster has however, increased the PHN's decision-making power in the local government system, thus new programs such as a mental health support program for mothers at the 18-month child health checkups, regular lectures on radiation-related topics for residents, and epidemiological assessments of child growth have been implemented since the Fukushima nuclear incident [10].

Although human resource and budget constraints exist, and the differing interests among stakeholders (such as upper boards of prefectural government, municipal office and universities) will need to be taken into account, continuous efforts to improve services that can enhance communication with the residents are required to address the social distrust caused in part by how the Japanese government has communicated with people immediately after the disaster [31].

## 10.4.5 STUDY LIMITATIONS AND STRENGTHS

A major limitation of the present study was the limited amount of qualitative data extracted from the child health checkup files and workshop discussion notes. Each case contained only a few sentences that were often fragments. Another limitation was how samples were only collected within a specific time period of each year (between April and May). However, the qualitative analysis of both parenting counseling records and discussion notes from PHNs' training workshops, although limited in amount and time-frame, can provide comprehensive information for PHNs and policy makers to understand community needs and to formulate appropriate strategies. Of note, a comparison between the present study and a previous study adopting a similar sampling strategy throughout a year in the sample city has indicated no differences in mothers and children's basic characteristics [32].

On the other hand, a methodological strength of this paper was that it has demonstrated the usefulness of the combination of text mining and SCAT for the analysis of text data that are readily available and accessible via currently available healthcare services.

## 10.5 CONCLUSION

The analyses of existing parenting counseling records and PHNs' peer discussions have provided a deeper understanding of the challenges pertaining to risk communication that exist in the community and the possible strategies that PHNs can act on following a disaster in Japan. These challenges include the need for mothers to be considerably informed on radiation risks as they can have impact on their relocation decisions, child safety concerns, and interpersonal conflicts within the family due to differing risk perceptions. In addition, this study has shown how PHNs perceive themselves as information channels within the community; yet they acknowledge their lack of capacity to provide information and to communicate in a way that facilitates an optimal delivery of healthcare services in a disaster setting. Our study has therefore suggested a three-tiered strategy at the resident, healthcare provider and health system levels to alleviate these challenges of risk communication: empowerment of local residents to assume more active roles in the understanding of their environment and subsequently making informed decisions about preventive measures against radiation exposure, capacity-building of PHNs in health literacy skills so as to allow them to be sources of reliable communication channels, and the expansion of health services to enhance communications between PHNs and communities. As our findings have provided a premise for the initiation of capacity-building specific to health literacy in PHNs, the Fukushima Medical University has in collaboration with some local government offices started to conduct health literacy training sessions for the PHNs. It is anticipated that the recommendations from this research will inform future efforts in disaster recovery and the strengthening of current health and social care systems during times of crisis.

## REFERENCES

1.  Perko T: Importance of risk communication during and after a nuclear accident.
2.  Integr Environ Assess Manag 2011, 7:388-392. The National Diet of Japan: The Fukushima Nuclear Accident Independent Investigation Commission. The official

report of the Fukushima Nuclear Accident Independent Investigation Commission. Executive summary. Tokyo: The National Diet of Japan; 2012.

3. Yasumura S, Goto A, Yamazaki S, Reich MR: Excess mortality among relocated institutionalized elderly after the Fukushima nuclear disaster. Public Health 2013, 127:186-188.

4. Takahashi S, Akabayashi A: Earthquake in Japan. Lancet 2011, 377:1653-1654.

5. McCurry J: Fukushima residents still struggling 2 years after disaster. Lancet 2013, 381(9869):791-792.

6. World Health Organization: Health risk assessment from the nuclear accident after the 2011 Great East Japan earthquake and tsunami, based on a preliminary dose estimation. Geneva: World Health Organization; 2013.

7. Apter AJ, Paasche-Orlow MK, Remillard JT, Bennett IM, Ben-Joseph EP, Batista RM, Hyde J, Rudd RE: Numeracy and communication with patients: they are counting on us. J Gen Intern Med 2008, 23:2117-2124.

8. Kitamiya C: Activities and awareness of public health nurses working at local government facilities and health centers regarding potential nuclear accidents. Japanese Journal of Public Health 2011, 58:372-381. (In Japanese)

9. Suzuki Y, Fukasawa M, Nakajima S, Narisawa T, Kim Y: Development of disaster mental health guidelines through the Delphi process in Japan. Int J Ment Health Syst 2012, 6:7.

10. Goto A: Academic institute: Parenting support strategies in areas surrounding evacuation zones. In Public Health in Nuclear Disaster. Edited by Yasumura S. Tokyo: Nanzando; 2014:333-338. In Japanese

11. Yoshioka K, Asahara K, Murashima S: Processes and strategies for developing public health nurse directed community health projects in municipalities of Japan: Focusing on setting agendas and making project alternatives. Japanese Journal of Public Health 2004, 51:257-271. (In Japanese)

12. Bromet EJ, Havenaar JM: Mental health consequences of disasters. In Psychiatry in Society. Edited by Sartorius N, Gaebel W, Lepez-Ibor JJ, Maj M. West Sussex: John Wiley & Sons; 2002:241-261.

13. Higuchi K: Analysis of free comments in a questionnaire survey: Quantitative analysis by KH Coder. Shakai to Chosa 2012, 8:92-96. (In Japanese)

14. Chong Ho Y, Jannasch-Pennell A, Samuel DiGangi S: Compatibility between text mining and qualitative research in the perspectives of grounded theory, content analysis, and reliability. Qual Rep 2011, 16:730-744.

15. Hachiken H, Mastuoka A, Murai A, Kinoshita S, Takada M: Quantitative analyses by text mining of journal articles on medical pharmacy. Japanese Journal of Drug Informatics 2012, 13:152-159. (In Japanese)

16. Otani T: "SCAT" a qualitative data analysis method by four-step coding: Easy startable and small scale data-applicable process of theorization. Bulletin of the Graduate School of Education and Human Development (Educational Sciences) 2007–2008, 54:27-44. (In Japanese)

17. Maeno T, Takayashiki A, Anme T, Tohno E, Hara A: Japanese students' perception of their learning from an interprofessional education program: a qualitative study. Int J Med Educ 2013, 4:9-17.

18. Bromet EJ: Mental health consequences of the Chernobyl disaster. J Radiol Prot 2012, 32:N71-N75.

19. Bromet EJ, Goldgaber D, Carlson G, Panina N, Golovakha E, Gluzman SF, Gilbert T, Gluzman D, Lyubsky S, Schwartz JE: Children's well-being 11 years after the Chernobyl catastrophe. Arch Gen Psychiatry 2000, 57:563-571.

20. Tateno S, Yokoyama HM: Public anxiety, trust, and the role of mediators in communicating risk of exposure to low dose radiation after the Fukushima Daiichi Nuclear Plant explosion. JCOM 2013, 12:A03.

21. Gustafson PE: Gender differences in risk perception: theoretical and methodological perspectives. Risk Anal 1998, 18:805-811.

22. Inter-Agency Standing Committee: ISAC Guidelines on mental health and psychosocial support in emergency settings. Available at: http://www.who.int/mental_health/emergencies/guidelines_iasc_mental_health_psychosocial_june_2007.pdf . Accessed February 14, 2014

23. Dubreuil GH, Lochard J, Girard P, Guyonnet JF, Le Cardinal G, Lepicard S, Livolsi P, Monroy M, Ollagnon H, Pena-Vega A, Pupin V, Rigby J, Rolevitch I, Schneider T: Chernobyl post-accident management: the ETHOS project. Health Phys 1999, 77:361-372.

24. Lochard J: Rehabilitation of living conditions in territories contaminated by the Chernobyl accident: the ETHOS project. Health Phys 2007, 93:522-526.

25. Sanders LM, Shaw JS, Guez G, Baur C, Rudd R: Health literacy and child health promotion: implications for research, clinical care, and public policy. Pediatrics 2009, 124(Suppl 3):S306-314.

26. Rudd RE, Comings JP, Hyde J: Leave no one behind: Improving health and risk communication through attention to literacy. J Health Commun 2003, 8(Suppl 1):104-115.

27. U.S. Department of Health and Human Services, Office of Disease Prevention and Health Promotion: National Action Plan to Improve Health Literacy. Available at: http://www.health.gov/communication/hlactionplan/ . Accessed October 5, 2012

28. Tokuda Y, Doba N, Butler JP, Paasche-Orlow MK: Health literacy and physical and psychological wellbeing in Japanese adults. Patient Educ Couns 2009, 75:411-417.

29. Maeda Y, Miyahara M: Determinants of trust in industry, government, and citizen's groups in Japan. Risk Anal 2003, 23:303-310.

30. Japanese Nursing Association: Review of health activities in municipalities. Available at: http://www.nurse.or.jp/home/publication/pdf/senkuteki/23-houkoku shichoson.pdf . Accessed Ma 6, 2013. (In Japanese)

31. Reich MR: A public health perspective on reconstructing post-disaster Tohoku: one year later. JMAJ 2012, 55:384-387.

32. Kawai T, Goto A, Watanabe E, Nagasawa M, Yasumura S: Lower respiratory tract infections and gastrointestinal infections among mature babies in Japan. Pediatr Int 2011, 53:431-445.

# CHAPTER 11

# Communication, Perception, and Behavior During a Natural Disaster Involving a "Do Not Drink" and a Subsequent "Boil Water" Notice: A Postal Questionnaire Study

GABRIELLA RUNDBLAD, OLIVIA KNAPTON, AND PAUL R. HUNTER

## 11.1 BACKGROUND

During times of major public health emergencies, good communication between the emergency response agencies and the public in affected areas is vital [1]. Effective communication is particularly important when it is essential that people take steps to protect themselves from injury or disease. When looking at why people did not evacuate the city prior to the arrival of Hurricane Katrina, Brodie and colleagues [2] found that about one-third did not get the message and a further one-third heard the message but did not understand how to evacuate. They also reported that people who did not evacuate were predominantly from the poorest and most marginalised sections of society. Further, following terrorist attacks, good communication with the public is essential not only to reduce acute morbidity and mortality but also in mediating the social and psychological impact of terrorist attacks [3]. Indeed, it has been argued that poor communication may itself pose a risk to health by heightening anxiety and the development of somatoform disorders [4].

The experience of Hurricane Katrina reported by Brodie and colleagues [2] illustrates the main issues associated with risk communication during natural disasters. Firstly, getting the message to all the people including the poor and marginalised sections of society, and secondly, ensuring that the message is understood and leads to appropriate responses. Typically, risk communication is considered to contain four components: message, source, transmitter and receiver [e.g. [5]]. Original theories of risk communication drew upon the concept of the individual as a "rational actor" who receives information from a knowledgeable authority source and then uses this information to manage and minimize their risk exposure [6]. Arguably, non-compliance is not necessarily driven by a lack of knowledge or an "information gap" between official sources and the public. Rather it is a combination of individual and other societal factors that leads an individual to make active choices concerning their behaviour. These factors range from demographics, knowledge and previous experience of similar situations, and general health beliefs and attitudes towards risks and preventative actions, to the particular transmitter(s) used to convey the message to the public. Previous transmitter studies have highlighted the impact of media [7-9] and interpersonal contacts with health professionals [10]. Compliance studies have, however, found that whether consumers received the advice from a leaflet or some type of mass media did not impact compliance [11,12]. In September 2005, a category 3 hurricane, Hurricane Rita, made landfall on the Texas/Louisiana border, US. The chaos brought about by Hurricane Rita was such that word of mouth proved more useful than media channels [13].

On the 19th-20th July 2007, the equivalent of two months of rain (125 mm) fell over Gloucestershire (total population 528,370) and neighbouring areas in the United Kingdom (UK), causing Britain's "largest peacetime emergency since World War II" [[14]:vii]. There was widespread flash flooding and fluvial flooding of the River Severn and the River Avon. Approximately two days later, Mythe water treatment works (which is one of the main water works in Gloucestershire and is managed by Severn Trent Water (STW)) was flooded and Castle Mead electricity substation had to be shut down, leaving 140,000 homes (ca. 340,000–350,000 consumers) without mains water [15] and 48,000 homes without electricity [16]. While electricity was returned within 48 hours, consumers were left without drinking water for up to 17 days. No UK water company has ever experienced loss of supply on such a large scale before [15]. Before mains water was restored to normal, alternative supplies were provided. A total of 40 million bottles of water were distributed and an average of 3 million litres of water per day provided by mobile water tanks (bowsers). The provision of bowser and bottled water generally overlapped. Water restoration began on 27th July, after confirmed delivery to all affected consumers of a non-standard "Do Not Drink" notice devised by the regional health authority (Gloucestershire Primary Care Trust). The "Do Not Drink" notice was replaced by a water industry standard precautionary "Boil Water" notice seven days later, at which point the bowsers were withdrawn. On 7th August, the water company (STW) declared the tap water safe to drink. The day before, the emergency phase of the Gloucestershire floods had been formally declared over and recovery begun [17].

When there is a risk that public health is threatened through contaminated drinking water, one of three standard notices may be issued: "Boil Water" (= water safe to ingest after it has been boiled), "Do Not Drink" (= water should not be ingested) and "Do Not Use" (= water should not be used). While "Boil Water" notices are relatively common, "Do Not Drink" notices are rarely issued, and the combination of two notices is exceptionally rare [18,19]. "Do Not Drink" notices are generally reserved to incidents where short-term exposure to contaminants is likely to have adverse health effects [20]; for the Mythe incident, the risk turned out to be minimal [15]. The issuing of a "Do Not Drink" and a subsequent "Boil Water" notice during the same natural disaster afforded us a unique opportunity to investigate compliance with public health advice and to investigate factors associated with risky and cautious behaviour to this advice (including the general advice always to boil bowser water before consumption).

## 11.2 METHOD

### 11.2.1 STUDY DESIGN AND SAMPLE SELECTION

A postal questionnaire study of 1,000 households supplied with mains water from Mythe waterworks and affected by loss of water and two subsequent water notices during summer 2007 was carried out in January-February 2009 (18 months after the incident). Assuming a response rate of 40%, 1000 questionnaires would yield a sample size of 400 which would give a standard error of less than 2.5%. Postcodes of affected households were provided by the Drinking Water Inspectorate. Full addresses were obtained using the Royal Mail Postcode Address File and 1,000 addresses were selected using a random number generator. Addresses were scrutinised and any businesses and schools were replaced with a further randomised selection of residential addresses.

Ethical approval was received from the King's College London Social Sciences, Humanities and Law Research Ethics Sub Committee.

### 11.2.2 QUESTIONNAIRE DESIGN

A questionnaire containing nine sections was constructed. A short section on demographics was followed by four sections that followed the chronological order of the incident: the initial period without mains water ("Water Loss"), the "Do Not Drink" notice, the "Boil Water" notice, and the time immediately after the water had been declared safe to drink ("Water Safe"). The sections for the four "incident stages' contained questions about the respondents' uses of water straight from the tap (if any), uses of boiled water (if any), types of cold water used for drinking, the advice that they remembered receiving and the information sources from which they got their advice. Following these "incident stages" sections, the questionnaire ended with several shorter sections concerning the use of temporary water supplies (in particular bowser water), use of information sources, information source preferences and previous experience and knowledge of water incidents. Mainly closed questions were employed. Open-ended questions were predominantly used towards the end of the questionnaire.

The questionnaire was piloted twice on undergraduate students from King's College London (N = 50), and minor revisions were made in order to improve clarity. The final questionnaire was sent out together with a detailed project description and a stamped, addressed return envelope. Non-responders were sent a reminder four weeks later.

## 11.3.3  CODING

Where respondents ticked rather than ranked options on the four ranking questions, one tick alone was coded as rank one. If a respondent ranked several options and then ticked one further option, the ticked option was coded as their lowest rank. If only ticks were used, these were given the same rank (e.g., three ticks were ranked as 2). Between 46 and 63 of the participants used ticks. For "tick only one" questions, multiple ticks were typically entered as inconclusive. However, for questions such as those asking what water notice participants remembered being in place during one of the incident stages, we coded multiple ticks as "believed more than one advice was in place" in order to allow analysis of uncertainty. For questions where respondents selected "other" and then qualitatively specified their answer, these were re-coded into the original categories where possible. Similarly for information sources, website usage was re-coded so that only sources that occur solely on the internet are in the category "websites", while e.g., "local radio" included listening, phoning and visiting the website of this source. Replies from between two and ten participants under the categories "other" and/or "websites" were re-coded into original categories. Open-ended questions were also quantified where possible; for example, occupations were translated into the binary categories "yes, currently employed" and "no, not currently employed". Across all questions, non-responses were coded as missing data and inconclusive replies were generally excluded from further analysis.

**TABLE 1:** Demographic comparison of study respondents with the 2001 census for Gloucestershire.

| | n | Study population % (LCI - UCI) | Census population % |
|---|---|---|---|
| Gender | | | |
| male | 62 | 40.0 (32.2 - 48.2) | 48.8* |
| female | 93 | 60.0 (51.8 - 67.8) | 51.2* |
| Age | | | |
| 29/30 or younger[a] | 10 | 6.3 (3.1 - 11.3) | 16.7* |
| 30/31 to 59/60[b] | 83 | 52.5 (44.4 - 60.5) | 42.4* |
| 60/61 or older[c] | 65 | 41.1 (33.4 - 49.2) | 22.4* |
| Ethnicity | | | |
| white UK | 150 | 96.8 (92.6 - 98.9) | 95.6 |
| white non-UK | 3 | 1.9 (0.4 - 5.6) | 1.6 |
| non-white | 2 | 1.3 (0.2 - 4.6) | 2.8 |
| Home ownership | | | |
| sole/joint owner | 138 | 87.3 (81.1 - 92.1) | 74.3* |
| renting from council | 13 | 8.2 (4.5 - 13.7) | 8.5 |
| renting privately | 7 | 4.4 (1.8 - 8.9) | 8.3 |
| Occupation[d] | | | |
| managers & senior officials | 14 | 15.1 (8.5 - 24.0) | 15.3 |
| professional | 24 | 25.8 (17.3 - 35.9) | 10.9* |
| associate prof. & technical | 12 | 12.9 (6.8 - 21.5) | 13.8 |
| admin & secretarial | 21 | 22.6 (14.6 - 32.4) | 13.6* |
| skilled trade | 8 | 8.6 (3.8 - 16.2) | 12.4 |
| personal service | 4 | 4.3 (1.2 - 10.6) | 6.5 |
| sales & customer service | 4 | 4.3 (1.2 - 10.6) | 7.1 |
| process & machine operatives | 4 | 4.3 (1.2 - 10.6) | 8.9 |
| elementary | 2 | 2.2 (0.3 - 7.6) | 11.5* |

[a] *Comprises our categories 20 or younger and 21-30 with the census categories 0-4, 5-9, 10-14, 15-19, 20-24 and 25-29.*
[b] *Comprises our categories 31-40, 41-50 and 51-60 with the census categories 30-34, 35-39, 40-44,45-49, 50-54 and 55-59.*
[c] *Comprises our categories 61-70 and 71 or older with the census categories 60-64, 65-69, 70-74,75-79, 80-84 and 85+.*
[d] *Occupation data collected through an open-ended question was re-coded on a nine point Socio-Economic Scale adhering to the British Standard Occupational Classification 2000 [40] and using the Computer Assisted Structured Coding Tool [41].*
*Census population estimate falls outside 95% confidence interval of census population.*

## 11.3.4 ANALYSES AND HYPOTHESES

The data were entered into Microsoft Access 2007 and then validated against the original questionnaires. For statistical comparison, data were transferred into SPSS version 16 and validated a second time, with the exception of demographic comparison which was performed using Stats-Direct. Some questions were not (fully) answered by all respondents, thus sample size often varied between questions.

We hypothesised apriori that non-compliance with water advice would be higher for the "Do Not Drink" phase compared to the "Boil Water" one. In addition, we predicted that demographic factors (such as age, gender, home ownership and employment), prior beliefs/experiences, use of information sources, and practical issues (e.g. loss of electricity) could have had an effect on participants' perceptions and behaviours; however, as no formal hypotheses were defined apriori, statistical outcomes should be interpreted solely as indicators of the potential strength of association. Quantitative analysis is mainly descriptive. Inferential analysis was carried out using chi-square, ANOVA, and for repeated measures generalised estimating equations (with and without prior factor analysis). For analyses with multiple outcome variables, initial analysis was done using multivariate ANOVA with all possible outcome and predictor variables. For all analyses with multiple predictor variables, only those variables that were significant at the $p < 0.2$ level in single predictor models were included in the multiple predictor models. The least significant variable was then removed from the model until all predictor variables were significant at the $p < 0.2$ level. The value of the model in predicting each dependent variable was then derived from the tests of between subjects effects in the corrected model. Throughout, the level of significance was set at 5% and only responses with at least 10 responses deferred from the median response were included as dependent variables.

## 11.4 RESULTS

### 11.4.1 RESPONSE RATE AND DEMOGRAPHICS

A total of 195 completed questionnaires were returned, giving a response rate of almost 20%. Thirty-six respondents stated that they did not lose their tap water during the incident. These were excluded from analysis, yielding a total sample size of 159 affected consumers.

To check for sampling bias, we compared the demographic characteristics of our respondents with those for Gloucestershire residents using the 2001 census survey (Table 1)[21]. Overall, our sample is representative. There is, however, an under-representation of younger and male participants, which is a common pattern in postal questionnaire studies [22]. There is also a disproportionate number of home owners and professionals versus people with elementary skills (e.g. farmers, porters, cleaners), which ties in with response rates typically being higher in the higher social classes than in the lower classes [23].

## 11.4.2 PARTICIPANT EXPERIENCES DURING THE 2007 FLOODS AND PARTICIPANT BACKGROUNDS

During the 2007 floods, 33 respondents (20.9%) lost their main electricity and two (1.3%) were flooded. Twenty-seven participants (17.1%) chose to leave their homes due to the disaster. Of these, 23 stated that the main reason for not staying was difficulties managing without mains water, with several highlighting that they had (young) children or were "vulnerable" due to ill health. Only one person left because of the floods, while no one stated loss of electricity or their home being flooded as their main reason.

Five households (3.2%) reported experience of flooding prior to the floods of 2007, but none of them were flooded during the Mythe incident. Forty-nine participants (31.6%) had previously experienced tap water loss; thirty-three of them recalled the cause being maintenance work and/ or burst mains pipes, whereas only four had experienced water loss due to natural events such as floods or snow/ice. For the majority of these previous experiences (79.6%), participants could not recall if a water notice had been issued or they did not specify. Eight participants were certain that they did not receive a notice, whereas one participant recalled a "Do Not Drink" notice and another a "Do Not Use" notice.

In their general everyday life (i.e. outside the context of the incident), our participants show a very strong preference for tap water (124/151 (straight from the tap 92/151, boiled or filtered 32/151)), with only 16.5%

preferring some type of bottled water and 1.3% stating that they drink other drinks than water.

**TABLE 2:** Use of information sources for all four stages of the incident.

| Information source | "Water Loss"[a] (N = 140) | | "Do Not Drink" (N = 144) | | "Boil Water" (N = 115) | | "Water Safe" (N = 137) | |
|---|---|---|---|---|---|---|---|---|
| | n | % | n | % | n | % | n | % |
| I turned on the tap and no water came out[b] | 19 | 13.6 | | | | | | |
| family/friend/neighbour | 42 | 30.0 | 22 | 15.3 | 12 | 10.4 | 28 | 20.4 |
| leaflet through the post[c] | 8 | 5.7 | 66 | 45.8 | 44 | 38.3 | 51 | 37.2 |
| local newspaper | 4 | 2.9 | 53 | 36.8 | 32 | 27.8 | 40 | 29.2 |
| national newspaper | 0 | 0 | 6 | 4.2 | 0 | 0 | 2 | 1.5 |
| local charity/volunteers | 1 | 0.7 | 4 | 2.8 | 1 | 0.9 | 2 | 1.5 |
| GP/nurse/health organisation | 0 | 0 | 0 | 0 | 2 | 1.8 | 1 | 0.7 |
| water company | 0 | 0 | 60 | 41.7 | 41 | 35.7 | 48 | 35.0 |
| TV | 15 | 10.7 | 40 | 27.8 | 19 | 16.5 | 32 | 23.4 |
| local radio | 43 | 30.7 | 88 | 61.1 | 64 | 55.7 | 78 | 56.9 |
| national radio | 3 | 2.1 | 5 | 3.5 | 2 | 1.7 | 5 | 3.6 |
| local government/council | 0 | 0 | 3 | 2.1 | 3 | 2.6 | 1 | 0.7 |
| website | 1 | 0.7 | 15 | 10.4 | 8 | 6.9 | 7 | 5.1 |
| other | 4 | 2.9 | 3 | 2.1 | 4 | 2.5 | 3 | 2.2 |

[a] For the "Water Loss" stage, respondents could only choose one option (i.e. the information source first used), whereas for all other stages multiple responses were possible.
[b] Option only available for the "Water Loss" stage.
[c] No leaflets were handed out during the "Water Loss" stage.

## 11.4.3 INFORMATION SOURCES

Generally, information about the (imminent) loss of tap water reached consumers via the local radio station (i.e., BBC Radio Gloucestershire) or they were told by family/friends (30.7% and 30.0%, respectively (N = 140)). As Table 2 shows, those who did not find out about the planned shutdown of the tap water beforehand usually became aware when they turned on their taps and no water came out (13.6%). When the water came back on, three consecutive notices were issued by the authorities: "Do Not Drink", "Boil Water" and "Water Safe". Although the authorities had official water notice leaflets delivered to all households, only an average of 40% used them as an information source. Instead, information about the notices tended to reach consumers through other channels; notably, local radio remained the primary information source throughout these three stages: 61.1%, 55.7%, and 56.9%, respectively. Similarly, when participants were asked to rank the information sources in order of preference for the incident, local radio was ranked highest (53.4%, N = 118), followed by family/friends (11.9%), local newspapers (11.0%) and STW (by telephone or internet) (10.2%).

**TABLE 3:** Final parameter estimates of MANOVA of predictors of information source use

| Dependent variable | Predictor variables | B | LCI | UCI | p |
|---|---|---|---|---|---|
| family/friend/neighbour | Intercept | 0.139 | -0.057 | 0.335 | |
| | Age | 0.024 | -0.02 | 0.069 | 0.287 |
| | paid employment | -0.094 | -0.228 | 0.039 | 0.165 |
| leaflet through the post | Intercept | 0.884 | 0.638 | 1.129 | |
| | Age | -0.113 | -0.169 | -0.057 | 0.0001 |
| | paid employment | -0.239 | -0.407 | -0.071 | 0.006 |
| local newspaper | Intercept | 0.079 | -0.166 | 0.324 | |
| | Age | 0.06 | 0.004 | 0.116 | 0.034 |
| | paid employment | 0.09 | -0.078 | 0.257 | 0.292 |

While information source use did not differ much between the three notice stages, the total number of sources used did differ. The total number of information sources utilised during the "Do Not Drink" stage was higher (M = 2.602, LCI = 2.320, UCI = 2.884) compared to the "Boil Water" (M = 2.019, LCI = 1.792, UCI = 2.247) and "Water Safe" (M = 2.146, LCI = 1.919, UCI = 2.372) stages, as confirmed by a repeated measures ANOVA with Bonferroni adjustment (F(1) = 10.747, p = .001).

In order to investigate whether our predictor factors were associated with consumers' choice of information source, we entered the information sources as well as the total number of information sources used during the incident into a MANOVA as dependent variables, with gender, age, home ownership and whether or not in paid employment as the independent variables. The final parameter estimates in the final analysis are shown in Table 3. The key observations are that increasing age and being in paid employment were negatively associated with using leaflets and using the local newspaper was marginally associated with increasing age. This would suggest that older consumers, in particular, but also those in paid employment do not seem to have used the leaflets. For example in the "Do Not Drink" phase 43 of 83 (52%) respondents under 60 years reported using the leaflet compared to only 23 of 60 (38%) of people over 60. In the "Boil Water" phase, these responses were 30/71 (42%) and 14/44 (32%) respectively.

## 11.4.4 ADVICE RECOLLECTION

Most consumers (75.6% (118/156)) were informed about the loss of tap water beforehand. The majority of consumers reported receiving tap water advice ("Do Not Drink": 138/155; "Boil Water": 110/154; "Water Safe":136/154), with 94 consumers (63.9%) reporting receiving all three notices. Several consumers reported not receiving advice about their tap water during one or more of the stages; notably, five consumers reported receiving no advice at all.

As Table 4 shows, there was a lot of confusion as to which water notices were in place during the "Do Not Drink" and "Boil Water" stages, with correct recall varying from 23.2% (33/142) to 26.7% (31/116). During the "Do Not Drink" stage, most consumers believed two notices were in place at the same time; alternatively the "Do Not Drink" notice was confused with "Do Not Use" and "Boil Water". Similarly, half of consumers - males in particular - recalled that when the first notice was changed, the new advice was that the water was safe.

We queried how clear the advice about tap water was using a five-point Likert scale (1 = "very unclear", 2 ="unclear", 3 ="understandable", 4 ="clear", and 5 ="very clear"). Twenty-three consumers (16.3%) stated that the advice was "very clear", 59 (41.8%) that it was "clear" and a further 41 (29.1%) felt that it was "understandable" (N = 141). Similarly, a four-point Likert scale (1 ="very uninformed" – 4 ="very informed") revealed that the majority of consumers felt "informed" (97/142) or "very informed" (22/142). Not surprisingly, consumers who left their homes during the crisis consistently gave lower ratings for clarity of advice and feeling informed.

We used a MANOVA to test the association between information source use (i.e. family/friends/neighbour, leaflet through the post, local newspaper, water company, TV, local radio, and the number of information sources used) and clarity of advice and feeling informed. The final model is shown in Table 5. Use of local newspapers as an information source was positively associated with increased clarity of advice. Water company use was associated with feeling informed. The association between use of the local radio and feeling informed was approaching significance.

**TABLE 4:** Advice recollection for the "Do Not Drink" and "Boil Water" stages.

|  | "Do Not Drink" (N = 142) | | "Boil Water" (N = 116) | |
|---|---|---|---|---|
|  | n | % | n | % |
| there was one advice: do not use | 23 | 16.2 | 1 | 0.9 |
| there was one advice: do not drink | 33 | 23.2 | 9 | 7.8 |
| there was one advice: boil | 24 | 16.9 | 31 | 26.7 |
| there was one advice: safe | 2 | 1.4 | 58 | 50.0 |
| not sure what the advice was | 10 | 7.0 | 9 | 7.8 |
| there was more than one type of advice | 50 | 35.2 | 8 | 6.9 |

## 11.4.5 WATER ACCESS AND PREFERENCES

For the incident as a whole, 21 of the 69 participants who used temporary water supplies reported serious problems securing access to temporary water supplies. Access failures were mainly due to empty bowsers and/or no available stock of bottled water (n = 15). Other reasons included problems travelling to and from the water sites (n = 6) or not being able to locate them (n = 7). Except for one participant who had to rely solely on water supplied by family/friends, consumers did on at least one occasion gain access to temporary water supplied by STW.

During the "Water Loss" stage, collecting bottled water from distribution sites was the most favoured means of procuring water (84.9%, N = 159), compared to bowser water (57.9%). In addition, 35.8% of consumers bought bottled water, or collected water from family/friends (8.2%). Consumers who found out about the water loss beforehand tended to refrain from buying bottled water, instead opting for supplied bottled water. Consumers who generally (i.e. outside the context of the incident) prefer to drink water straight from the tap also tended to refrain from buying bottled water, with many of them choosing to get water from family/friends in unaffected areas.

**TABLE 5:** Final parameter estimates of MANOVA of predictors of clarity of advice and feeling informed

| Dependent variable | Predictor variables | B | LCI | UCI | p |
|---|---|---|---|---|---|
| clarity of advice | Intercept | 3.204 | 2.894 | 3.513 | |
| | local newspaper | 0.559 | 0.134 | 0.983 | 0.010 |
| | water company | 0.278 | -0.111 | 0.668 | 0.160 |
| | local radio | 0.232 | -0.142 | 0.606 | 0.222 |
| feeling informed | Intercept | 2.627 | 2.406 | 2.848 | |
| | local newspaper | 0.193 | -0.11 | 0.496 | 0.210 |
| | water company | 0.314 | 0.036 | 0.592 | 0.027 |
| | local radio | 0.255 | -0.012 | 0.522 | 0.061 |

For the "Do Not Drink" and "Boil Water" stages, consumers were asked to rank different types of drinking water in terms of frequency of use. Based on these data, we can discern popularity in terms of how many respondents used a particular source as well as its mode rank and the total number of rank 1s that it received (Table 6). Both in terms of users and ranks, tap water was the least preferred water source for both stages, including tap water from family/friends, while bottled water was clearly the favoured type of drinking water. Although many households did collect water from bowsers for drinking purposes, rank data shows it to be quite unpopular.

**TABLE 6:** Water drinking preference for the "Do Not Drink" and "Boil Water" stages.

| Popularity of water sources | "Do Not Drink" (N = 155) | | | "Boil Water" (N = 108) | | |
|---|---|---|---|---|---|---|
| | No of Users | Mode rank | Rank 1s (%) | No of Users | Mode rank | Rank 1s (%) |
| bottled water from distribution site | 133 | 1 | 70.0 | 90 | 1 | 69.9 |
| bought bottled water, still | 73 | 1 | 20.0 | 46 | 2 | 16.3 |
| water from bowsers | 34 | 2 | 3.8 | 18 | 2 | 3.3 |
| bought bottled water, sparkling | 21 | 2 | 2.3 | 9 | 2 | 1.1 |
| chilled boiled tap water | 17 | 2 | 0.0 | 8 | 2 | 2.2 |
| water straight from the tap | 13 | 8 | 0.8 | 21 | 2 | 3.3 |
| tap water from family/friends | 12 | 1 | 3.1 | 4 | 1 | 2.2 |
| filtered tap water | 8 | 7 | 0.0 | 9 | 1 | 2.2 |

We also found that 28 participants (17.6%) carried on using temporary water sources after the tap water was safe, because they were not convinced that it was safe, and some also commented that the water was dirty, cloudy and smelly, or tasted strange.

## 11.4.6 TAP WATER BEHAVIOUR AND COMPLIANCE

Participants were asked to specify their use of tap water during the "Do Not Drink" and "Boil Water" stages (Table 7). Of particular concern is the high proportion of consumers who ingested (i.e. brushed teeth, prepared food/cook and drunk) unboiled tap water; a risky behaviour which increased substantially when the advice changed to "Boil Water". Ingestion of boiled water during the "Do Not Drink" stage was also risky and prominent. Table 7 also reveals that some consumers refrained from using tap water for safe actions such as hand washing, showering/bathing and toilet flushing, or they used boiled tap water for these purposes. Thus, individuals' tap water actions commonly included both risky and over-cautious behaviour.

Regarding compliance with water advice about drinking, 47.2% (75/159; based on respondents drinking water straight from the tap and/or boiled tap water during the "Do Not Drink" stage) versus 29.3% (34/116; based on respondents drinking unboiled tap water during the "Boil Water" stage) of respondents did not comply with the notices. Looking at overall compliance with water advice, i.e., including brushing teeth and preparing/cooking food, non-compliance increases to 62.9% (100/159) and 48.3% (56/116) for the "Do Not Drink" and the "Boil Water" notices, respectively. The higher non-compliance rates for "Do Not Drink" are predominantly attributed to the high use of boiled tap water.

**TABLE 7:** Use of tap water during the "Do Not Drink" and "Boil Water" stages.

| | "Do Not Drink" (N = 159) | | "Boil Water" (N = 116) | | p |
|---|---|---|---|---|---|
| | n | % | n | % | |
| Using unboiled tap water for | | | | | |
| flush toilet | 148 | 93.1 | 105 | 90.5 | 0.439 |
| shower/bathe | 120 | 75.5 | 97 | 83.6 | 0.102 |
| wash hands | 83 | 52.2 | 81 | 69.8 | 0.003 |
| prepare/cook food with[a] | 34 | 21.4 | 49 | 42.2 | $2.0 \times 10^{-4}$ |
| brush teeth[a] | 26 | 16.4 | 44 | 37.8 | $4.9 \times 10^{-5}$ |
| Drink[a] | 15 | 9.4 | 34 | 29.3 | $2.1 \times 10^{-5}$ |
| Using boiled tap water for | | | | | |
| flush toilet | 4 | 2.5 | 5 | 4.3 | 0.409 |
| shower/bathe | 6 | 3.8 | 5 | 4.3 | 0.823 |
| wash hands | 17 | 10.7 | 6 | 5.2 | 0.103 |
| prepare/cook food with[b] | 75 | 47.2 | 41 | 35.3 | 0.050 |
| brush teeth[b] | 61 | 38.4 | 29 | 25.0 | 0.020 |
| drink hot[b] | 67 | 42.1 | 45 | 38.8 | 0.577 |
| drink cold[b] | 34 | 21.4 | 23 | 19.8 | 0.753 |

[a]*Action not safe with unboiled water if a "Do Not Drink" or "Boil Water" notice is in place.*
[b]*Action not safe with boiled water if a "Do Not Drink" notice is in place.*

In order to test our hypothesis that non-compliance would be greater for "Do Not Drink", we used a generalised estimating equation with drinking water compliance and overall compliance as dependent variables and with incident stage, demographics and participants' general drinking water preference and previous experience of loss of tap water as predictor variables. The final model is shown in Table 8. It can be seen that the main factor associated with both drinking water compliance and overall compliance is incident stage (i.e. "Do Not Drink" stage versus "Boil Water" stage), confirming our hypothesis. Drinking water compliance was, in addition, associated with employment, i.e. those in paid employment were less likely to comply. There was some suggestion that females were more likely to be compliant, but this association was not significant.

Furthermore, respondents' reported use of unboiled and boiled tap water during the "Do Not Drink" and "Boil Water" stages was analysed by rotated Equamax factor analysis followed by generalised estimating equation analysis with demographics, sources of information used and participants' general drinking water preference and previous experience of loss of tap water as predictor variables. No significant associations were identified.

## 11.4.7 BOWSER WATER BEHAVIOUR AND COMPLIANCE

Ingestion of unboiled bowser water was limited (Table 9). In contrast to tap water compliance, only six of the 53 participants (11.3%) who utilised bowser water for drinking during one or more stages of the incident failed to comply with the advice to boil it before drinking it, while overall non-compliance was 27.3% (21/77). Numbers were insufficient to determine factors associated with compliance with advice on bowser water.

## 11.5 DISCUSSION

The world faces unprecedented changes in climate and environment, and an increased risk of natural disasters, which for the UK will include floods, droughts and heat waves [24]. Natural disasters, whether hurricanes or floods, potentially pose a risk to drinking water and consequently public health. After Hurricane Ami hit an island of Fiji, nearly 75% of water samples taken showed contamination [25]. Due to scarcity of safe water during large emergencies, high incidences of fever, diarrhoeal illnesses and skin infections are common place, at least in low income countries [26]. Isolation from medical care further increases rates of morbidity and mortality. Where drinking water is still available, albeit not safe to drink (with or without treatment), water advice is issued. Public health communication is key to safe water behaviour and compliance with advice.

**TABLE 8:** Final parameter estimates of generalised estimating equation of predictors of compliance with water advice

| Dependent variables | Predictor variables | | B | LCI | UCI | p |
|---|---|---|---|---|---|---|
| drinking water compliance | incident stage | Do Not Drink | 1 | | | |
| | | Boil Water | 1.35 | 1.11 | 1.64 | 0.002 |
| | paid employment | No | 1 | | | |
| | | Yes | 0.81 | 0.68 | 0.97 | 0.024 |
| | gender | Male | 1 | | | |
| | | Female | 1.154 | 0.96 | 1.40 | 0.137 |
| overall compliance | incident stage | Do Not Drink | 1 | | | |
| | | Boil Water | 1.79 | 1.34 | 2.34 | $2.3 \times 10^{-5}$ |

Compliance studies have varied in methodology with some focusing on unboiled tap water and others on boiled water, reducing comparability across studies and across notices. With the exception of the Hurricane Rita study [13], previous studies have focused on human error and everyday incidents, and for the absolute majority of these, the notice investigated is "Boil Water". This study is the first to contrast advice recollection, information use, water behaviour and compliance during an incident involving two notices. It is also the first to investigate a "Do Not Drink" notice issued due to a natural disaster, and the first to include compliance with the general advice to boil bowser water.

It should be noted that the study took place 18 months after the incident. This may have resulted in a lower than normal response rate. Compliance surveys sent out within one month of the incident have yielded response rates around 65% [e.g. [12]]. However, risk perception studies normally attract response rates just below 20% [e.g. [27]]. The time delay may also have impacted consumers' recall of actions and events. However, the 2007 Gloucestershire flood incident was unique and highly memorable; our study has shown that consumers' main concern revolved around their tap water; and in focus groups carried out after the postal questionnaire, consumers shared very detailed accounts of the incident and their quest to access safe drinking water. The time lag, nevertheless, does place some restrictions on the results and conclusions presented here.

**TABLE 9:** Use of unboiled bowser water during the first three stages.

| Use of unboiled bowser water | n/Nª | % |
|---|---|---|
| prepare/cook food with[b] | 16/72 | 22.2 |
| brush teeth[b] | 11/47 | 23.4 |
| drink cold[b] | 5/50 | 10.0 |
| drink hot[b] | 5/31 | 16.1 |

*ª The number of participants who said they used unboiled bowser water (n) out of the number of participants who used boiled and/or unboiled bowser water (N). In total, 77 participants used bowser water for some purpose, but not all of them replied to each bowser water question.*
*[b] Action not safe.*

Consumers relied on a range of sources for information about safe water behaviour, and use of sources differed somewhat between the first and the subsequent three stages, with the exception of local radio which remained the primary source through the whole incident. Information usage was at its highest during the "Do Not Drink" notice stage. In situations of lots of uncertainty, the public commonly seeks out more information sources [27].

During natural disasters, water advice has commonly not reached consumers. In the aftermath of Hurricane Rita, as few as 31% of people issued with a "Boil Water" notice were aware of it [13]. In the present study, 3%

of participants reported not receiving any water advice at all when the tap water was returned. In addition, several consumers reported not receiving one of the advices. Due to the nature of the crisis, Severn Trent Water was not able to inform consumers before the water supply failed. Similarly, printed media and media websites were unable to deliver advance warnings. Official water notices were, however, issued during the three subsequent stages. These were consulted by only about 40% of consumers. Notably, older participants and those in paid employment hardly used them. For an information source that did reach all households, a 40% efficacy is very worrying, and it is essential that we evaluate how official advice is provided to the general public; especially since we also found that receiving information from the water company was positively associated with feeling informed. The apparent discrepancy most likely stems, in part, from the fact that the first water notice was not a standard water industry notice; thus, it is therefore essential that standard water industry protocol be upheld in future incidents. This is also the recommendation of the Drinking Water Inspectorate in their Incident Assessment Letter [20]. Another reason may be the close collaboration between Severn Trent Water and local media, which we discuss further below.

As printed information could not be made available when the tap water was turned off, family/friends and direct media such as radio and television featured prominently during the first incident stage. In New South Wales, 67% of people found out about severe storm warnings through television, but during the storm they relied more on radio and family/friends [28].

Personal dissemination networks have been shown to be particularly vital for vulnerable sub-populations [29], and interpersonal information is often perceived as more credible and efficient than official information sources [10,30]. Decisions on how to respond to flood warnings have also been found to rely to some extent on the behaviours and attitudes of people close by [31]. In the present study, we found that family/friends/neighbours were the second most preferred source along with local newspapers (which was significantly used by older consumers) and the water company, despite a drop in use after the initial stage which presumably is due to the availability of printed media from then onwards. Dissemination plans should be revised in order to tap into family/friends/neighbours as a potential information stream, e.g. personal networks and nomination of local 'disaster contact persons' can be established through local community organisations, and dissemination through these networks should be given prominence.

Reflecting the complexity of the event and the combination of two subsequent notices, consumers' advice recollection was noticeably affected, leaving consumers highly uncertain about which notice was in place when, with significant proportions believing two notices were in place at the same time. Clearly, the public is not aware of the exclusive nature of notices (i.e. only one can be in place at a time) or that there are several different types of notices. This could indicate that they construe water as either safe or not safe.

Typically, non-compliance with "Boil Water" advice ranges between 9% and 20% [11,32] whereas after Hurricane Rita, only one-third reported boiling water for drinking [13]. If unsafe actions such as using unboiled water for brushing teeth or preparing/cooking food are considered, non-compliance increases dramatically to 57% and 77% for human error and natural disasters, respectively [13,32]. Our data show high non-compliance for the "Boil Water" notice (29.3%), and when including other unsafe behaviours, it rises to 48.3%. Comparison of "Boil Water" compliance for this incident with preliminary results from a recent UK human error "Boil Water" incident tentatively confirms that natural disasters are associated with higher degrees of non-compliance compared to human error incidents (Knapton, Hunter & Rundblad; submitted 2010).

The first water notice issued was "Do Not Drink". To date there is only one previous study of this advice, a human-error incident in Israel in 2001. Non-compliance was estimated to 18% [33]. We found that non-compliance for drinking was significantly higher for the "Do Not Drink" notice (47.2%) compared to the "Boil Water" notice (29.3%). Similarly, overall non-compliance was also significantly higher: 62.9% versus 48.3%. By contrasting participants' use of unboiled and boiled tap water, we can see for the first time that the higher use of contaminated water during the "Do Not Drink" notice stage is due to consumers boiling the water, presumably due to a belief that it renders it safe to drink and use. These results are in line with Rundblad's [34] hypothetical "Do Not Drink" scenario study which predicted that 39.3% of consumers would boil and drink contaminated water. In the Mythe incident, there were attempts to neutralise this common folk belief by including additional information on notices and in material supplied to media and the public. It is beyond the scope of this study to evaluate if this addition did impact consumer behaviour; however as the high degree of non-compliance here suggests, this measure alone is far from sufficient. It is highly likely that this folk belief in boiling is linked to the aforementioned binary folk classification of water. The higher degree of non-compliance for "Do Not Drink" is not because consumers acted differently for the two notices, but rather that the protective measures they took were more or less the same, and as such, they were not sufficient for the more restrictive notice.

It should be noted that many consumers varied in their behaviour such that they displayed a mixture of safe and unsafe behaviours. Some also engaged in over-cautious behaviour such as flushing the toilet with boiled tap water or avoiding to flush. The mixture of risky and over-cautious actions can be attributed to consumers not being aware or being unsure of what actions are unsafe. The title of the notice "Do Not Drink" is highly misleading as it fails to highlight all ingestion actions listed on the notice [34]; an alternative title, such as 'External Use Only' could prove more informative. In addition, the Drinking Water Inspectorate were strongly critical of the notice issued by the health authorities because it did not follow water industry standards and the messages were unclear [20]. We also found that 17.6% carried on using temporary water supplies after the tap water had been declared safe, which is similar to the 10% of consumers continuing to boil water after the "Boil Water" notice was lifted in Willocks and colleagues' study of 2000 hospital employees in the North Thames region, UK, in 1997 [32]. Information and reassurance that water is safe or that certain water actions are safe during a particular notice are as important from a health point of view as informing about unsafe actions. Worries about potential health hazards can cause severe anxiety and, like detection of discolouration and odour in the water, causes increases in reports of symptoms of waterborne illness [35]. It is vital that the titles of notices be reviewed and that the public's classification of water and beliefs about precautionary actions such as boiling be addressed through public health education.

It is important to separate the public's perception of information sources and their behaviour. While media has been found to impact general risk perceptions because these perceptions are impersonal, they do not necessarily impact the personal risk perceptions that would initiate behaviour responses [36]. In the present study, media did not affect consumer behaviour. However, BBC Radio Gloucestershire came to take up a rather unique position. Throughout the incident, it remained the primary information source, both in terms of usage and preference, and its association with feeling informed was approaching significance. BBC Radio Gloucestershire estimates that roughly half the population of Gloucestershire kept up-to-date about the crisis by listening in, and their website saw a 159% increase of users (personal communication). We believe that its apparent success rested on more than radio being easily accessible. Other local mass media was also favoured; notably, local newspapers were positively associated with clarity of advice. This could indicate a need for geographic-specific information [28]. Severn Trent Water followed standard water industry practice and issued frequent and regular bulletins to the local media in parallel to issuing notices. BBC Radio Gloucestershire was quick to broadcast not only about the mains water loss, but also about locations of distribution sites. Users of local radio therefore knew there was no need to buy bottled water. Another important step taken was the broadcasting of the daily press conferences with updates from Severn Trent Water and Gloucestershire Constabulary. Altogether, BBC Radio Gloucestershire was able to establish themselves as a timely and trustworthy information source. Building on the example of BBC Radio Gloucestershire, it is essential that local media be pre-prepared and, during an event, be continuously up-dated to maximise their role in ensuring public safety.

Although a potential key player in public behaviour response, no information source was associated with water behaviour. We did, however, find that those in paid employment were significantly less likely to comply with drinking water advice. Demographic factors such as socioeconomic status have previously been found to influence behaviour during natural disasters [37-39]. In order to ensure appropriate and safe behaviour during natural disasters, public health education needs to reach all income quartiles, at home or at work.

Lack of electricity contributed to non-compliance after Hurricane Rita [13]. In this incident, approximately 20% of our participants were without electricity, but loss of mains electricity occurred at the same time as consumers were without main tap water and only lasted for 24 hours. Consequently, electricity could only have impacted boiling of bowser water. However, compliance with bowser water advice was very high: 88.7% (drinking) and 72.7% (including food preparation, etc.) Bowser advice is more consistent and thus less open to interpretation as it is water industry practice for every bowser to bear a clear permanent "Boil Water" message at the point where consumers draw water. Even so, whether consumers conceptualised the instruction to boil the water as relating to use of unsterilised collection vessels rather than unsafe bowser water could not be ascertained in the present study.

Whilst bowser water was used, it was not popular for drinking. Instead, bottled water was preferred during both notices. It has been suggested that bowser water and bottled water serve slightly different purposes, with the former to be used for personal hygiene and cooking, and the latter for drinking. However, it was not clear from the study whether consumers understood such a distinction, or whether there is a general distrust in the quality of bowser water. Thus in future incidents, bottled water should be considered a priority over bowser water, where supply, distribution and recycling allows. More than half of consumers bought bottled water even though the Security and Emergency Measures Direction 1998 requires all water companies to provide a minimum of 10 litres of water per person per day in case of supply failure [15]. We trace buying of bottled water to the public not being aware of this provision duty, especially since consumers who found out about the water loss beforehand tended to refrain from buying bottled water. It is also possible that consumers did not trust the water company to supply enough water and in time.

## 11.6 CONCLUSION

A high proportion of consumers, especially elderly, reported not having used the official leaflets containing advice on safe and unsafe water behaviour. Instead, local media and family/friends functioned as main information channels. Contacts with local media and community/personal networks should be established, maintained and kept up-to-date with drinking water standards and emergency protocol, so that when an incident occurs official advice can reach all consumers of all demographic backgrounds in a timely fashion. High degrees of non-compliance, especially for the "Do Not Drink" notice, are the result of consumers employing insufficient protective measures, presumably due to incorrect folk beliefs regarding water contaminants and boiling. Unsafe behaviour was commonly coupled with over-cautious behaviour illustrating that consumers are equally unaware of what actions are safe. Current public health education provision should be evaluated and drinking water knowledge be included, in order to minimise risky behaviour and avoid unnecessary stress from over-caution during incidents.

## REFERENCES

1.   Glik DC: Risk communication for public health emergencies. Annu Rev Public Health 2007, 28:33-54.
2.   Brodie M, Weltzien E, Altman D, Blendon RJ, Benson JM: Experiences of Hurricane Katrina evacuees in Houston shelters. Am J Public Health 2006, 96(8):1402-1408.
3.   Rogers MB, Amlot R, Rubin GJ, Wessely S, Krieger K: Mediating the social and psychological impacts of terrorists attacks: the role of perception and risk communication. International Review of Psychiatry 2007, 19(3):279-288.
4.   Hunter PR, Reid M: Poor communication during a contamination event may cause more harm to public health then the actual event itself. In Water Contamination Emergencies. Edited by Thompson KC, Gray J. Cambridge: RSC Publishing; 2006:156-164.
5.   Renn O: Risk Communication and the social amplification of risk. In Communicating Risks to the Public: International Perspectives. Edited by Kasperson RE, Stallen PJ. Amsterdam and New York: Kluwer Academic; 1991:287-324.
6.   Alaszewski A: Risk communication: identifying the importance of social context. Health, Risk & Society 2005, 7(2):101-105.
7.   Griffin RJ, Dunwoody S, Zabala F: Public reliance on risk communication channels in the wake of a cryptosporidium outbreak. Risk Anal 1998, 18(4):367-375.
8.   Doria MF, Abubakar I, Syed Q, Hughes S, Hunter PR: Perceived causes of sporadic cryptosporidiosis and their relation to sources of information. BMJ 2006, 60:745-750.
9.   Hunter PR, Syed Q: Community surveys of self-reported diarrhoea can dramatically overestimate the size of outbreaks of waterborne cryptosporidiosis. Water Science and Technology 2001, 43(12):27-30.
10.  Griffin RJ, Dunwoody S: The relation of communication to risk judgment and preventive behavior related to lead in tap water. Health Communication 2000, 12(1):81-107.

11. O'Donnell M, Platt C, Aston R: Effect of a boil water notice on behaviour in the management of a water contamination incident. Communicable Disease and Public Health 2000, 3(1):56-59.

12. Karagiannis I, Schimmer B, de Roda Husman AM: Compliance with boil water advice following a water contamination incident in the Netherlands in 2007. Eurosurveillance 2009, 14(12):8-10.

13. Ram PK, Blanton E, Kinghoffer D, Platek M, Piper J, Straif-Bourgeois S, Bonner MR, Mintz ED: Household water disinfection in hurricane-affected communities of Louisiana: Implications for disaster preparedness for the general public. Am J Public Health 2007, 97(Suppl 1):S130-S135.

14. Pitt M: Lessons from the 2007 floods: what people need. London: Cabinet Office; 2008.

15. Severn Trent Water: The Impact of the July Floods on the Water Infrastructure and Customer Service. Gloucestershire; 2007.

16. Knight K: Facing the challenge. London. 2008.

17. Gloucestershire Constabulary: Operation Outlook narrative and analysis: Chief Constable's report to the Gloucestershire Police Authority. Gloucestershire; 2008.

18. Drinking Water Inspectorate: Incidents in England and Wales 2006. London. 2007.

19. Drinking Water Inspectorate: Incidents in England and Wales 2007. London. 2008.

20. Drinking Water Inspectorate, Health Protection Agency: Drinking water safety - Guidance to health and water professionals. London. 2009.

21. Census 2001 [http://www.gloucestershire.gov.uk/inform/index.cfm?articleid=94726]

22. Murray SA, Graham LJC: Practice based health needs assessment: use of four methods in a small neighbourhood. BMJ 1995, 310:1443-1448.

23. Sheikh K, Mattingly S: Investigating non-response bias in mail surveys. J Epidemiol Community Health 1981, 35(4):293-296.

24. van Aalst MK: The impacts of climate change on the risk of natural disasters. Disasters 2006, 30(1):5-18.

25. Mosley LM, Singh S, Sharp DS: Effects of a tropical cyclone on the drinking-water quality of a remote Pacific island. Disasters 2004, 28(4):405-417.

26. Rashid SF: The urban poor in Dhaka City: their struggles and coping strategies during the floods of 1998. Disasters 2000, 24(3):240-253.

27. ter Huurne E, Gutteling J: Information needs and risk perception as predictors of risk information seeking. Journal of Risk Research 2008, 11(7):847-862.

28. Cretikos M, Eastwood K, Dalton C, Merritt T, Tuyl F, Winn L, Durrheim D: Household disaster preparedness and information sources: rapid cluster survey after a storm in New South Wales, Australia. BMC Public Health 2008, 8:195-203.

29. Spence PR, Lachlan K, Burke J, Seeger MW: Media use and information needs of the disabled during a natural disaster. J Health Care Poor Underserved 2007, 18:394-404.

30. Parker DJ, Handmer JW: The role of unofficial flood warning systems. Journal of Contingencies and Crisis Management 1998, 6(1):45-60.

31. Drabek TE: The social factors that constrain human responses to flood warnings. In Floods. Volume 1. Edited by Parker DJ. London: Routledge; 2000::361-376.

32. Willocks LJ, Sufi F, Wall R, Seng C, Swan AV: Compliance with advice to boil drinking water during an outbreak of cryptosporidiosis. Communicable Disease and Public Health 2000, 3(2):137-138.

33. Winston G, Lerman S, Goldberger S, Collins M, Leventhal A: A tap water turbidity crisis in Tel Aviv, Israel, due to technical failure: toxicological and risk management issues. International Journal of Hygiene and Environmental Health 2003, 206:193-2000.

34. Rundblad G: The semantics and pragmatics of water notices and the impact on public health. Journal of Water and Health 2008, 6(Suppl 1):77-86.

35. Fowle SE, Constantine CE, Fone D, McCloskey B: An epidemiological study after a water contamination incident near Worcester, England in April 1994. J Epidemiol Community Health 1996, 50(1):18-23.

36. Wåhlberg AA, Sjöberg L: Risk perception and the media. Journal of Risk Research 2000, 3(1):31-50.

37. Blendon RJ, Benson JM, DesRoches CM, Lyon-Daniel K, Mitchell EW, Pollard WE: The public's preparedness for hurricanes in four affected regions. Public Health Rep 2007, 122:167-176.

38. Tierney K, Lindell MK, Perry R: Facing the Unexpected. London: Altamira Press; 2001.

39. Phillips BD, Metz WC, Nieves LA: Disaster threat: preparedness and potential response of the lowest income quartile. Environmental Hazards 2005, 6:123-133.

40. Office for National Statistics: Standard Occupational Classification 2000 [http:/ / www.ons.gov.uk/ about-statistics/ classifications/ archived/ SOC2000/ index.html]

41. Warwick Institute for Employment Research: CASCOT [http://www2.warwick. ac.uk/fac/soc/ier/publications/software/cascot/]

# Author Notes

## CHAPTER 1

### Competing Interests
The authors declare that they have no competing interests.

### Author contributions
LMD performed the surveys and theme-generating data analysis. GBK contributed to the project methodology and design. LMD and GBK wrote the manuscript. All authors read and approved the final manuscript.

### Acknowledgments
The authors will like to acknowledge Carey S. Kyer, Gustav Asp, and William Frank Peacock. While the cost of this project was minimal, all funding was provided by WHO Department of Communications.

## CHAPTER 2

### Funding
This work was supported by the National Natural Science Foundation of China under Grant No. 71173128, 91224008, and the Ministry of Science and Technology of the People's Republic of China under Grant No. 2011BAK07B02. The funders had no role in study design, data collection and analysis, decision to publish, or preparation of the manuscript.

### Competing Interests
The authors have declared that no competing interests exist.

### Author Contributions
Conceived and designed the experiments: NZ HH. Performed the experiments: NZ JZ BS BZ. Analyzed the data: NZ BS. Wrote the paper: NZ HH. Contributed software programming: BS NZ.

## CHAPTER 3

### Funding Statement
Salary and fees for DTB were paid by the Public Health Agency (Northern Ireland)

### Competing Interests
One of the authors (Mike Clarke) is on the editorial board of PLOS Currents Disasters. The authors have declared that no other competing interests exist.

## CHAPTER 4

### Acknowledgments
The authors wish to thank the workshop participants for their insightful comments and Ms Liana Formichella for conducting the background literature searches.

## CHAPTER 5

### Disclosure
This paper is an extended version of the work originally presented at the 7th International Conference on Innovative Mobile and Internet Services in Ubiquitous Computing (IMIS2013), Taichung, Taiwan, July 3–5, 2013.

### Conflict of Interest
The authors declare that there is no conflict of interests regarding the publication of this paper.

## CHAPTER 6

### Competing Interests
The authors declare that they have no competing interests.

### Author Contributions
All authors contributed equally on developing the concept described in this paper and read and approved the final manuscript.

## Acknowledgments

The authors would like to thank the reviewers and those who worked in the field of emergency rescue and social networking for their efforts in coordination of the study.

## CHAPTER 7

### Author Contributions

WJA conceived the essay and wrote the first draft. WJA, CSP and GRA contributed to the writing and with ideas, revised and approved the final version.

### Acknowledgments

We thank Lewis Kim, Ellis McKenzie, Bing Kung, Eduardo Beltrame and Alicia A. Levinsky (National Institutes of Health Library) for their valuable comments on manuscript. This research has been made possible by the support of the Fogarty International Center, National Institutes of Health.

### Competing Interests

The authors have no financial competing interests to declare. Dr. Ghassem Asrar currently serves as Editor-in-Chief to Earth Perspectives.

## CHAPTER 8

### Data Availability

All relevant data are within the paper and its Supporting Information files.

### Funding

This work was supported by National Science Foundation awards CMMI-1031853 (CTB) and CMMI-1031779 (JS), and IIS-1251267 and by Office of Naval Research award N00014-08-1-1015 (CTB). The funders had no role in study design, data collection and analysis, decision to publish, or preparation of the manuscript.

### Competing Interests

The authors have declared that no competing interests exist.

## Author Contributions

Analyzed the data: CBG ESS. Contributed reagents/materials/analysis tools: JS ESS CL SF. Wrote the paper: JS CBG ESS CL SF CTB. Conceived and designed the study: JS CTB.

## CHAPTER 9

### Conflict of Interest

The authors declare that there is no conflict of interests regarding the publication of this paper.

### Acknowledgments

This work is supported by the Ministry of Higher Education (MOHE) and University of Malaya (Project no. HIR-MOHEB00009) and by the BK21+ Program of the National Research Foundation (NRF) of Korea. Also, this work was supported by the 2013 Yeungnam University Research Grant.

## CHAPTER 10

### Competing Interests

The authors declare that they have no competing financial interests.

### Author Contributions

AG designed the study, analyzed data and wrote the manuscript. RER and AYL contributed to data analysis, interpretation and manuscript writing. KY contributed to data collection and data management. YS conceived of the study and collected data. DDH contributed to manuscript planning and writing. HK supervised the workshop and contributed to manuscript writing. MRR contributed to data interpretation and manuscript writing. All authors read and approved the final manuscript.

### Acknowledgments

We thank the public health nurses of Fukushima City Health and Welfare Center for their contribution in data collection, and journal reviewers for improving the manuscript. This work was supported in part by the Japan Foundation for the Promotion of International Medical Research Cooperation.

## CHAPTER 11

### Competing Interests

PRH is Chair of Science Board to Suez Environment, Paris, Chair of Board of Directors of Institute of Public Health and Water Research, and acted as consultant to Danone Beverages. All other authors have no competing interests to declare.

### Author Contributions

GR designed the study, contributed to literature review, contributed to questionnaire design, participated in data analysis, wrote the manuscript. OK contributed to literature review, contributed to questionnaire design, participated in data analysis, contributed to manuscript. PRH contributed to study design, participated in data analysis, contributed to manuscript. All authors read and approved the final manuscript.

### Acknowledgments

We would like to thank the Drinking Water Inspectorate for their help and support. Special thanks to Jo Van Herwegen for help with data entry. Drinking Water Inspectorate reports are Crown Copyright material. Census data is Crown Copyright material and is reproduced with the permission of the Controller of HMSO and the Queen's Printer for Scotland. Data from the Office for National Statistics are Crown Copyright material and are reproduced with the permission of the Office of Public Sector Information. This research was funded by a Leverhulme Trust grant to GR and PRH.

# Index